ALSO BY SY MONTGOMERY

Journey of the Pink Dolphins
Walking with the Great Apes: Jane Goodall, Dian Fossey, Birute Galdikas
Spell of the Tiger: The Man-Eaters of Sundarbans
The Curious Naturalist: Nature's Everyday Mysteries
The Wild Out Your Window: Exploring Nature Near at Hand

FOR CHILDREN

The Snake Scientist
The Man-Eating Tigers of Sundarbans
Encantado: Pink Dolphin of the Amazon

SEARCH FOR

THE GOLDEN

MOON BEAR

Science and Adventure

in Southeast Asia

SY MONTGOMERY

Simon & Schuster

New York   London   Toronto
Sydney   Singapore

SIMON & SCHUSTER
Rockefeller Center
1230 Avenue of the Americas
New York, NY 10020

Copyright © 2002 by Sy Montgomery
Maps copyright © 2002 by Liddy Hubbell
All rights reserved,
including the right of reproduction
in whole or in part in any form.

SIMON & SCHUSTER and colophon are registered trademarks
of Simon & Schuster, Inc.

For information about special discounts for bulk purchases,
please contact Simon & Schuster Special Sales:
1-800-456-6798 or business@simonandschuster.com

Designed by Jeanette Olender
Manufactured in the United States of America

1   3   9   5   7   9   10   8   6   4   2

Library of Congress Cataloging-in-Publication Data is available.

ISBN 0-7432-0584-7

To my mother,
Mrs. Willa Brown Montgomery,
aviatrix and adventurer

CONTENTS

Banded Palm Civet

Binturong

C·H·I·N·A

Hainan

V·I·E·T·N·A·M

Annamite Mountains

Lak Xao

Louang Phabang

OU RIVER

L·A·O·S

MEKONG R.

Vientiane

MEKONG RIVER

T·H·A·I·L·A·N·D

Mae Hong Song

Chiang Mai

Mae Sariang

SALAWEEN R.

B·U·R·M·A

Author's travels through Southeast Asia

PART ONE

A First Encounter

The Golden Moon Bear

A PALE FACE stares out at us from the darkness, looming from the close, damp shade. At first we see only the lobed, moist nose, the small, brown eyes circled in black like a panda's—features set against the ghostly cream fur of her muzzle like a mask that a Siamese dancer might wear for a *khon* drama.

"Ahhhhh!" Sun Hean sighs softly. "She's here!"

The bear moves slowly toward us, padding on leathery, in-turning paws. As she steps heavily from the leafy shadows in back of her outdoor pen, she reveals herself to us by inches. Now we see her round ears, sticking up like two unfolded oriental hand fans. They are light inside, but fringed with dark fur like eyelashes. The ears swivel toward us, then back, consulting both directions, considering as she paces forward. Now we see her deep black mane. Thick as a lion's, it covers the top and sides of the neck and head. On her chest is a crescent etched in white fur. And now we see the rest of her body, and it takes our breath away. The legs, the back, the belly, the haunches—even the claws—are various shades of gold: the gold of wild bee honey, the gold of the ginger's root, the gold from the throat of a rain forest orchid. A spectrum of gold—topaz, buttercup, amber, tigereye—the colors seem to change with the light filtering through the feathery leaves of the mimosas in her enclosure. On the upper part of her back, the hair is nearly orange.

No bear like her is known to science.

She was captured one dusky evening in the wet season, a year and a half before. She was living wild only a kilometer from where she is now caged. A hired guard hoped to please his boss with the gift of this unusual cub. She lives now confined within bars of orange-painted steel. To the wealthy man who considers her his property, she is merely a beautiful curiosity.

But to us, she is the entryway to a labyrinth of mysteries.

We have come from half a world away to learn who and what she is. We look to her to show us the secrets of her kind. With the help of a laboratory full of machines and enzymes that chop, sort, and compare subcellular information, we will try to follow her back in time.

She could be a link to a past when Neanderthals roamed Europe, when Homo sapiens was confined to Africa, and when Homo erectus was still alive in Java, a human backwater. Most of Southeast Asia's rain forests, oldest in the world, at that dry, turbulent time had shrunk to tiny, verdant oases surrounded by dry thorn scrub. Most of its bears, if there were any, may have been restricted to mountain refuges. She could help lead us to a vanished refuge—or help us to create new ones.

She could help reveal to us a map of her ancestors' travels. If we could read it, we might be able to help conservationists repopulate now-empty forests with once-captive bears like her.

For a scientist, she could be the Eureka of a lifetime. For a conservation official, she could provide an emblem as compelling as World Wildlife Fund's panda. For a storyteller, this bear could be the starting point of a tale of historic discovery—or the frustrating saga of a mystery unsolved.

She is smaller than we expected. She weighs perhaps 125 pounds, and she is thin for her age. Yet so much rests on her.

The air is heavy with our hopes, heavy with the febrile heat, heavy with the southwest monsoon. The weight of it all seems to slow down time.

Perhaps this is the pace the bear lives by—an ancient pace, graceful and considered, like the way her long tongue emerges from her mouth to examine a morsel on the ground. Like a separate, private creature, the pink ribbon slides from between her black lips, taking five full seconds to extrude its full length, stretching seven inches longer than her muzzle. It does not seem like something that would inhabit the cavernous, yellow-toothed mouth of a bear. The tongue hovers like a hummingbird over the husk of a small nut. The tip can fold, acting like the two fingers of an African elephant's trunk, capable of plucking a grape. She touches the nut, releases it, withdraws the tongue. She considers its information in the most ancient, mysterious, emotional part of the brain, where the oldest bear-knowledge is stored.

Bear-time seems slow to us, perhaps, because we do not have the patience for such a life. In the winter, in the country where I live, a bear can slow her heart to eight beats a minute, and spend a quarter of a year waiting in the darkness. Bears are not made for speed. They do not stand on their toes, in order to run fast like tigers and wolves, but on their soles. Their stout limbs and short backs are built for strength. Bears are meant for long lives. If as cubs they are not killed by predators, or as youngsters by malnutrition, or as adults by hunters, they can live more than thirty years. Such a long lifespan testifies to the value of knowledge carefully accumulated and considered. There is a close, deep, den-dark patience to their movements, their senses, their knowing.

The golden bear lifts her head and opens her nostrils to our scent. She lives in a flood of odors. The area of her nasal mucosa is one hundred times ours. To her, the world is radiant with scent: she can smell the vapors rising from the soil, the ions escaping from the earth. Some scientists believe that bears navigate, often over ranges of many hundreds of square miles, by mapping and memorizing the different odors of their world.

Her nostrils quiver, pink and wet inside. She breathes in our identities: she reads the stories redolent in our sweat, our breath, our hair. She can smell the eggs in our stomachs.

But of her story, we know next to nothing. Her gaze comes to us as if from across many lifetimes—slow, wise, patient, and wondering. Her eyes seem tiny, as if they look out from the soul of a smaller creature hidden within this shambling body. You look into her eyes as you would look at the stars, their light crossing eons, alien, eternal and mute.

For now, she keeps her secrets.

Chapter One

In the Market for Bears

As we pull over at the market at Kampong Som—a street fragrant with French bread and roasting swallows, crammed with wedding dresses, live lobsters, chain saws, flyswatters, cooking pots—our Toyota is thronged with children trying to sell us snails and clams. Our companion, Sun Hean, chats in Khmer with a pregnant woman in a blue pantsuit. Does she know where we might find a moon bear?

The name of the animal evokes the luminous night. Its original Latin moniker—*Selenarctos thibetanus*—honors Selene, the Greek goddess of the moon, because of the white crescent mark on the animal's chest. Otherwise, the moon bear, big and shaggy, with prominent, round, upright ears, and often, a thick mane like a lion's, is black as the tropical night—and as mysterious.

Rudyard Kipling called it "the most bizarre of the ursine species." It doesn't look like it belongs in the tropics. In fact, the first specimen described by science came from the foothills of the snowy Himalayas. Though moon bears are found from northeastern Russia and China to Afghanistan, they are little studied. Not until the 1960s did scientists realize these dark, heavy beasts, panting beneath their thick coats, padded through the heated, steamy stillness of Cambodia's jungles.

Yet in the same forests where grasses grow into trees one hundred feet high and banyons spill curtains of hair-fine aerial roots from treetops, the moon bears of the Himalayas scratch and snuffle. At dawn and dusk, they shift like shadows among gingers and bamboos. Their imprint is unmistakable. On the straight-boled, spotted trunks of bee trees, they carve their five-fingered signatures with black, recurved claws. In the crotches of tropical oaks, they break tree limbs to create springy resting platforms for their up to 325-pound bulk. In glossy monsoon soils, they leave their footprints. With five rounded toes and a long heel pad on the back foot, their footsteps look like those of giant humans.

But you could spend years exploring these tangled rain forests and never see a moon bear. Instead, you would find them, as we did, caged in back of tourist hotels, chained outside of city pharmacies—and at markets like this one.

The pregnant woman doesn't ask what two young, well-dressed Cambodians, a sunburned blonde, and an American professor might want with a moon bear. She is an animal dealer. She knows that here in Cambodia, people buy bears for many reasons. They are treasured as household pets and kept as roadside attractions. They are sold for their meat and for their teeth. People eat their paws in soup and use their gall for medicine.

What *we* want from a moon bear, though, is stranger than the woman could possibly imagine. We want only to pluck out, with my eyebrow tweezers, a few of its hairs.

We already have a small zoo of hairs tucked in vials inside the professor's camera case. Each vial holds the genetic information of a bear captured from a different, known site. It is not the hair, per se, but its base, the living cells of the bulb, that contains the information we seek. After we return to the States, a laboratory in Idaho will extract from these specks of flesh the genetic information contained in each bear's DNA, and compare them.

In this way, we hope to document what could be the first new bear species to be reported in over a century.

But in order to do so, we need the hair of a black moon bear who has been captured in this province, a bear from the fragrant, misty forests of the Elephant Mountains.

The animal dealer says she *had* a moon bear for sale—but just that morning she'd sent it to Phnom Penh. For what? I ask Sun Hean. "For pet. For restaurant. I don't know," he answers. But the dealer does confirm that the bear had come from the rain-forested slopes of the Elephant Mountains. And there will be more where it came from.

Two mountain systems comprise most of the wilderness left in mainland Southeast Asia: with the adjoining Elephant Mountains and Cambodia's highest peak, Phnom Oral, the Cardamom range, occupying much of western Cambodia, huddles in the shape of a Q beneath a cloak of monsoon clouds. The rainfall here is the highest in Cambodia, and the jungles the most dense. The spice-scented forests harbor creatures beautiful, deadly, and ancient: clouded leopards, with spotted coats soft and thick as mist; tiny primitive deer called muntjacks, their upper jaws curiously spiked with fangs. There are more tigers here than anywhere else in the country, and, possibly, more wild elephants than anywhere else in Indochina. In similar habitat in neighboring Vietnam, scientists discovered in 1989 fresh tracks of the Javan rhinoceros species thought extinct on the mainland for nearly half a century; some think it might yet survive here, too.

The other, wildest mountains are the Annamites. In a great igneous spine, they run for more than six hundred miles from the northeastern corner of Cambodia up along the border of Vietnam and Laos. A mosaic of rain forest, dry evergreen woods, cypress and old-growth pine, the Annamites preserve, in the words of the great American wildlife conservationist George Schaller, "a living lost world." Four hundred species of birds have been cataloged here, a count only cursory. Of the roughly dozen large mammal species discovered in the world since 1900, nearly half of them—including a two hundred-pound antelope with spear-like horns, a giant, barking deer, and a zebra-striped rabbit—have been found, since 1992, in the Annamites.

Eventually our quest will lead us into both these mountain jungles. But before we would step into that wild and leafy realm, we would need to search its looking-glass opposites: private zoos, hotel menageries, and noisy, crowded streetside markets.

In Kampong Som, it appears that most of the wildlife is destined for the dinner plate. Along the street, where dentists advertise their services with large paintings of white, extracted teeth, a beautiful young woman, her hair tied up neatly beneath a conical hat, tends a charcoal fire over which skewered bats are roasting. In a pink plastic bowl beneath a dome of woven rattan, live frogs, tortoises, and cobras await the soup pot. In the palm oil of a neighboring vendor's wok, three-inch grasshoppers sizzle.

"Is there any animal that people don't eat here?" I asked Sun Hean.

He thought for a moment. "The vulture," he answered solemnly.

The scent of pigs' blood mingles with the fragrance of temple marigolds. To be looking for a new species here seems irreconcilably absurd.

But it is no more unlikely, really, than the way our expedition had begun.

*   *   *

The route that led to the market in Kampong Som was circuitous, winding from China to the Amazon, from Hancock, New Hampshire, to Bangkok, Thailand. I had come to Cambodia thanks to extraordinary coincidences and extraordinary people.

Dr. Gary J. Galbreath was one of them. A professor of evolutionary biology at Northwestern University and a research associate of the famous Field Museum, Gary had been president of the Chicago-based Rainforest Conservation Fund when it took on funding the Tamshiyacu-Tahuayo Community Reserve in Peru in 1991. We met there in 1997 when I was researching a book on the Amazon's pink river dolphins.

"Did you know," Gary asked me as our boat chugged up the tea-colored river, "this place used to be full of giant, carnivorous Terror Birds?"

No, I did not. This he quickly remedied.

"They were feathered dinosaurs, essentially, long after the dinosaurs went extinct," he began. "It's possible a human being even saw one. They were the dominant predators in South America during the Age of Mammals. The Terror Birds even made it to Florida—to Daytona Beach! They found some fossils there. But only twenty months ago their *arms* were found—and it turns out they weren't winged like we thought."

This modest, green-eyed, middle-aged professor had me mesmerized.

"They had evolved tearing arms, with two fingerlike projections to grab their prey," he continued. "The fingers are fused bones, like the panda's thumb. Terror Birds began to decline when dogs, cats, and bears came down from North America, three million years ago or so. And if that didn't do them in, then people came eleven to thirteen thousand years ago and killed off their prey, the giant ground sloths and zebras . . ."

I was next surprised to learn that zebras arose in North America; that horses are more closely related to dogs than pigs; that a friend of his had shot for dinner, and thus discovered, a new species of pig, the sweet-smelling Chacoan peccary, and that, as a graduate student, Gary had acquired a pair of armadillos who liked to sleep with him in his bed. But I was not surprised to learn—much later and from another biologist—that at Gary's last lecture of the year, his students gave him a standing ovation.

After each day's fieldwork, when the others' talk often turned to jobs or family, photography or politics, Gary and I would take a canoe out on the dark waters of the Tahuayo and talk about animals and evolution.

It was on one of those starry, timeless nights that he told me about the golden moon bear.

Gary had been a delegate of the American Society of Mammalogists for the group's first official meeting with its Chinese counterpart in Beijing, back in 1988. Afterward, he had traveled south, to explore the tropical rain forest of Yunnan Province with a small contingent of other biologists.

"We were in this little town in Yunnan called Simao. My friend, Penny, called me over. She said there was something I should see. And there, in this little cage—it was sort of like a town mascot, and taking peanuts, very gently, from people's hands—was this young male bear, maybe ninety kilos, with tall, round ears and a white V on the chest. But what was remarkable was, its coat was golden. I had never seen anything like it."

In fact, Gary was stunned. The biologist was facing a creature he could not identify.

Quickly, he sorted through his encyclopedic zoological memory. There were only eight known species of bear on Earth. Obviously this was not a polar bear, or a panda. Nor was it an American black bear—although "black bears" can be brown, cinnamon, blond, or even white, the ears on this animal were too big for an American black bear. It couldn't be a spectacled bear, a native of South America's Andean highlands. It looked nothing like one, having a longer snout than this short-faced bear, and lacked the circular white markings around the eyes that make the spectacled bear look like it is wearing glasses.

Besides the panda, four other bear species are known in Asia. Sun bears—named for the patch, often sunrise orange, on the chest—barely range into tropical Yunnan. But this clearly wasn't one. Sun bears, the smallest and most tree-loving of bears, have inconspicuous ears, short, jet fur, long claws, and huge, stout canines. Nor was this a sloth bear, also known from Asia's tropics—it has masses of fluffy, messy, black hair, unusually mobile lips, with which it sucks termites out of their hills like a vacuum hose, and nostrils it can slam shut to keep termites from crawling in. The only Asian bear with a coat that ever comes close to blond is the brown bear, the same species (although a different subspecies) as the American grizzly. But it is unknown from the tropics. The only Asian bear with big ears like this was a moon bear—but Gary had never heard of one with a golden coat.

He took photos, and so did his friend and colleague, physician Penny Walker. "I was photographing it in case it wasn't known," he said. "But what were the chances of my discovering a new bear? For all I knew, someone in the literature long ago described a blond bear like this."

The next day, at the Kunming natural history museum, Gary looked through the collection of moon bear skins. All of them were black. But during China's Cultural Revolution, all the specimens' tags were destroyed, so he had no idea where they came from—or even whether moon bears had ever before been recorded living in Yunnan.

"It was enough to excite interest," he said. "This was of potentially significant biological import." Variation in coat color is important to document, Gary explained; one of the biologist's principal tasks, after all, is to describe the natural world. An unreported color phase in an existing species is an exciting finding, akin to making the first reports of a black panther (which is a dark form of the normally black-and-gold spotted leopard) or a white tiger (a pale-coated form of the Royal Bengal tiger). But the golden bear could be a discovery far more spectacular. Gary knew from his postdoctoral work on New World owl monkeys that, in the absence of genetic analysis, coat color alone can serve as a way—sometimes the only way—to tell different species apart. If the golden bear represented a new species, it would be the scientific finding of a lifetime—the first new bear reported since the panda more than a hundred years before. "This could be a major biological discovery," Gary realized. "But I was telling myself, I'm sure these things were known . . ."

When he returned from China, Gary made an exhaustive search of the scientific literature. He checked explorers' accounts of zoological expeditions throughout Asia. He laboriously translated manuscripts from French and German. He discovered only one account of a bear from Southeast Asia that wasn't black—a 1906 report of a young male bear with brown hair tipped with gray. Secured from an animal dealer, it was said to have come from the Shan States of upper Burma and thought to be a kind of grizzly. It was tentatively given the subspecies name *Ursus arctos shanorum*. There was no mention of a blond bear. Anywhere.

Gary had always wanted to go back to Simao and find out more, he told me. But his demanding teaching load at Northwestern was compounded by his administrative duties as associate director of the undergraduate biology department. Besides, what were the chances that bear was still there? Several times, he had started to write up an account of the golden bear for scientific publication, then abandoned the idea. "This was just one specimen. It could have been a mutant individual—not a new color phase, not a new species, not anything."

Still, the image of that bear stayed with him for nine years. Like a siren, it beckoned him, nagged him, teased. He could not forget it—but he did not see how to pursue it, either: "There was only one," he said, "just one, weird bear."

Or so we thought—until one year later, when I met Sun Hean.

At a birthday party in the small New Hampshire town where I live, a friend brought a guest whose power and importance went largely unappreciated by the others. Shy and unsure of his English, with a round, boyish face, Sun Hean looked like a foreign graduate student, which he was. But he was also, although still in his twenties, the deputy director for the Wildlife Protection Office of Cambodia—the equivalent of the second in command of the United States' Fish and Wildlife Service.

I asked him about bears. Had he ever heard of a bear in his country that wasn't black?

His dark eyes widened. Yes—in fact, a member of his staff had just sent him photographs of a strange bear. It was the color of gold.

It was living in a cage just east of Kampong Som, the captive of a wealthy palm oil plantation owner. Sun Hean was fascinated by it; he didn't know what it was. Cambodia had two known species of bear, the sun and the moon bear. This one, with its mysterious golden coat, looked to him like neither.

I arranged for Sun Hean and Gary to meet. I, too, flew to meet Sun Hean at the University of Minnesota, where he was next sent for graduate studies as part of the Fulbright scholarship that had brought him to the United States. The two men compared their photographs of different animals, taken a thousand kilometers and eleven years apart. They were virtually identical.

We began to plan our expedition.

* * *

Few travel guides were available for Cambodia. The country was usually included in larger volumes mostly devoted to the safer and more alluring Thailand, or sometimes with Vietnam and Laos. The sections on Cambodia did not begin on a hopeful note. *Travelers' Companion* noted that the Phnom Penh English-language newspaper, *Bayon Pearnick,* carried helpful articles for visitors, such as "Keeping Your Head While Losing Your Wallet," and a story on the latest public safety effort, the designation of February 24 as National Mine Awareness Day. (In the 1980s, the government had also declared a National Hate Day, setting aside May 20 as a day for everyone to reaffirm his hatred of former Khmer Rouge leader Pol Pot.)

Cambodia is the most heavily mined country on earth, with four to eight million land mines, according to one estimate—at least one land mine for every man, woman, and child still left alive when the Khmer Rouge were overthrown in 1979. The Communist forces had seeded fields and forests with explosives, fashioned from 60-mm and 82-mm mortar shells and from sections of iron water pipes stuffed with TNT, sugar, fertilizer, and shrapnel. These were supplemented with Chinese pressure mines, small as a lady's compact but capable of blowing off a leg. They were hung from bushes, buried along paths, placed near wells, at riverbanks and around fruit trees—anywhere people would go. As a result, 1 in 236 Cambodians is an amputee. An Australian Red Cross doctor called the one-legged man "the most obvious characteristic of national identity." Some thirty-five thousand of Cambodia's citizens have lost a limb to a land mine, and according to the reports we read, another three hundred to seven hundred more injuries were being added to the list each month.

Compounding the injuries from land mines was the fact that doctors could do little to help. Cambodia had no decent medical care, we read. Foreigners who get hurt or sick in Cambodia are advised to evacuate to Bangkok. Most of Cambodia's doctors were killed by the Khmer Rouge, who also destroyed most of the hospitals. Those who remain have no pharmaceuticals. The local life expectancy listed in our guide was 40. "According to this, we should both be dead already!" Gary noted when he read the statistic.

In his thorough manner, Gary had searched for travel information before we departed that summer. He had printed out, among other things, a report on Cambodia by The Control Risk Group Ltd., which prepares what it touts as up-to-the-minute online advisories for business travelers. In June 1999, it rated Cambodia thus:

> Political Risk Rating: *high*
> Security Risk Rating: *high*
> Travel Risk Rating: *high*

In the mid-nineties, the Khmer Rouge had been the main safety concern for foreigners in Cambodia, as the infrequent Western visitor was an easy target for terrorists. In 1994, the Communist rebels had kidnapped, in two separate incidents, four Britons, an Australian, and a Frenchman, three of whom were tourists. All were later murdered.

But by the time we were planning our travels, Sun Hean had assured us the Khmer Rouge were "no problem." When we had met in Minnesota, he had mapped out our route: from Phnom Penh, we would drive west, through the Elephant Mountains, to Kampong Som. We would then take a ferry to Koh Kong, and further explore the Cardamom range.

"Road travel outside cities is not recommended," Gary read to me from his risk report—not only because of land mines, but also because of antigovernment guerrillas. The Communist guerrillas' field forces had swelled to eighteen thousand in the early 1990s, and supplied with Chinese weapons, were said to be concentrated at our destination—the Cardamom Mountains. And the road to the port of Kampong Som, the report said, was potholed and thronged with bandits.

I had heard about the bandits. "Government soldiers, as well as Khmer Rouge rebels, sometimes resort to highway robbery," I read to Gary from a 1996 travel guide. "Bandits regularly hold travelers at gunpoint as they point torches into the eyes of long-distance taxi drivers—who now build the extortion money into the cost of a trip."

"The bandits might take our money," Gary resolved, "but they're not getting our bear hairs!"

Later, we found Cambodia listed in the 2000 edition of *The World's Most Dangerous Places*. "Don't be fooled," wrote its author, Robert Young. "With the demise of the Khmer Rouge, the violence simply doesn't make as many headlines." A pamphlet that the United Nations–sponsored peacekeeping unit had issued its soldiers and workers in 1992 contained Khmer phrases Young felt would be still useful to travelers today:

"That's a very nice gun, sir. I'd be honored to give you the gift of my truck."

* * *

We got a good deal on air tickets from Korean Air Lines—no doubt because we would fly roughly the same route that the ill-fated KAL Flight 007 had plotted before it was shot down over Kamchatka in the 1980s. Surely every passenger on board had the same thought as we watched the map on our personal video screens showing our plane skirting Russian airspace—all except Gary. "Look," he said cheerfully. "We're flying over Kamchatka—where the really giant bears live!"

For thirteen hours, on our flight from Chicago to Seoul, and then on the five-hour flight from Seoul to Bangkok, we talked bears.

"According to Ognev," he said, citing the great Russian zoologist, "there are two kinds of grizzlies on the Kamchatka Peninsula: one the size of the American grizzly, the other the size of a Kodiak." These bears were giant enough—an American grizzly can weigh 700 pounds, and a male Kodiak, 1,800 pounds. But there could be a third, even larger. Siberian hunters claim that Arctodus-like bears may also survive there—bears twice the size of a Kodiak.

Arctodus simus, the giant short-faced bear, was the largest terrestrial carnivore that ever lived. On long legs, it raced after zebras, camels, and bison and brought them down with a bite from canines larger than a leopard's. It would have been far swifter than a grizzly (who can, for short periods, run forty miles an hour) and more ferocious than a cave lion. For the first humans who invaded North America, Arctodus would have been a horrifying predator. "No kill by hunters would have been defensible against this beast, no hut would have been safe at night; no human would have been able to outrun this bear; and few trees would have been present or tall enough to climb for safety in the open country where it roamed," the wildlife biologist Valerius Geist wrote of the creature. In fact, the Canadian scientist suggests that it was this bear that slowed the immigration of humans from Asia to the New World. So agile and predatory a beast, he writes, would have "made human life in North America impossible. Only when this fauna collapsed did humans make inroads."

Arctodus was believed extinct by the late Pleistocene, twelve thousand years ago. Might it still survive? "Occasionally a hunter shows a TV crew what he claims is a skin of one," Gary said. He doubted it; but we both savored the thought. We wanted more bears.

Bears were special animals to both of us, for a variety of reasons. Gary had always been impressed by their size and ferocity. "They're big, and even as a youngster I liked that about them," he said, his green eyes glowing with childhood daydreams. "You think of them as being, in the temperate zone, at the top of the heap, like the lion in Africa or the tiger in Asia."

Besides, for Gary—whose passion for mysteries extended to devouring whodunits and even to loving algebra (since it required solving for the unknown)—the bear clan offered a fascinating taxonomic puzzle. "Nearly everywhere there have been bears, there have been arguments about how many different types there are," he said.

The varied appearance of grizzlies shows the common name for the species, brown bear, is a misnomer. He prefers to call them all grizzlies. For instance, the so-called red bear or Himalayan grizzly, also known as the Isabelline bear, *Ursus arctos isabellinus,* can be reddish, brown, yellow, or even white. There's a blue bear, also considered a grizzly, *Ursus arctos pruinosus,* who lives on the Tibetan plateau, whose coat is grayish-black, with a blond face. In Turkey, Iran and Iraq survive the last of a lighter-coated grizzly, *Ursus arctos syriacus.* And there are grizzlies of all different shapes, sizes and habits in between. A dwarf grizzly survives in the Gobi Desert of Mongolia; ten-foot-long grizzlies patrol the taiga of Russia's Vladivostok area. On Admiralty Island live huge, coal-black grizzlies. They, DNA studies now show, are the closest relatives of the polar bears—who are among nature's more recent inventions. The polar bear is a species less than half a million years old.

"And what about moon bears?" I asked. "Where do they fit in?"

"Ah!" said Gary. This was his favorite sort of question, for it required him to travel back in time. "Moon bears are the least changed of all the Old World bears," he said. "You could even argue they are the lineage from which most other Old World bears evolved." Four million years ago, a small bear now known as *Ursus minimus* ("small bear") appeared in Eurasia—an animal about the size of a modern sun bear, perhaps a hundred pounds. But other than its size, "*Ursus minimus* probably looked much like a moon bear," Gary said. "So much so, in fact, that except for the age of the bones, it would be extremely difficult to distinguish fossils of *Ursus minimus* from the skeleton of a living moon bear."

In the temperate and subtropical forests of Eurasia, this early bear was a generalist, able to thrive in a variety of habitats, Gary explained. It could climb trees but was not restricted to thick forest. It could eat meat, but could survive on plants, too. As the climate continued to cool and the world became seasonal, the descendants of *Ursus minimus* were able to outlast the Eurasian lions and hippos who had been its cohorts in the Pliocene and Pleistocene. It was this moon bearlike creature—not the ferocious, short-faced Arctodus—that gave rise, in the turbulent ice ages of the Pleistocene, to all the modern bears except the South American spectacled bear and the enigmatic panda.

Gary took his greatest delight in exploring the origin of things. By the time he was in second grade, he had already memorized the geologic time scale, as well as the scientific names for most of the major animals in each. He kept an extensive collection of plastic dinosaurs, as well as a scrapbook for clippings about rare and vanishing animals: rhinos and elephants, a living legacy of the Pleistocene—like bears are.

As a child, Gary's deepest wish had been for a time machine. But as a grown-up scientist, his greatest dream was to discover and to name a new species in our own time. The golden bear offered him a shot at every biologist's Holy Grail.

For me, bears held a different fascination. I knew several personally. In New Hampshire, a friend of mine, wildlife rehabilitator Ben Kilham, had rescued several litters of orphaned American black bears when they were so young that their noses were still pink and their eyes still blue. I had held some of these babies in my arms. When they were youngsters, I had watched them gambol in the northern woods, smelling and licking their way through a realm no human can experience. Their world is a symphony of scent, so rich in information, Ben came to understand, that bears may even be able to assess the nutritional and perhaps medicinal properties of plants with nose and tongue. I would return home feeling blessed by another world, redolent with the heady, musky, rich-earth smell of their fur, the caress of their wet, ribbonlike tongues still tingling my skin.

With Ben and with other wildlife biologists, I had also tracked wild, radio-collared black bears through the woods of Massachusetts and Vermont. One of the bears I followed was a ten-year-old female known as Number 125. Bear biologist John McDonald and his colleagues had studied her for eight years, tracking her each winter to her den to tranquilize, weigh, and examine her and her generations of cubs.

One February, we had followed the beep of the telemetry receiver to Number 125's shallow den beneath a slab of granite. Before John had a chance to warn me, and before the veterinarian had tranquilized her, I wedged my face into its opening. I looked directly into the mahogany eyes and tan muzzle of a fully alert mother bear and her two cubs.

My face was inches from her jaws. But I was never for a moment afraid. I knew that American black bears, unlike grizzly bears, almost never attack people. They do not consider us prey and are far more likely to flee than to strike out, even in defense of cubs. I knew that this female was probably more mortified than angry to see me, a hideous human, invading the sanctity of her nursery. But I knew something else as well. Meeting her eyes, I recognized in her brown gaze an ancient knowing, a cognizance remarkably humanlike, and yet more-than-human.

Humans have known this about bears since the dawn of our kind. For possibly as long as fifty thousand years, festivals of the bear ceremonies have celebrated the bear as a sacred messenger and mediator, a teacher, a traveler between worlds. Throughout human history, people have claimed kinship with them. Bears are strikingly humanlike: when they stand on their hind legs, when they sit, back against a tree, their postures look like ours, their front legs hanging down like arms. Their hands are dexterous enough to peel a peach. (The Blackfoot Indian word for the human hand is the same as the word for bear paw.) They are so intelligent that skilled trackers like Pennsylvania-based bear biologist Gary Alt has documented them outwitting people by causing their own tracks to vanish—by carefully backtracking. Ben Kilham considers bears at least as smart as chimps, though the animals are very different. In so many ways, bears mirror, then exceed us: in strength, in size, in sensory acuity. So we have made them our teachers, our mentors, our inspiration. The Khanty and Mansi people of Siberia say they received fire and weapons from the world's first bear. Many Native American tribes say the bear taught them the use of medicinal herbs. (And bears may in fact number among the animals documented to use plants as medicine. Just one example: an Alaskan hunting guide watched, puzzled, as a grizzly methodically stripped the bark from a willow shrub, which bears don't normally eat. He shot the bear and noticed the bear had an abscessed tooth—around which was packed willow bark, the source of salicylic acid, the active ingredient in aspirin.) The fierce Germanic warriors, the Berserks, took their name from the beast, and wore its skin in an effort to take on bear magic.

These northern peoples saw bears perform the impossible each spring. Emerging from the deathly still of hibernation out of gravelike dens, bears rise, Christlike, from the dead. The wise female bear, like the grandmother I had met in her den, brings forth her young from the earth itself, a netherworld Genetrix. Perhaps it was the bear who taught us to expect miracles. Some researchers suggest this is why humans bury their dead, trusting the bear's promise of transformation.

The Ostyaks, of western Siberia, say the bear began as a heavenly force, born of a union between the sun and moon. The bear still dwells in the sky. Ursa Major dominates the northern night, making its passage around the Pole Star in Ursa Minor, the star that has guided our kind for millennia, and given us our aptly named "bearings." At both ends of the universe, from the underworld den to the sky, the bear helps us find our place in the renewing cycle of the cosmos.

So, for our different reasons, Gary and I both saw, in this bear, opportunities as golden as its mysterious and intriguing coat. Whether we would describe a new species or an unknown color phase; whether we would witness miracles or achieve transformation; whether our story would lead to renewal or frustration—of course we could not know. But we were willing to follow a bear into a mine field to find out.

* * *

If he had anything like a totem animal, Gary mused on the plane, it would be the bear. The sole emblem on the Galbreath family crest, he said, is the head of a bear in a muzzle.

The symbol suggests controlled power. The Montgomery family crest, on the other hand, suggests unbridled rage: it shows a woman holding up the severed head of her enemy. This might have alarmed another traveler about to spend six weeks with a member of such a clan. But Gary, ever generous and optimistic, took this as a good sign. He noted that Galbreath means "foreign mercenary" and Gary means "spear-carrier." On paper, at least, we made a ferocious combination. "Considering where we're going," Gary had told me, "we should make an exceptionally successful team."

But in the fever-dream jumble of the market at Kampong Som, I have my doubts.

In the migrainous heat, an old woman spits blood on the dirt. No; she is chewing betel, the nutmeg-sized fruit of the graceful *Areca* palm. It produces a mild narcotic that reddens the saliva and stains the teeth black. The woman looks up at me and, parting bloodied lips, offers me a shocking, generous, grandmotherly smile—and then returns to tending a brace of skewered songbirds on the grill. Their eyes have melted, their beaks burned black.

We drive on to seek another bear.

CHAPTER TWO

The Bears of Phnom Penh

Finding bears usually proved alarmingly easy, as we had discovered long before we reached Kampong Som.

On our very first day in Cambodia, Sun Hean had insisted on chauffeuring us around Phnom Penh—a kindness we feared we might not survive. A flotilla of four motorcycles passed our car on the left to run a red light. "In United States," Sun Hean mused, "at a light like this, you stop . . ."

A homemade, two-wheeled carriage soldered to the front half of a motorcycle rattled past us, crammed with five passengers. In Cambodia the contraption is called a cyclo. (In the Laotian town of Savannakhet, the three-wheeler is more ominously called a "Skylab" after the doomed space station that crashed into Australia.) It screamed into the impossibly narrow space in front of us, between a taxi and two bicyclists, one of whom was balancing several shopping bags and a baby. A truck barreled toward us, in our lane.

" . . . and if you turn," Sun Hean continued, "in America, you have to wait. Here, the way you want to go, you go." It was only two years before, Sun Hean explained, that the government began to restore traffic lights to Phnom Penh after an absence of thirty years. "Now, no one remember them," he said. Drivers regard them as they might Christmas tree decorations, with no idea what they're for.

Sun Hean's calm behind the wheel was dazzling, especially considering the Camry he was driving had been borrowed from his future father-in-law. But in his short life, Sun Hean had confronted challenges even more dangerous and demanding than driving in Phnom Penh traffic.

He had seen an uncle murdered by political enemies. As a young man, he had to live in a shack the size of a toilet stall, and learned to sleep through the sound of exploding land mines.

In high school, when Cambodia was under Vietnamese rule, Sun Hean had been forced to study Russian, as English was prohibited. After the Vietnamese left, Russian became useless and English essential. So he learned English too—so well that he was hired, after graduating from forestry college in 1992, as a translator for the United Nations Traditional Authority. He was sometimes sent to areas occupied by Khmer Rouge guerrillas, where his nights were punctuated by gunfire and exploding land mines. But he earned two hundred dollars a month, most of which he sent home to his family.

His association with foreigners paid off in other ways. In 1995, impressed with his intellect and drive, American mentors recommended him for a conservation training course sponsored by the Smithsonian Institution—a course that sent him outside Cambodia for the first time, to Thailand and Malaysia. It was then that wildlife conservation piqued his interest. "Before that time," he told us, "I don't care about wildlife conservation. The government give you fifteen dollars a month. Conservation can't make you rich."

But he soon fell in love with wildlife, with wilderness, and the idea of preserving his country's rich natural heritage. His travels changed him. The son of a rice farmer in a country where most people don't leave their native province, before his thirtieth birthday he had visited fifteen countries. "In other countries, everybody is interested in Cambodian wildlife conservation," he told us. "I go into the forest and see animals. This make me more comfortable with conservation."

What about getting rich? "I don't care about that now," he said. "I can survive."

In 1992, Cambodia created the Wildlife Protection Office within its

Department of Forestry and Wildlife. Sun Hean was quickly promoted to the head of its Wildlife Conservation Department. In 1997, he was named deputy director of the entire office. In 1998, he was awarded the Fulbright scholarship that brought him to America. I happened to know Sun Hean's academic adviser at the University of Minnesota. David Smith studied tigers and sloth bears for more than twenty years in Royal Chitawan National Park in Nepal, the site of an innovative and respected conservation program. David is not extravagant with praise, but he said this about Sun Hean: "I think he's maybe the leading light for conservation in Cambodia."

Many Americans now associate Cambodia with the sound of machine gun fire; but to Norman Lewis, the very name Cambodia "was always accompanied in my imagination by tinkling, percussive music," as he wrote after his visit there in 1950. Its capital, Phnom Penh, was the beguiling beauty of Southeast Asia. French colonial villas and elegant monuments were set along gracious boulevards shaded by flowering trees. Beneath the glittering green, gold, and blue tile roofs of the royal palace, monks knelt and chanted in the Pagoda of the Emerald Buddha; in a pavilion called the Shadow of the Moon, classical dancers in brocades and jewels performed for the king.

Now the dancers and their king are gone, as are most of the city's old graces. The royal palace is still there, but the Khmer Rouge damaged or destroyed two thirds of Phnom Penh's housing, including most of the beautiful old mansions. They also systematically dismembered the city's plumbing network before they left in 1979. Everywhere, along crumbling streets lined with yellowing cement buildings, the smells of mangoes, fried pastries, and car exhaust mingle with the stench of human excrement.

Sun Hean called it "people mud." When we got out of the spotless Camry—scented aggressively with vanilla from the half-pint of car perfume on the dash—he advised us, like a museum guide warning tourists to stay behind the velvet rope, to be careful where we stepped.

But there were to be no museums or monuments on this city tour. We had come for bears, so our solicitous host would provide them. He was, in fact, taking us on a tour of bears in residence around the city.

On our first day in his country, he would not only give us a glimpse of our quarry but also an idea of what he, a wildlife conservationist in a country where most people don't know the concept or the word, was up against.

* * *

We stopped first at a tiny dirt street. Here, next to a noodle stall, a skinny yearling bear lived imprisoned in a wretched little wire cage with a chain around her neck. She reminded me of a street waif. She put a tender, orange-soled paw up to the wire of the cage, as if begging for her freedom. She stared at us with haunted eyes. Sun Hean shuttled us back into the car. We next drove to a pharmacy, Nakor Thom, whose successful French proprietors lived next door in a palm-shaded mansion. In front, protected by a barbed-wire overhang, lived an adult male bear, sleeping on a shaded platform inside a nineteen-foot enclosure overhung with blooming pink bougainvillea. Across the street, Sun Hean said, lived two more bears—but the gate to the residence was locked, so we couldn't see them.

We visited the Hotel Goldiana, popular with American travelers with budgets more generous than our own. We skipped its restaurant and spacious, mirrored lobby; we went straight to the dingy, cement-floored corner between the basement and the backyard. There, in filthy cages scarcely bigger than their bodies, we found two magnificent crested porcupines, huge rodents with bewildered, beaverlike faces. They weighed perhaps fifty pounds, their hindquarters arrayed like peacocks' tails with thick, banded, black-and-white quills nearly a foot long, capable of disabling a tiger. In another cage we found a banded palm civet, an agile, striped carnivore with retractile claws like a cat's. She stared at us defiantly. Another cage held a crowd of rabbits piled atop one another like laundry, with eyes lifeless as lead.

Worst of all was the pileated gibbon. She was, like us, a tailless ape. We shared an ancestor perhaps only twenty-five million years ago. Though speechless, her voice was richer than ours. At dawn, these apes whoop elaborate, elastic songs that seem to coax the sun to rise in the sky on their escalating notes. The songs are usually duets between pairs, mates for life. Her arms were as long as ours—nearly the length of the rest of her body, built for swinging from branch to branch in rain forest trees. In the wild, she could have covered ten feet in a single swing of an arm. She was confined, alone, to a cage so small she could barely stand. She looked out from its bars, stunned and hopeless.

The hotel also had a bear once, Sun Hean told us, but now it was gone. We were glad.

We drove on. We passed vendors selling stacks of fried pastries, plastic buckets, and huge ceramic piggy banks shaped like rabbits, symbols of good luck. We pulled up at a fancy restaurant. Sun Hean led us to the back, where a fifteen by fifteen-foot cage with a dirty cement floor housed two female bears. They had lived here for three years. A young man who worked as a keeper spoke with us as Sun Hean translated: "When the bear is well, he is nice animal, like a friend," he told us. But the bears are not always well. As we stood talking, a little boy—perhaps four years old—toddled with his parents to the back of the restaurant. Seeing the bears, he tossed a rock into their cage. The boy shrieked with delight that he hit one of the captives on her side.

"The people poke them with sticks," the young keeper told us. "They make them crazy." He pulled up the leg of his left trouser to reveal a series of scars from puncture wounds along his ankle and shin, where one of the bears, crazed with frustration, had bitten him. He had been hospitalized for a month.

All the bears we saw that day were sun bears. With small ears, wide, round faces and short velvety coats, they are the least bearlike bears on Earth, and among the smallest. They typically weigh less than a hundred pounds, about the size of a big dog. I have shown pictures of sun bears to people, even Cambodians, only to have them insist they are really dogs. The loose skin of the face makes them look rather like Rotweillers. Light and lithe, sun bears are excellent tree-climbers and also stand frequently on two legs. When they saw us approach their cage, the two sun bears in the restaurant both rose to their feet, as you would to greet a guest. They staggered forward like sleepwalkers, their long-clawed paws held out in front of them.

Sun bears prefer lowland rain forest, while moon bears prefer mountains. Sun bears are more numerous in Cambodia than moon bears, Sun Hean said. But there were plenty of moon bears around the city. The locked residence across the street from the pharmacy had a moon bear, and the vanished ursine at the Goldiana had been a moon bear, too. It was just bad luck we hadn't seen any that day.

Keeping bears as pets, hunting them in the wild, or selling them to others is illegal in Cambodia, Sun Hean explained. But these regulations, like most others, are largely ignored. Later, we secured an interview with His Excellency the Undersecretary of State of the Ministry of Agriculture, who was also Chair of the Management Authority of CITES, the Convention on International Trade in Endangered Species, to which Cambodia was a recent signatory. Speaking through Sun Hean, Chhun Sarreth was charming and affable, a smiling man with a prominent scar shaped like barbed wire on his right temple. Near the end of our conversation about the need to protect Cambodian wildlife, we learned to our astonishment that His Excellency owned a sun bear—who, until recently, had lived in the house. It got along well with his dog but had begun to tear up the furniture. Now, he wanted to give it away. There was no room for it at the zoo, and the paperwork to export it to a foreign zoo was too clumsy. Perhaps, he asked us hopefully, he could just let it go?

There were many other bears in the city we did not see. "Twenty, thirty bears I know, live in Phnom Penh," Sun Hean said. He made it clear these were just the individuals he knew of personally; "Many more, really." How many, no one knew. Perhaps hundreds.

Gary and I gasped. Even with its bad plumbing and crumbling buildings, Phnom Penh is still a nation's capital. We tried to imagine Washington, D.C., with hundreds of people keeping bears in their apartments.

* * *

Bears have been kept as pets for centuries in Asia. Because they are so agile and intelligent, and because they can walk and stand up like us, they have been trained to dance, roller skate, ride bicycles, and walk on stilts, sometimes dressed in coats and top hats. In Russia, there was an Academy for Training Young Bears in Samourgun in the nineteenth century. In China, performing giant pandas were the centerpiece of the traditional circus. One photo we have seen shows a panda riding a giant rocking horse in a circus ring. In Turkey, India, and Greece, despite humane agencies' efforts to stop the practice, bears still dance alongside street performers, and live with their owners in traveling caravans. Moon bears are particularly prized because they can be trained to walk upright for more than a quarter of a mile.

Despite laws against keeping wildlife captive, bears are often kept as pets in Chinese villages. They serve as watchdogs, deterring strangers and warning of their approach. They sometimes even help with household chores, carrying laundry with their owners from river to home. In Thailand, Buddhist monks sometimes keep bears at their temples, believing they will earn merit for the next life for their kindness to animals. In Taiwan, Westerners are surprised to find people walking pet sun bears on leashes and riding in taxis in downtown Taipei.

But even as they are valued as companions and performers, bears are coveted far more in Asia for a different purpose: to be cut up, sometimes while still alive, so their body parts can be eaten as delicacies or sold as medicine.

So prized are bear parts that forty live sun and moon bears were smuggled out of Thailand into South Korea, where their meat, blood, and gallbladders were used to fortify the Korean 1988 Olympic team. So effective are the bear remedies thought that Hyundai Corporation's elderly ex-president, Jung Ju Young, publicly credits his excellent health to regular supplements of bear bile. And so accepted is the eating of bears that a *Singapore Business Times* reporter found soft-fried bear paw served at the state-run restaurant in the Beijing Zoo in the early 1990s. In response to his questions, a waiter replied, "This is the place where people come to see animals, so doesn't it make sense that you can also try them?"

In Native American tradition, the bear is said to have taught man the use of medicinal herbs; in oriental tradition, the bear *is* the medicine. Bear blood is believed to cure nervousness in children. The bones are said to treat rheumatism. The fat is prescribed to cure baldness, remove pimples, treat colds, darken hair, sharpen wits, and prevent hunger. Eating the paw is said to ward off colds, cure beriberi, and generally revitalize the body, especially the hands. The gallbladder is the part most prized. Along with rhino horn, it is the most coveted medicine in the oriental pharmacopoeia. For three thousand years, the Chinese have considered the bile salts in bear gall a "cold" medicine, believed to extinguish the "heat" of illnesses like diabetes, high blood pressure, burns, eye infections, sprains, hemorrhoids, tooth decay, cirrhosis, and heart problems. It is especially valued as a treatment for serious liver disease, in a part of the world where hepatitis is rampant and rates for liver cancer can run thirty-five times that of the United States. And in fact, the medicinal properties of bear gall are real: ursodeoxycholic acid (UDCA), its active ingredient, was isolated in 1927, and chemically synthesized in 1955. It is now used in a number of prescription and over-the-counter remedies around the world, including Summit Pharmaceuticals' drug Actigall, which dissolves gallstones without surgery. Synthetic UDCA is pure and cheap—about sixteen cents per pill. Yet, in many areas of China, captive bears are actually "farmed" for their bile, confined to small cages with tubes or needles stuck in their sides. The proprietors of 247 bear farms collect more than 15,400 pounds of bear bile a year. Bears often chew their paws to cope with the pain. Despite the availability of synthetic UDCA, despite the practice of farming bears for their gall, most of Asia looks to wild bears for this product—it is widely believed bile from a bear is better, and bile from a wild bear is best. Collected from wild animals that are shot, trapped, and snared, bear bile salts, looking like broken pieces of brown glass, are ground up and mixed into ointments, decocted into wine, and stuffed into capsules, often with other ingredients such as civet musk and ground pearls.

"At one time," wrote Judy Mills and Christopher Servheen in a report for TRAFFIC USA, the wildlife trade monitoring program for World Wildlife Fund, "there were so many bears and so few people that using bears as medicine, food and pets probably did little harm to the sustainability of wild bear populations." But now there are over 1 billion potential bear consumers in China alone. And with a surge in wealth, during the 1980s, in countries like Hong Kong, Japan, Singapore, and Taiwan, prices for bear products skyrocketed: on the black market, bear gall is as valuable as China White heroin, sometimes bringing eighteen times the price of gold.

This lucrative trade "has put a price on the head of every bear, making all of them worth more dead than alive," concluded Mills and Servheen. In response to the growing scarcity of Asia's sun and moon bears, some sources say Asian wildlife traffickers are now poaching grizzlies, polar bears, and North American black bears. Summarizing their year-long investigation of the Asian bear trade, Mills and Servheen called the trade in bears and bear body parts "a blueprint for extinction."

Sun Hean knows well the extent of the trade in endangered species. "One company ask me to sign a permit to export thirty thousand python skins," he told us as he drove. "They just want my signature—and they pay me for each piece! To sign that document, I can make fifteen thousand dollars! But no—I can't."

The greed that Sun Hean eschews feeds an illegal trade so widespread in Cambodia that endangered animals and their body parts are sold openly on the streets of the capital.

One day, he took us to Rue 166, a street once paved but now crumbling, thronged with motorcycles, cars, pedestrians, beggars, shoppers, just a few minutes' drive from our hotel. We stopped at the open storefront of Number 47. Sun Hean told us to leave our cameras and notebooks behind. We should not ask questions, he told us; and he warned us not to cry out at what we would see.

At first glance, Number 47 seemed an ordinary Third World market on an ordinary street. Flickering fluorescent lights bounced off the tile floor. Burlap sacks brimmed with fragrant leaves and chips of wood. A bamboo basket held dried mushrooms, big as cantaloupes. But in the next basket, we saw strips of what appeared to be warty, shriveled skin. These were pieces of the hides of highly endangered—and internationally protected—Asian elephants.

Our inventory continued: Large bowls of dried starfish, platters of tiger and bear teeth, stacks of flattened bodies of tiny primates called lorises, dozens of antlers and horns from deer and wild cattle, a pile of elephant penises. A large tiger skin and the skins of three sun bears were pinned to the back wall. Dried snakes coiled like wire hung overhead, while from a rafter sheets of python skins stretched floor to ceiling like curtains. On a shelf we saw six, nine-foot-long strips of gray leather, pierced with coarse black hairs longer and thicker than boar bristle. These were the severed, dried tails of Asian elephants. They were supposed to bring good luck. A glass case held four sun bear skulls—mere curios. Two of them had been cubs, Gary said, noting the sutures of their skulls had not yet fused.

The proprietor, a woman my age, smiled at Sun Hean and greeted him with a nod. She knew perfectly well he was the deputy director of the nation's Wildlife Protection Office. She also knew the status of the goods she was selling according to both Cambodian and international law.

"All is *il*-legal!" Sun Hean said in disgust when we got back into the Camry.

"But why," Gary asked, "can't you confiscate this?"

"This is private residence," Sun Hean said with a sigh, "so we cannot confiscate." To transform your "store" into a "private residence," all you have to do is sleep there. In this way, you are subject to an entirely different set of laws.

Because of this loophole, officers from nearly half a dozen local and national agencies must sign papers in advance of a raid on a house. Then, a posse of up to ten people must be organized to arrive at the residence. Of course, this takes weeks. Word of this complicated plan invariably reaches the shop owner in advance. Forewarned, the shop owner may also be forearmed. "They can kill you," Sun Hean said. Interpol considers wildlife the second-largest illegal trade in the world, after drugs, and many illegal wildlife traders are also involved in arms dealing. Wildlife dealers are as well organized as Mafia gangsters, and as dangerous.

"There is restaurant I know that serve bear paw," Sun Hean told us. "But they know very well who you are. If you are new people, they have bear paw to serve you." But when Sun Hean comes through their door, the item vanishes from the menu.

This culinary practice is particularly gruesome because the bear is not always killed before the paw is removed, Sun Hean told us. The left front paw is usually amputated first; it is said to be the sweetest because with this hand, the people believe, the bear scoops out honey. Being expensive commodities, the other paws stay freshest on a living creature. The doomed animal is left to limp on bloody stumps until all four paws are eaten. Friends of ours in Bangkok confirmed that this was true there, too; friends of theirs lived next to a Korean restaurant, and their nights were sometimes rent by the horrifying, humanlike screams of suffering bears. After they complained, the noise stopped. They later found the restaurant owners had changed their procedure. Now they cut the bears' vocal cords so they could not cry out loud.

International humane agencies find this cruelty so distressing that several operate within Phnom Penh to try to rescue captive bears. "People complain to my office, why don't you do something about that?" Sun Hean said. "But it is very difficult."

He organized a group to try to raid that restaurant and confiscate the bear for the zoo. "But by that time," Sun Hean said, "the bear is gone!" Even on the rare occasions that such raids succeed, first-time offenders are punished only by confiscation; there is not even a fine.

* * *

Of course, Gary and I realized, the fact that there were so many bears in captivity was a boon for us. We had little hope of blundering into the jungle just in time for an undiscovered bear to amble past our cameras. In the nearly two decades I have lived in New Hampshire, a state so full of bears they've been known to steal cooling pies off back porches in bad acorn years, I have never happened on a wild bear in the woods; I have found them only in the company of biologists following collared bears with radio-telemetry. In all his years growing up in rural Kentucky, Gary had never seen one there; they had long been exterminated from his state. The only wild bears he had seen were at Yellowstone, during family vacations. Black bears walked up to cars to beg food from tourists. He had also once seen a single grizzly, on a hillside next to the road where his father had pulled over the car. Seeing the family, the bear crashed away through the brush.

In fact, most of the new mammals recently discovered in Southeast Asia have not been found in the wild. "Discoveries are made not in the depths of the forest," as George Schaller has observed, "but in village huts and markets." With fellow Wildlife Conservation Society field biologists, Schaller discovered two species of barking deer, living in a private menagerie run by an army general in the Annamite Mountains, on different trips there in the mid-nineties. One was a new, giant muntjack unknown to science; another was a rediscovery of a species of which only a single, dubious specimen was known from sixty years before. With a Laotian colleague, Schaller documented a species of yellowish, long-snouted pig after his party had dined on its meat in a villager's hut. The scientists saved the bones; the unique measurements and DNA analysis later showed they had rediscovered the Vietnamese warty hog, not seen by scientists since 1892 and known, at the time, only from two skulls in the Shanghai Museum, one of which had disappeared. (Biologist Colin Groves had relocated it, unregistered but labeled in the same nineteenth-century biologist's handwriting, in the collection of the Institute of Zoology in Beijing in July 1996.) British biologist Rob Timmins found a new species of short-eared, zebra-striped rabbit by noticing its pelt for sale while shopping for groceries at a Laotian market in 1998. The first of the new large mammals to be discovered that decade was the Sao la, an oryxlike antelope described by biologists Do Tuoc and John MacKinnon in 1992 after finding sets of its horns in villages in Vietnam.

So why should we not be able to find a new species under similar circumstances here in Cambodia? Sun Hean was understandably miffed that all these Southeast Asian discoveries had been made in Vietnam and Laos, but not Cambodia. "Cambodia is better than Vietnam," he told us with patriotic pride. "That has a very long shape. Laos: a long shape. Thailand: long. But Cambodia is perfect. It's, like, round, you know."

Sun Hean's auspiciously shaped homeland certainly held much promise for conservation. Cambodia retains much of its forest, covering more than 60 percent of the nation—the largest extent of natural forest in mainland Southeast Asia. It is sparsely populated: just over eleven million people in a country the size of Wisconsin. Yet, of the nations of Indochina, Cambodia is the least surveyed by wildlife biologists—because, notes a 1998 World Wildlife Fund report, "the uncertain security situation . . . limits the ability to implement conservation recommendations from surveys." Cambodia, as Sun Hean saw it, was overdue for its share of biological discoveries, and for the prestige and conservation dollars that would flow as a result.

To that end, he had good news for us: since we had met in Minnesota to talk about the Kampong Som bear, he had heard of yet another golden bear. It was living in a zoo founded by a one-armed senator in the province of Prey Veng, just 100 kilometers east of Phnom Penh. We would be able to see it before we left Phnom Penh for Kampong Som. We made plans to go there the next day.

* * *

The morning we set out for Prey Veng, I was nervous. Gary was the senior scientist on our expedition; Sun Hean was our logistical chief. My contribution to science was to stick my hand into a cage with a live bear in it, and pull out some of its hair.

I was the logical person for the job. My hands were smaller than those of my companions, and I was skilled at fine motor skills like embroidery (my first badge in Girl Scouts had been for Needlework). But I didn't think the bear would like it.

I'd tried to prepare for my task, using my own eyebrows for practice. In front of the bathroom mirror, I experimented with different techniques, hoping to discover what would be least annoying to the bear. An annoyed bear is something best avoided. As a bon voyage gesture, a friend who had worked as a geologist in Alaska lent me her copy of *Alaska Bear Tales*—a chronicle, basically, of bears people had annoyed, and the human body parts that had been removed as a result. "The fact is," wrote its author, Larry Kaniut, "when bears attack, blood usually flows."

Bears can hurt you even without meaning to. Ben Kilham was constantly bruised and bleeding from the attentions of his cubs. They sliced him with their claws as they climbed him like a tree. They also gave him huge hickeys from sucking on his neck, trying to nurse. Later they switched to his ears, and he worried he would end up looking like Vincent van Gogh. As they got older, when annoyed, they would not infrequently deliver what Ben called "message bites." What was a message bite? "If you weren't getting the message," Ben explained, "they'd bite you."

American black bears are known for their gentleness. Moon bears, on the other hand, have a reputation for aggression. Local people fear encountering them in the forest, and reports of killings and maulings are common. Bear trainers say that in captivity, moon bears are as dangerous as polar bears—the largest and most predatory bears of all—but for a different reason. Moon bears are "exceptionally clever," writes biological anthropologist Alison Ames, a scientific officer for the Universities Federation for Animal Welfare in Britain, "and will try to lead their trainer into making critical errors. They are quick to spot a mistake and take advantage of it, such as a trainer turning his or her back, or approaching an animal from the incorrect direction."

My plan was to keep the bear's mouth too busy to bite. So along with field clothes and water bottle, malaria pills and first aid kit, notebooks, pens, and batteries, I had packed treats bears find irresistible: a big bag of marshmallows, and two cans of sweetened, condensed milk. The maverick Minnesota-based black bear researcher, Lynn Rogers, has found bears so relish this last treat that he's actually been able to put radio collars on wild bears by hand, without tranquilizers, while they're lapping it up.

But Lynn's were bears he knew well and had observed at close range for months, sometimes years. Gary and I would have, at best, probably just part of one day to come to know the bears before I would try to touch them. Lynn's wild bears came to him freely. The bears Gary and I would work with were all born wild, but had been taken captive. Were their mothers killed? Did they remember? Were they caught in painful snares? Had they faced taunting children, tiny cages, prodding strangers? There was no way we could know what might be in their hearts.

* * *

It was a relief to escape the city. On a paved but potholed road, we drove south and then east in air-conditioned comfort toward Prey Veng. At the wheel of the Camry, Sun Hean aptly dodged motorcycles, bicycles, and cyclos piled with children, wreathed in bananas, quilled with bamboo poles, and pulling carts full of people, chickens, and pigs. Sometimes baby pigs are packed like melons into cylindrical bamboo baskets. Large pigs travel singly to market, strapped upside down on the back of motorcycles or cyclos, pink bellies burning in the sun, trotters akimbo. The breeder boars are luckier. They travel in style, in a cart drawn by a cyclist. People pray to be reincarnated as a male pig, said Sun Hean: "They get sex and money, too!"

Sun Hean translated the joke for Lina, his fiancée, sitting next to him in the front seat. She smiled shyly. Fine-boned, porcelain-skinned, and unaware of her own beauty, Lina was an accounting student at the university, and only nineteen. Perhaps she was uncomfortable with the ribald joke. Sun Hean had spent little time with her outside the company of her family. Throughout the day, Sun Hean's cell phone would issue its signature ring: an electronic rendition of the first eleven notes of the "Sailor's Hornpipe." It was Lina's father calling, checking to make sure his daughter was safe.

Cambodia, it is said, was born of such paternal love. Its national creation myth tells us that it was once almost entirely covered with water. It was inhabited only by the Nagas, magical beings half-serpent, half-human, who could transform themselves at will into either. One day, a handsome prince from another land set out on a voyage, inspired by a dream. He sailed until he sighted a slip of shore, on which he found standing the most beautiful maiden he had ever seen. She was the daughter of the Naga-king, the seven-headed cobra who rules the waters. The prince and the maiden fell in love. As a wedding gift, her father drank so much of the surrounding waters that mountains appeared, clothed in forest, and then in the center, like a bowl, vast, fertile plains— the land that is now Cambodia.

As we drove deeper into the countryside, it was easy to believe this land was born of a miracle of generosity. The world seemed radiant with tranquility. Lush rice paddies stretched heartbreakingly, dazzlingly green beside us along the road, tender with promise. On this day, the sky was the color of blessing, and the waters, the color of the people's skin. The irrigation channels, the ponds blooming with pink lotuses, and the rivers crowded with catfish, all shimmered like bronze mirrors, rich with life-giving silt. Their source, the Mekong, is known as the Mother of Waters in Thai and Lao, and honors the Naga in Vietnam, where it is called Nine Dragons. In Cambodia, it is simply called Great Water. It ferries nutrients for 4,320 kilometers, from the rock pinnacles of eastern Tibet, from China, from Laos, to deposit these gifts in the bodies of these fish, these grains of growing rice. We watched the people tread, like Nagas, half in, half out of the rich, brown water. In a land where so many promises have been broken, they follow the plows pulled by their endlessly patient water buffalo, reconsecrating the ancient covenant of the people and the water and the emerald fields of rice. We could almost hear the tinkling of percussive music.

* * *

When we arrive at the Bayab Farm Zoo, it's nearly noon. Gary and I check our cameras, test batteries for video and tape recorder, and ready the tweezers, surgical gloves, centrifuge tubes, markers, and marshmallows. "Let's go!" says Sun Hean, sounding rather like a sergeant.

The heat hits me like a wrecker's ball. The Camry's air conditioning is cold enough to keep lettuce crisp. The cool, vanilla-scented sphere of the car and the hot noontime air outside are separate incarnations, as disorienting as stepping from a dark room into blinding sunshine. Sun Hean and Lina are used to this; but Gary doesn't seem bothered, either. But then, he also said nothing earlier when Lina closed the car door on his hand. Gary is the uncomplaining sort.

The bear cage is less than a hundred yards from where we park, but at the end of this short walk I am drenched in sweat. The heat overwhelms my senses; it seems my peripheral vision is gone. Straight ahead, though, I see the bear inside: a black, maneless moon bear with a white chest V like a college sweater. He approaches us to sniff. He sticks most of his head out through the bars with no difficulty. The blue-painted bars are spaced nearly a foot apart.

But where is the golden bear? "There!" says Sun Hean. "Oh, my!" says Gary. Her face looks strikingly pale as she approaches us from the back of her cage. She has little mane, but the hair on the side of her neck is black, as are parts of her back, shoulders, and rump. Her eyes are lightly rimmed in black, like an Egyptian princess wearing kohl. She is darker than Gary's Yunnan bear, and darker also than the bear in Sun Hean's photo. Gary doesn't know quite what to make of her.

We both long to simply watch her, to notice and discuss every nuance of her feet, her nose, her stumpy tail. But this is not to be.

"Quickly, please!" Sun Hean says urgently. He has just paid a zoo-keeper a princely five-dollar bribe to let us pluck hairs. But we must do this before our activity is discovered by the other keepers.

And now we realize that the golden bear and black one are not in ad-joining cages, but in the same one.

Do we want hair from the dark bear, too? "Why not?" says Gary. The black bear, the keeper tells us, was captured as a cub in the Cardamoms' Mount Oral. We can use his hair for comparison with his golden com-panion's. The golden bear was captured in a different area of the same mountain chain, near the border between Koh Kong and Kampong Speu provinces.

The keeper, at Sun Hean's suggestion, has found some bananas and is feeding them to the black bear through the bars, causing him to stand on his hind legs and rest both front paws on the bars. I grab a single hair in my tweezers from the back of his right paw. He moans in irritation, ex-actly as a human might, and withdraws the offended appendage. The op-posite paw shoots out to try to swat me. I stuff the hair, with its attached bulb, into Gary's waiting test tube. "Please be careful!" warns Gary. Now the golden bear comes over, drawn by the bananas or by her cagemate's distress. She thrusts her paw through the bars, probing. Her reach can easily extend through the bars for well over twelve inches. The keeper distracts her with one of my marshmallows. I pluck a second hair from the back of the black bear's paw—where he'd just warned me not to touch. His jaws lunge out between the bars with a growl and a snap. "Watch out!" cries Sun Hean. "He's angry now!" I consider the ignomin-ious possibility of being mauled by a bear *in a cage*.

To our horror, a crowd of people has gathered behind us. They're not looking at the bears. They're looking at us. Few foreigners come to this zoo, fewer still are trying to pull hair out of the caged zoo animals.

The crowd grows and edges closer. The bears have eaten their fill of bananas and now my marshmallows are starting to run out. Sweat sheets from my face, stinging my eyes. Both animals are now pushing their paws and snouts through the bars. I have only harvested two hairs from one of them. We need a dozen hairs for a good sample.

"I'm going back in," I announce.

"Don't!" cries Gary. "That bear almost bit you!"

"Let me try." Sun Hean takes the tweezers chivalrously and tries for another sample from the paw. The bear jerks away. The tweezers come up empty. Next Sun Hean tries to grab hair from the head—and with a single pluck, nabs half a dozen hairs. Clearly this is what I should have tried in the first place. Sun Hean takes over the harvest, while I switch to taking photos and video. Gary is delighted. I am thinking: better not quit my day job.

* * *

We would end up leaving Phnom Penh for Kampong Som never having entered the royal palace, the Pagoda of the Emerald Buddha, or the National Museum. But first, a delay brought on by a minor accident gave us half a day in which to visit one of the capital's historic attractions.

While parked outside Sun Hean's office, the exterior rearview mirror of the borrowed car had been broken. For this reason, we would not be able to leave for Kampong Som that morning, as we had planned, Sun Hean explained. Our departure would be delayed till the next day. But that afternoon, once the mirror was fixed, he could take us sight-seeing.

He decided to show us Tuol Sleng.

"Museum of Genocidal Atrocity," he explained. "Give you some idea of how we lose our human resources."

The museum's crumbling bulk of yellow cement looked like many of the buildings we had already seen. Most of all, it looked like the place where Sun Hean had been sent away to school in Prey Angh. He had taken us there on the way back from the zoo. He was only fifteen when he left the family farm to continue his education. He had nowhere to live at the school, so, in the school courtyard, he had built his own house out of bamboo: "Small, like a toilet," he had told us. He had been miserable. "For two years, I no laugh."

In fact, the museum had originally been a secondary school, we read on a plaque as we entered the complex. After his takeover of the capital, on April 17, 1975, Khmer Rouge leader Pol Pot (who had himself worked as a schoolteacher while an underground revolutionary in the Cambodian Communist Party) transformed the school to the largest prison in the country, surrounding its buildings with a double wall of corrugated iron and dense barbed wire. The school bulletin boards were used to post rules for the prisoners, such as "Do not cry out loud while being tortured."

The torture was meant to elicit confessions of disloyalty to the Cambodian Communist Party, of which the elite and bourgeoisie were particularly suspect. In reality, the crime for which these people were imprisoned was their education.

"The educated people, they hear an announcement from the Khmer Rouge to come and help them develop our country," Sun Hean told us. Cambodian intellectuals who were abroad flew back to their homeland to help. "Ph.D. people, professor, scientist, student—good sources for Cambodian development." Physicians and nurses, engineers and architects, artists and writers, monks and missionaries, anyone who spoke French, anyone who wore glasses. People like us.

When the educated elite answered the Khmer Rouge's call, they were arrested. "And they keep them here," Sun Hean said as we entered the first classroom. It had been partitioned into cells. In each was a set of leg irons, a metal box that served as a toilet, a metal bed, and a photograph of the corpse found on that bed. More than twenty thousand people had been taken prisoner. Those who died here under torture are buried in mass graves on the grounds. Most of the prisoners, though, were taken to the killing fields of Choeung Ek, 16 kilometers to the southwest. When that camp was discovered in 1980, 8,985 corpses were counted. The victims had been bludgeoned to death. It saved on bullets. The last fourteen of Tuol Sleng's prisoners, though, were murdered here on January 7, 1979—as the Vietnamese arrived to liberate the capital.

"I first come here when I was fifteen," Sun Hean said. "Bad. I keep a strong memory. When I get back, I don't sleep. I tell my brother, don't come, don't come. I have all night bad dream."

Two other buildings were filled with photographs. One room showed photos of torture. Another was devoted to individual portraits: a boy whose upper lip had been split by a blow from an unseen weapon, revealing his upper gum and incisors; a young woman with a sleeping infant in her arms; a round-faced boy who looks at the camera astonished, as if just awakened from a dream; a Western student wearing long sideburns, an Elvis hairdo, and a big-collared polka-dot shirt. Some of the captives were in military uniform. "Soldiers of the Lon Nol Army," said Gary, referring to Cambodia's former army commander in chief, prime minister, and president, who fled when the Khmer Rouge seized power. The soldiers were U.S. allies in the Vietnam War. "People we trained."

A broken mirror had brought us here, a mirror that forced us to look back into a past we had helped to create.

The long-dead victims stared out at us from the past, eyes wide with terror, defiance, bewilderment.

We felt we had seen their eyes before.

CHAPTER THREE

The Sorrow of the Forest Spirits

On the drive to Kampong Som, we had expected potholes and bandits. Instead, we got the magnificent Road 4.

Built with American money two years before, it unfurled like a black satin ribbon for 250 kilometers, from Phnom Penh directly to our destination. Apparently, the authors of Gary's risk assessment report had not yet learned of it.

"Good road!" I said to Sun Hean.

"Not a *good* road," he corrected, "the *best* road!"

Yet, though our way was smoothed by American asphalt, our safety was still not assured. For this, we were told, one must stop at the shrine at Pichnil Mountain.

Our new companion, Heng Kimchhay, a tall, slender tiger specialist on Sun Hean's staff, had journeyed this route to the Elephant and Cardamom mountains many times before. He assured us this was an important stop. Clearly, other travelers agreed. At least twenty-five cars, plus a number of bicycles and motorcycles, were already parked beside the series of small shrines that stretched for a hundred yards along the side of the road. Most were small pagodas the size of dollhouses. Each sat on a pedestal, its pitched, tiled roof curling up to the sky. The largest, though, was as big as a suburban garage and built on a base of brick. It housed the life-sized image of a blue-skinned woman, robed in yellow silk and wearing a red towel on her head—the image, Kimchhay tells us, of Yimao.

"Yimao married a husband," Kimchhay says with Sun Hean's translation help, "but he left her for another girl. Yimao is pregnant. She crosses the sea looking for the husband, but the waves break the boat. As she is dying, she says, 'My blood sprays out in all directions.'"

Her blood, the price of a promise broken, still drenches these coasts. The land is stained forever with betrayal; only with her blessings can we safely pass.

Sun Hean buys each of us three sticks of incense to offer as we kneel before Yimao. Her shrine has been sumptuously appointed. It is crowded with colorful silk banners and garlands of peppery-smelling marigolds. Bowls overflow at her feet with offerings of money, fresh-baked sweets, polished rice, and fragrant fruits: hands of tiny, sweet bananas; aubergine globes of mangosteen, which smell like apples; starbursts of crimson, hairy rambutan, whose slippery opalescent flesh tastes like lychee. Yimao, once spurned, is now adored with earthly pleasures. Someone has even given her a cigarette, still smoking in between the red-painted lips of her clay mouth.

As trucks and cars whiz past us on the magnificent Road 4, we kneel and pray silently to her spirit. The scent of incense rises in the hot, mid-morning air, our prayers riding its smoke like words on a song.

* * *

As we drove on toward the goal of our scientific expedition, we spoke of gods and ghosts.

How did Kimchhay come to know the story of Yimao? He said it was told to the old people by her ghost, speaking through a medium, here called a *baromey*. The dead are not silent in Cambodia. Ancestral spirits called *Teak Na* inhabit certain trees, hills, and mounds, and must be propitiated with offerings, lest they cause sickness, flood, or drought. Even on city sidewalks, often you will see a banana, some flowers, a cup of wine, or sticks of incense someone has left for the *Teak Na*. Like the living, the dead can be fearsome or kind. Some spirits make babies cry; some wake you up to warn of disaster; some, the mischievous spirits of young Buddhist acolytes, hang around temples and cause the faithful to trip over stones. Some spirits are such welcomed guests that their human relatives are honored to host the visitor in their own bodies. In this way, Sun Hean told us, his grandparents often visit the family, choosing to speak through their daughter.

"When my grandmother use my mother to say something, the behavior is quite different," Sun Hean reported. For instance, his mother doesn't smoke, but when his grandmother inhabits her body she enjoys cigarettes without coughing. When his grandmother uses his mother's body to speak, his mother puts on lipstick just like her mother did, although she seldom wears it herself.

When the grandmother visits in this way, she sometimes reveals news that the mother does not know, Sun Hean told us. "She says to my brother: 'You have a girlfriend.' And he has a girlfriend! Or, 'Be careful—you're going to have a big accident!'—and the next month you have a big accident."

For some years, especially since he began his scientific training, Sun Hean has tested the efficacy of prayers and prophesies, like a pharmaceutical company might test a new drug. Sometimes they do appear to work. He told us about the time his cousin, an unusually tall and handsome fellow whom we would later meet, was traveling some years ago to Kampong Som, where he now lives, in a taxi truck. He prayed at a shrine before the journey. He got into one taxi, but then something told him to choose another. The first car left immediately, while the second was delayed. He was annoyed with his decision. But when he finally made it to Kampong Som, he discovered that the first car was attacked by Khmer Rouge insurgents. The passengers were murdered for their luggage.

On the other hand, Sun Hean said, he has observed that the traditional beliefs are sometimes wrong, and traditional spiritual remedies do not always work. "One guy close to my house was bitten by a cobra," he told us. Instead of getting the patient to the hospital for a shot of antivenom, a shaman was summoned to call the cobra to the scene. If the cobra can be convinced, according to traditional belief, the snake will take its poison back.

"I wait all day," said Sun Hean. "I want to see the snake! But the person say, something is wrong with the spirit of the forest, so the cobra not come." A more famous shaman was then summoned, but still the snake did not return. The person died at the end of the day. "Stupid!" said Sun Hean.

Sun Hean's parents tell him he has a guardian spirit watching over him. "My parents encourage me to pray every night. I go to pagoda; I am Buddhist. I do not want to lose my culture. But in my mind," he said, "I don't believe."

Nonetheless, we all prayed at the shrine to Yimao—even Gary, who, though raised Protestant, does not believe in gods or spirits or even (to my continuing and ill-concealed Christian dismay) in the historical veracity of Jesus' human existence. Science is god enough for him. Still, the professor admitted, when he learned, four years ago, that his father had cancer, he prayed. After chemotherapy, the cancer went into remission. "It's good, I think, to play it safe," Gary told us. "There's nothing to lose by praying if it might help."

Later, I was grateful for our prayers at the shrine. Sun Hean's snake shaman, as it turns out, was right: something *is* wrong with the spirit of the forest.

* * *

Shortly after our stop at Pichnil Mountain, we drove through the gates of Mong Reththy's oil palm plantation. We had seen billboards advertising his venture along the road: "Mong Reththy Cambodia Oil Palm Investment Co., Ltd." Long before we approached the gate to the compound, we saw a sprawling company town of wooden houses on stilts adorned with blue metal roofs. "Mong Reththy must be like the Cartwrights in *Bonanza*," Gary said.

The inner compound was surrounded by a sturdy gate. A uniformed guard with an AK-47 spoke brusquely with Sun Hean before he let us pass.

"What did you say to him?" I asked.

"He wants to know what party we are from," Sun Hean replied.

"The Free the Bears party!" suggested Gary.

Sun Hean allowed as to how that was not the right answer.

Within a hundred yards, we came to a square metal cage, large as a courtyard and roofed in the same material as the workers' houses. Inside, among the feathery leaves of low-growing mimosas, was the beautiful creature we had come so far to see.

"AHHH!" cried Sun Hean. "Yes! Right there!"

She was more beautiful, more golden, and more fragile than we had imagined. Her face was ghostly pale, like the moon's, or an angel's, and framed by a dark thick mane, black on the sides and gold on the top, where it shone like a halo. Except for the pale face and the dark at the mane and the edge of her ears, she was arrayed all in gold, golds of different hues—like a royal raiment a princess might wear. In fact, she *was* a captive princess—a sovereign stolen from her home realm, seized by an alien race for her very rarity and beauty. So was the radiant Sita, the incomparably beautiful wife of Prince Rama, kidnapped by the ten-headed King of Demons in the greatest of the sacred Hindu epics, the *Ramayana*, scenes from which are depicted on every Buddhist temple's walls.

The bear's gorgeous golden fur hung loosely on her frame. She was at least one and a half years old, but weighed perhaps only 125 pounds—so thin we could see her ribs. Through Sun Hean, we learned from a guard that she hadn't eaten for a week.

Everything we learned about her caused us more distress. Earlier, we had heard she had a male black cagemate. Where was he? We had planned to pluck hair from him, too, for comparison with her DNA. But, we learned from the guard, two months ago he had severed his tongue; he had died within days.

The golden bear's mate was dead, and now she was sick. In the *Ramayana*, Sita is ultimately rescued. Her freedom is won, in large part, thanks to the help of millions of animal-warriors—monkeys called Vanars, and bears called Bhallukas. In the folk epic, Prince Rama is also able to bring the animals who had died serving him in battle back to life. But

Rama was a god on earth. To perform miracles was his dharma—his life's work, his destiny. Our dharma is of a different nature. We cannot free the golden bear, or revive her mate. But Sun Hean, working to strengthen and enforce laws to protect animals like her, is perhaps Rama's human equivalent. And Gary, as a scientist, can bestow upon her a sort of immortality. She will be among the first of her kind to be described by science—whether she turns out to be a color phase, a new species, or a new subspecies—and Gary's account in the scientific literature will outlive both her and us.

Gary speaks his notes into the tape recorder: "The snout is patchy grayish white, the chin also, perhaps just pure white. The mane is black and all along the side of the neck down to the head and the back of the ears is black, and it looks like it gets yellowish on the chest . . . it looks kind of reddish yellow on the head, and the V on the chest is slightly lighter than the light yellow . . . a yellowish black mixture of hairs, I would say, behind it, and the much deeper reddish yellow hairs in front of it . . ."

Now Sun Hean reports an incredible stroke of luck: he has met the very man who captured her, a security soldier who works for the plantation. From him, we can confirm precisely where she came from, and perhaps glean other details that will help us to determine who and what she is.

He tells us he was hunting nearby in Prey Nup District, around six-thirty one evening, in the rainy season of 1997, when he first saw her: a small golden cub, perhaps ten kilograms (22 pounds), running, by herself, across a recently cleared patch of land. At first, he thought she was a forest pig. He had never seen a bear like her. He came close, thinking to capture the cub as a gift for his boss. At one point he feared the cub would bite him. He told us without shame that he then struck her so hard that he broke her teeth, bloodied an eye, and knocked her unconscious for two days.

Did he ever see the mother bear? Gary wants to know. A black-haired moon bear with a golden youngster would answer our question immediately: the golden bear would have to be an unknown color phase, not a new species. But the mother, says the guard, was never seen.

Has the bear changed color since her capture? Gary asks. There is no data on color change in moon bears, and very little on their likely closest relatives, American black bears. About 80 percent of American black bear cubs are born with a white patch on the chest, but many of these fade. Brown or cinnamon-colored American black bear cubs sometimes turn black or dark brown within two years. If the golden bear were growing darker with age, it could be a sign that her unusual color was a growth phase. But no, the guard answers: "Impossible."

Has he ever heard of anyone else seeing other golden bears? Well, said our informant, the well-guarded private compound doesn't get many visitors; but yes, he remembers once when people came from another part of the country; they said they had seen a bear like this before. Where were they from? asked Gary. "Koh Kong" came the answer—the huge province to the north, which encompassed the heart of the Cardamom wilderness.

When we finished our interview, Sun Hean and I asked Gary what he made of this information. "I don't think it tells me one way or another," he answered. "It could be a very rare species of bear. It could be an occasional color morph. We really need to have the DNA information to tell."

With some difficulty, we enticed the bear over to us with bananas, marshmallows, and sweetened condensed milk so that Sun Hean, Kimchhay, and I could take turns plucking hairs from her head. She loved the sweet milk. Sun Hean, squatting close to her cage, withdrew the can to enlarge the opening for her. She grew impatient, and her head lunged out between the bars with astonishing speed. She snapped at his knee with a snarl. "If I get a scar, I show my professor in America this is how the wildlife thinks about me!" he joked. Miraculously, she had not even broken his skin.

But without hair from a black bear caught from the same area for comparison, the hairs we obtained from her would be irrelevant.

*   *   *

"No problem," says Sun Hean. "Many people have bear." We first visited the Lie Phnom Hotel, one of the fanciest in Kampong Som, built during the city's heyday as a seaside resort. Among its lush plantings and land-scaped paths, the hotel has an impressive zoo with twenty spacious, green-painted steel cages housing a sleeping golden cat, four playful sun bears, colorful, shrieking pheasants, several kinds of monkeys and gib-bons swinging from tires and ropes—but no moon bear. Next, we spoke with the pregnant woman in the blue pantsuit at the market—only to learn she had just sold her moon bear that morning. We traveled a bit farther. We stopped at a fruit farm, on newly cleared land planted with mango and jackfruit. Next to the owners' veranda, where you might ex-pect to find a large shade tree with a spirit house beneath, we found, in-stead, a yellow bulldozer, its jaws caked with forest.

We spoke with eight of the farm laborers—gaunt, sinewy men with broken toenails and callused feet. Yes, they said, they could tell us where to find a bear. One of their friends snared a bear in the forest, right here, about seven kilometers from where the Mong Reththy bear was cap-tured. He plans to sell it for much money, they said. For a day's work on a fruit farm, the men explained, a laborer can make five thousand riels—about $1.37—but a wild pig caught from the forest, whose flesh is a deli-cacy, can bring thirty thousand riels, a week's salary, at the market. A bear garners much more. Awaiting a buyer, the friend is keeping the bear at his forest camp in the mountains, not even a day's walk from here.

But what kind of bear have they captured? A sun bear would be use-less to us scientifically. But if it is a moon bear, we could not ask for a more perfect comparison with our second golden specimen. Animals of the same species who live far apart geographically are likely to have marked genetic differences; but if two from the same area show large ge-netic differences, this can reflect the wider, deeper separation of different species or subspecies.

Discovering what kind of bear it is proves unexpectedly difficult. The Khmer word for bear, Sun Hean explained to us, is *kla khmum,* or "honey-eating tiger." In traditional literature, the moon bear is called *kla khmum thom,* "large honey-eating tiger." The smaller sun bear is *kla khmum touch,* "small honey-eating tiger." In the province where Sun Hean grew up, though, the people call the moon bear *kla khmum chkai,* the honey-eating tiger-like-a-dog, or dog bear—even though it looks less like a dog than the sun bear. The sun bear, however, is called the honey-eating tiger-like-a-pig, *kla khmum chruk,* or pig bear. But our informants do not know these terms. They use a different word to describe this bear: *Kla khmum krabei,* the honey-eating tiger-like-a-buffalo.

Sun Hean gesticulates as he quizzes them on the buffalo bear's characteristics: does it have large or small ears? Small ears, they say—like a sun bear. Does it have a short or shaggy coat? Shaggy, they answer—like a moon bear. Both species might be found in the Elephant ranges.

Which is it? Or is it a new bear species? Is it a bear at all? Many Southeast Asians consider the dark, fluffy, tree-dwelling binturong, closely related to civets and mongooses, as a kind of bear. In Thai, the binturong is called *mii khor,* or "hook bear" for its grasping tail. In Guangdong, China, certain hunters consider the hog badger (which is a species of badger, not a hog) as a type of bear, naming it the "dog bear." The Bamar of Burma call the red panda (which unlike the giant panda, a true bear, is thought to be related instead to raccoons) the "catlike bear"—whereas the binturong there is called the "bearlike cat." In many languages, an animal goes by a name that suggests a false identity—like the American prairie dog, which is not a dog at all but a stout, short-tailed, short-legged ground squirrel. Canadians used to call the wolverine the "devil bear," although it is not a bear and certainly no devil; it is a huge, tree-dwelling weasel.

"This thing could be anything!" I say.

"Including sold," says Gary.

There is only one way to find out. We hire one of the workers to take us to the forest camp the next day.

* * *

At dawn, rain clouds hang over the Elephant Mountains like dragon's breath. We are eager to enter the forest, to immerse ourselves in a world teeming and unexplored. Besides sun and moon bears, there are thought to be more than four hundred tigers, and perhaps three hundred elephants, scattered among the Cardamom and Elephant ranges. Clouded leopards, with fur soft as mist, hide in the trees, waiting to spring on ground-prey. Fishing cats, with strange, nonretractable claws, and webbed paws, haunt shallow streams and scoop out fish. Rare, red Asian wild dogs called dholes hunt in packs, whistling to keep the family together. Prey are diverse, from the sambar, at seven hundred pounds southern Asia's largest deer, to wild boar and muntjack, to the tiny chevrotain, a mouse deer that grows just over a foot long and can weigh as little as three pounds. Rarer hoofed animals can be found here, too, including two, perhaps three kinds of white-stockinged wild ox: the gaur, huge and hump-shouldered, the banteng, whose dark coat gleams almost blue, and possibly the even rarer kouprey.

In interviews with hunters, Kimchhay reported some of them claim the presence of an even more exotic hoofed animal: the Khting vor. Sun Hean had told us about it when we had visited him in Minnesota. No museum has ever acquired its corpse, skin, skull, or photograph. It is known to science only for its unique, annulated horns. But the horns alone were evidence enough for biologists, in 1994, to bestow on it a scientific name, *Pseudonovobos spiralis,* and to classify the unseen creature as a new type of wild goat.

American collectors obtained the first horns known to science from Vietnam in 1929, but the specimens were misclassified as the horns of a female kouprey. The kouprey is now thought extinct in Vietnam, and there, hunters may have exterminated the Khting vor, too—but the creature, Sun Hean believed, might well have found refuge in Cambodia.

"The local people, they say they know this animal," Sun Hean had told us. Eight of thirty-one hunters Kimchhay interviewed in the Elephant and Cardamom mountains said they had seen it. Indeed, one man said he had last seen one in 1998: a buffalo-like animal with black or gray pelage, weighing perhaps 660 pounds, but capable of leaping like a goat.

What else is known of this enigmatic animal? Sun Hean told us what the people say: that the beast uses its horns to spear poisonous snakes, which it eats; that the snakes, attempting escape, may coil onto the horns; and that in so doing, the serpents carve the characteristic ringlike, spiraling ridges, and leave the horns imbued with a powerful antidote to snake venom. For this reason, the animal has two Khmer names: Khting vor, "wild cow with horns like lianas" as well as *Khting si puoh*, "the wild cow who eats snakes."

"Maybe we make another expedition—search for Khting vor!" Sun Hean had suggested. As we set out that morning, we all fantasized about seeing one, even getting a photograph. Kimchhay mentioned that tigers in these forests are known to kill people in chance encounters, and told us to watch out for cobras.

* * *

We began our journey along a track as wide as a suburban American house, the yellowish soil corrugated with the metal tread of earthmoving equipment. Sun Hean clucked his disapproval. This track had not been here when he last visited, two years before. Elephants used to cross the road here, he said. He reckoned that elephants might soon be gone from the mountains that bear their name.

The track ran through a wasteland of charred stumps and blackened earth. The destruction did not abate for miles. We followed our ragged guide, a hunter wearing flip-flops, who had known the forest that once stood here well. He was a friend of the worker we had met at the farm the day before, who had also joined us, bringing up the rear. The plantation worker carried a machete—to clear our path through the jungle. It seemed absurdly unnecessary.

Finally, after an hour or so, we could see the raped land struggling to reclothe itself in green. Loggers had cleared this portion of the land perhaps fifteen years ago, and now small saplings, scrub, and lianas scrambled toward the light. Actually, Sun Hean told us, degraded forest like this often makes excellent habitat for bears. Some of the early plants that re-colonize a logged area are berry-bearing brambles. Fire-hollowed trees provide excellent nests for tasty bees, ants, termites, and their high-fat larvae. All of these are foods bears love. Perhaps, in addition to solving the mystery of the captive cub, we might see signs of wild bears today, he said: claw marks on trees, holes clawed in the dirt, the platform-like "nests" bears make in tree branches as they feed on nuts and fruits. Cricket song rose around us like heat exhaled from the earth.

The track became more muddy until we came to a knee-deep stream. Sun Hean was not pleased.

"Wah-ter," he lamented, letting the word go reluctantly, like a sigh. "Many leeches, maybe." I hoped not. I had encountered many of these while working on a book in Borneo several years back. One of the more unwelcome discoveries of my literary career was plucking one of these black, slug-shaped parasites, bloated with my blood, out of my bra.

Gary has no such prejudices. When he was a graduate student taking a field course in Costa Rica, he had graciously hosted a parasitic maggot in his flesh. He named it George. George's mother had glued her egg to a fe-male mosquito, who had then bitten Gary on the back of his upper left arm. Warmed by his skin, the egg had hatched immediately, and George had burrowed into his skin. Soon the bot created an itchy swelling as big around as a nickel, from the center of which George would periodically poke out a snorkel-like breathing tube. Gary observed his parasite with interest until it grew to the size of a lawn grub and unfortunately died.

"You put the leg in the water, and leeches are coming," Sun Hean tells us dejectedly as we cross the stream. Leeches locate their prey by sensing body heat. But if any have found us, we won't know until later. Their saliva contains both a natural anesthetic and an anticoagulant, so the first sign of a bite is often blood soaking from a painless wound.

Soddenly, we mount a small rise. Fat, white geese, which many people keep as watchdogs or doorbells, herald our arrival with deafening honks. We have reached the hunters' camp. Beneath a tin roof held aloft by log pillars, we find two little wire cages. One, on the ground, houses a miserable muntjack. In the other, raised above the ground on blocks of wood, is a small black bear with tall, rounded ears and a white chin.

"Oh, *yes*!" cries Sun Hean in delight. "Asiatic black bear!"

We have our comparison bear.

She is about the size of a cocker spaniel—perhaps a year old, Sun Hean says. She has a white, triangular chin patch and a white V on her chest. She seems dazed with terror. She has been here for many weeks. A ring of naked skin around her neck testifies that not long ago, she was held captive by a collar or chain. We offer her a treat of sugarcane, which she shyly accepts. She doesn't seem to mind when we pluck her hair. For her, life is boredom punctuated only by food and fear.

Summoned by the geese, one of her captors appears. Attempting to be gracious to his visitors, he opens the door of her tiny cage to display his prize. Seeing him, her fan-shaped ears slam back, like an uncertain dog. As he shouts at her, brandishing a stick, she steps forward gingerly, as if her footsteps hurt her. She has clearly been hit before. She does not know what he wants. At her first opportunity, she hurries back into the horrid little cage.

Why is he keeping her captive here? What does he propose to do with her? Sun Hean asks at our request. The man answers, improbably, that he plans to start a zoo. We doubt it.

All of us wish desperately that we could rescue her. We could certainly buy her—like many of the captive bears we've seen. But then what? The national zoo outside Phnom Penh is already full of moon bears and can accept no more. Let her go? Baby bears cannot survive in the forest without their mothers any better than a human baby could. Older bears loosed in new territories would likely die also. Wild females in their second spring of life share their range with their mothers and sisters. Other bears are driven away. Young male bears must establish new territories, wandering sometimes for hundreds of miles to find them, running a gauntlet of older established males, roads, dangerous terrain, and hunters' guns and snares.

The little bear at the camp reminded me of the dilemma of the caged wild birds at many Buddhist temples. The pious purchase them to set them free—an act of kindness to "make merit" and improve one's lot in the next life. But the freed birds, weakened by their captivity, are almost invariably captured before the day is over, and again sold in order to make humans feel more noble by freeing them.

We took away her hairs for science, and left her behind in her prison.

* * *

We continued to walk toward the forest, as if immersion in the wild lands where the little bear should have roamed free could cleanse our hearts.

"Quick, quick please!" Sun Hean called to us from up the trail. "Very large, very big!"

Excitedly we hurried toward him. Could it be a wild bear? A monkey? A muntjack?

No—our wildlife encounter lay on the mud beside Sun Hean's boot. At first the creature appeared to be as long as a man's thumb, but then, sensing the heat of our bodies, it stretched toward Gary's foot. Green on the bottom, brown on the top, with a black stripe down the middle, it was a slippery mucous-coated muscle as long as a banana—the most monstrous leech any of us had ever seen.

* * *

"Sun Hean, what's the matter?"

As we walk, Gary and I have been listening for the trills and chirps of unseen birds, the rumble of approaching thunder. But our Cambodian companions are holding an animated discussion. In the nasal singsong of their voices, we hear deep concern.

"Three people on the road," Sun Hean says. "Don't know who they are."

We don't understand.

"The guy with the red shirt," Sun Hean says, referring to our guide, "he was arrest a few months ago."

Arrested?

"He get hit and he have to pay five thousand bhat. And he's a worker, not a rich people, but he came with a rich people who have a lot of money and they going to buy land here, and he was arrest in this area."

"They paid that money not to get arrested?" Gary asks.

"To be *released*," says Sun Hean. "Mixed together with Khmer Rouge are other people who will kill."

Sun Hean, who is extremely brave, is clearly rattled by the news. Slowly, the garbled story begins to unfold: two months ago, as our guide was escorting some Cambodian land speculators through this very forest, he and his party were attacked by bandits. They were blindfolded, beaten with sticks, and held for days in the jungle for ransom. His family had paid the equivalent of $140—four months' of a day-laborer's salary—for his release. The families of his rich companions each paid fifty thousand Thai bhat—an astronomical $1,315. And now, the guide is concerned, because he has spotted three strangers on the road into the forest. He is worried they might be bandits. Bandits in this area are well armed, and also have radios to alert companions in deeper parts of the forest that good ransom bait might be coming their way. They could be lying in wait for us now.

"With skin like us," says Sun Hean, "who will believe we have no money? We are the targets."

He means, of course, with skin like mine and Gary's.

"At least we outnumber them," I note, trying to sound very calm.

"Not necessarily," said Gary, who is carrying all of our cash in the front pocket of his cargo pants. "We don't know how many there really are."

"I wish he had shared this with us before he took us into the forest," I say.

Gary's wish is more practical: "I wish we had a gun."

"If you have a gun, they also have gun," said Sun Hean. "Long gun, strong gun . . ."

We walk along silently with our wheeling thoughts. The gallant Gary is trying to figure out how he will subdue the bandits and save us all. I am irrationally planning to convince the bandits to just take me but let the

others go; then I will somehow escape. Sun Hean is pragmatic and re-
signed. "Where," he asks, "will Lina's parents get fifty thousand bhat?"

* * *

We see no other option than to continue on. Standing still we are sitting
ducks. To turn back now would take us to where our guide so recently
saw the strangers. To go deeper into the forest at least affords us a chance
to see bear habitat and bear sign. And besides, now it is raining, and the
young trees are large enough to provide some shelter. On the wide logging road we'd be soaked.

The decision feels right. To me, the forest means safety. In dreams, it's
always to the forest that I run to escape the faceless, human dangers of
my fears. True, the forests of my dreams are always New England's:
stately, ordered, cool—not the tangled, humid jungles of Southeast Asia.
And it's true that no jungle is particularly safe. Part of the operatic
majesty of the rain forest is its voluptuary dangers, its sweet poisons and
hidden jaws. I had discovered in Borneo that in Southeast Asia's jungles,
fruits spiked like maces fall from trees and can kill you. A moment sitting
on the wrong log can burn the skin black with toxic sap. Unseen biting,
stinging ants may erupt from holes in the ground, venomous caterpillars
can drop from branches, vipers might coil beneath your feet. But these
are innocent cruelties. There is purity even in their menace. There is no
greed, no duplicity in the cobra's bite. Only the humans were evil enough
to be sent away from Eden; God in His wisdom let the snake stay.

It is raining insistently now, making a sound as if all the souls in
heaven and hell were whispering at once. But what are they telling us?

What to do? Again, Sun Hean's idea is practical: "Let's eat lunch."

Our guide leads us to a small platform beneath a thatched roof.
Drawn by the smell of food, two yellow, ridge-backed hunting dogs appear from the wet gloom. I toss them a bit of rice. To my sorrow, they
cower from my offering. Like the little bear, they have been hit before,
and expect humans to harm them.

The dogs and the shelter belong to our guide. Gary and I ask how he
hunts, and he shows us eagerly. He holds up a coil of wire the circumfer-

ence of a dinner plate with two metal loops; one loop attaches to a flexed pole. The snare is set on the ground and covered with duff. When an animal trips the trap, the loop closes, the pole straightens, and the creature is hoisted up into the air by a leg, where it will hang until the hunter checks his snare. The hunter smiles broadly as he portrays these events with his gestures.

What sorts of animals would he catch in this way? Kimchhay translates for us: "Pig, deer, barking deer . . ." Some species in Cambodia are protected against hunting by local tradition. It is believed in certain areas that to kill an elephant, a wreathed hornbill, or the tiny, wide-eyed slow loris brings bad luck to the hunter. To slaughter a fish eagle (which mates for life) causes divorce. Killing a tiger can bring depression or disease to wife and children. But these snares make no choices. They tighten around any hand or foot, paw or hoof that steps on them. And even if a large animal, like an adult bear, can break free, the loop will continue to tighten, wire chewing into flesh, slowly disabling the creature until it dies of gangrene. Primatologist Dian Fossey considered snares like this one the primary killers of the endangered mountain gorillas she studied in Rwanda. And although the crime is unsolved, many agree that her murder may well have been committed by one of the men who lived by setting such snares.

Yet this is neither the most lethal way of hunting, nor the most hideous. A report by Cat Action Treasury, authored by Sun Hean's friend, the expat American Hunter Weiler, mentions animals in Cambodia are routinely hunted with machine guns. In Cambodia's Veal Veng District, farther north in the Cardamoms, the police chief told Hunter that Thai merchants were supplying hunter groups with high-velocity magnum elephant guns with telescopic sights, capable of dropping an elephant at five hundred meters for the illegal ivory trade. Tigers, whose bones are sold as medicine, are often killed by placing mines under monkey carcasses. In many areas, the illegal wildlife trade is supported by gangs of traders, widespread availability of guns, illegal logging, deforestation (which both makes the forest more accessible and the capture of wild animals easier), and an utter lack of law enforcement. All hunting, even for food, is illegal in Cambodia—but the absurd law is impossible to enforce. Especially for cheap snares like these: they cost pennies to buy, can be set anywhere, and are so well hidden that even the animals can't find them.

How many snares like this has our guide personally set in this forest, we ask through Kimchhay? How many are out there now?

The answer: about one hundred and eighty. Just by this one hunter. In this forest, there are certainly thousands.

For its innocent residents, this Eden has become a hell.

* * *

After lunch, we slog on through the mud. We hear nothing but the hissing rain, our sucking footsteps, and the zippery squeal of our nylon ponchos. We see little beyond the blinders of our hoods and the curtains of rain.

Sun Hean tells us there is little chance of finding sign of bears or anything else. Sensibly, the animals are hiding snug in thickets, in holes, or beneath logs or rocks. Their footprints have dissolved in the rain. So reluctantly, we decide to turn back. Tomorrow, he suggests, we will take the ferry to Koh Kong, and there venture into a much wilder area, in the heart of the Cardamom range.

We never saw the strangers again. But on the way back, we heard an explosion in the direction from which we had just come. Thunder? I asked Gary. No, he said; and answering my unspoken question, neither was it the sound of a gun. "What was that?" we asked Kimchhay.

He knew the sound well. He answered matter-of-factly: "Land mine."

CHAPTER FOUR

Year Zero

The next morning, Gary and I found ourselves distractedly watching a giant squid dismember people in a foaming pool of blood.

The video was the most pleasant scene available at the time. If we looked to our right, we would see, out the porthole, the ten-foot jade waves of the Gulf of Siam slamming against our ferry. If we looked to our left, we would see Sun Hean throwing up beside us into a red plastic wastebasket.

The monsoon had come on like a child's tantrum. On gusts of maniacal wind, rain crashed down as if hurled from angry fists. Water had poured through the holes in the roof of the little restaurant where we had awaited the ferry that morning, puddling in the orange plastic chairs and soaking our pants. Oblivious, Sun Hean and Kimchhay devoured vast breakfasts: soup, noodles, eggs, fish, and rice seasoned with mint, garlic, and chiles. Gary and I had abstained, considering the four-hour boat ride ahead of us.

During the meal, I had wondered aloud about the ferry. I hoped it would have a roof.

"Oh yes!" assured Kimchhay, who had taken this ferry many times. And walls? "Yes—and air conditioning!" In fact, the sleek, red-and-yellow-striped craft that slid up beside the dock was, to my surprise, as modern as any airplane—and besides roof, walls, and air conditioning, even featured free, extremely violent, Khmer-captioned Grade B movies. The first movie had been about Satanic possession among high school students. Before the start of the squid video, as the craft bucked epileptically on the waves, vendors staggered down the aisles, offering candies, drinks, and fruit. Shortly afterward, many of the passengers began to throw up.

By the time the squid had eviscerated most of the movie's cast, we still had two hours to go before we reached Koh Kong. If we ever got there, Gary and I would be the second group of Westerners in thirty years to enter its rain forest. It was amazing we had even gotten this far, considering the night before.

* * *

After we had returned from the Elephant Mountains to our hotel that evening, I had been transcribing notes while Gary was trying to figure out how to operate Sun Hean's new Global Positioning System unit. This handheld device taps information transmitted from orbiting satellites to determine your location. We had hoped to use it for the first time in Koh Kong.

"'Step 1: Plug in your latitude and longitude,'" Gary read aloud from the unit's unhelpful manual.

"If you know your latitude and longitude already," I huffed, "what do you need with a GPS? I thought that was what the thing was for."

"Hmm," he agreed. He read further. The manual did not seem to address this conundrum. However, although it appeared the GPS could not determine our location, unless we psychically intuited its coordinates, the unit was not useless. Gary read aloud: "It can also be used as a clock alarm."

"And it makes an excellent doorstop," I added.

"It could also be thrown at a pig if it's misbehaving," Gary noted.

A knock came at the door. Gary answered. From the writing desk, I could hear it was Kimchhay, but couldn't hear their exchange.

What did Kimchhay want? "He was just reminding us to meet Sun Hean at six," Gary said after he had shut the door. "He seemed very insistent, though."

A few minutes later, Kimchhay was back again. It seemed Gary and he talked for several minutes. What did he want this time?

"He kept saying, 'Mr. Sun Hean at six.' He kept just standing there," Gary reported. "He repeated it over and over. I finally said, 'Fine! We'll see you at six then,' and shut the door. Very strange."

We went back to transcribing our notes.

At six, we met Kimchhay on the stairs leading to the dining room. Where is Sun Hean? we asked.

"Mr. Sun Hean *sick*!" he wailed. "Mr. Sun Hean is *sick*!"

Apologizing frantically, we rushed to Sun Hean's room. There we found our friend lying on the bed in his shorts, clutching his stomach and writhing. He looked at us, the closest things to mother and father figures he could find, and asked pathetically, "How come?"

We tried to piece together what was wrong. Sun Hean would sometimes get out of bed, only to squat leaning against the wall in an attempt to find a position that didn't hurt. Periodically he would go into the bathroom and throw up. Then he would crawl back to bed again. Finally we managed to glean some information, and what we learned left us further alarmed.

Feeling queasy and tired after our trek in the Elephant Mountains, Sun Hean had gone to visit his tall cousin in town. There, he was given "Chinese medicine" that was "too hot." Feeling worse, next he had sought, with Kimchhay, a "doctor"—who, we discovered after some discussion, had a bed literally on the street—and who had given Sun Hean two injections.

Dear God, I thought, where had that needle been before it was plunged into the flesh of our friend? Was it even possible to find a clean, disposable needle in southern Asia outside of Bangkok? I remembered meeting a cyclist in rural India who had needed the rabies series after being bitten by a dog. In order to sterilize the local doctor's only needle, he had sent her pedaling off to the nearest hot springs.

And with what had Sun Hean been injected? What did the doctor think was wrong? This no one could say. The doctor had also dispensed six pills. Gary and I examined them and recognized two of them as antibiotics ("A mighty short course," Gary observed). The others we could not identify. And they weren't exactly working miracles: Sun Hean had been lying here for an hour, pleading with Kimchhay to go get us to help—but we had continued to transcribe notes and fiddle with equipment just yards away from his room.

Gary's bad hearing was as notorious as my own. Gary has tinnitus and some deafness in his left ear from shooting cans in Kentucky with his dad as a kid. I lost much of my hearing to years of traveling with loud Third World boat motors. We often have phone conversations like: "How's your mother?" "It's raining here—how's *your* weather?" But when our deafness combined with Cambodian English, the results could be bizarre—like the time in Phnom Penh, after a short phone conversation, Gary informed me that Sun Hean had asked permission to bring a special musical instrument to the hotel.

"A special musical instrument—what kind?"

"He said it was some kind of flute."

I didn't realize Sun Hean was a musician. And why would he ask us permission to bring a flute?

Then it dawned on me: Sun Hean was talking about a *fruit*. And there was but one fruit so controversial that Sun Hean would have asked permission to bring it: the durian—a celebrated, football-sized, custard-fleshed treat, with one significant drawback—when cut, it releases a stupefying stench. It smells like onions rotting in an unventilated latrine. Hotels throughout southern Asia post signs at their entrance doors featuring a picture of a durian within a slashed red circle, and the English admonishment NO DURIANS IN ROOMS. I had raced down the stairs to intercept disaster.

But now we faced a problem far more serious. Sun Hean might have appendicitis, or a ruptured spleen—in which case we would have to evacuate him, somehow, to Bangkok. Describing the nature of pain is difficult in one's mother tongue, and virtually impossible in a foreign language. So I presented Sun Hean with a Chinese menu of agonies from which to choose: Was it like his guts were on fire? Was it like being hit with a fist? Being clubbed with a truncheon? Being stabbed with a knife?

Like something chewing through his stomach? At each of my suggestions his eyes grew wider, as if he were experiencing, thanks to my intervention, all of the above in turn.

The pain, he said, was in his middle—indicating, according to our limited medical knowledge, that it was not appendicitis. I went back to my room and fished out of my toilet kit two Pepto-Bismols—a product Sun Hean had never seen or heard of before. Although he had lived for nearly a year in America, while he had attended the University of Minnesota he had rented a room from a Cambodian family. They used traditional Cambodian medicines and ate traditional Cambodian foods. Though he had spent five days a week in university classrooms listening to and speaking in English, when he came home every night he spoke Khmer.

With a foot in both worlds, Sun Hean had absorbed an astonishing amount of Western knowledge—and managed to apply it in his own country. In graduate school in Minnesota, Sun Hean had managed to master concepts he had never heard of before. His Cambodian university schooling had not prepared him well for American graduate studies. When we had flown to Minnesota to plan our expedition, Gary had mentioned, of course, the need to pluck hairs from the golden bear.

"Why need the hair?" Sun Hean had asked.

"To sample its DNA," Gary replied.

"What," Sun Hean had then asked, "is DNA?"

Now he had taught his staff all about the spiral-shaped chains of nucleotides that are the blueprints of all life. And later we would learn from David Smith that Sun Hean had used this knowledge in yet another way: he had posed, in a dangerous undercover investigation, as a genetics student in order to obtain samples of tiger skin to collect evidence of the illegal wildlife trade.

But no one had told him that spicy Chinese herbs might further inflame an upset stomach, that he should never get an injection from some guy on the street, or that two little pink pills available at any Western drugstore might help him through his anguish.

I stroked his head and held his hand. I told him everything would be all right. I promised we would look after him, as he had looked after us. Again I remembered how young he was, how committed, and how brave.

*   *   *

Within an hour of taking the Pepto-Bismol, Sun Hean started to feel better. Then his tall cousin appeared at the room. With Kimchhay translating, we decided together that Sun Hean should see a Western doctor. We drove in the rain to the home of a thin, French-speaking woman who, her diploma said, had earned her medical degree in Paris. As small children peered in from an outside window, Sun Hean was shown to a little twin bed, at the foot of which was a medicine cabinet containing bottles of drugs adorned with pictures of different human organs. He was feeling almost well by now. She thought he might have an ulcer, but she gave her okay for him to make the ferry trip the next day.

*   *   *

Sun Hean rallied a second time once our ferry delivered us to the shores of Koh Kong. In fact, he was ebullient again. So was Gary. Within minutes of our arrival, the two men were talking about guns.

"Tomorrow we are in command of our own private army!" exclaimed Gary.

"Three AK!" chortled Sun Hean. "No kidnapping—no way!"

After the scare in the Elephant Mountains, Sun Hean had made arrangements via his cell phone for five soldiers to accompany us on our next expedition, along with a forestry department officer with a radio. On our trip in the Cardamoms, three of the soldiers would carry AK-47s, weapons of which both Gary and Sun Hean were devoted fans.

"These are incredibly rugged firearms," Gary said with enthusiasm. "They make U.S. military rifles look terrible. You can do anything to them you want and they'll still shoot."

"Horrors!" I said. "Surely we're not going to *shoot* people?"

No, answered Sun Hean. The soldiers, the forestry official, and the guns were to impress the security police.

"But what are the security police for, then?" I asked.

"For illegal logging."

"To stop illegal logging?"

"No—not that," he answered. The security police, he explained, were there to prevent people from asking questions about it.

* * *

After dropping us and the luggage at our mildewing hotel, Sun Hean and Kimchhay left us to pursue a number of errands. First on Sun Hean's list was to phone Lina and her parents. "They will be worried about the ferry," he told us.

Why would they be worried about the ferry?

"Sometimes," he said, "they sink."

They *sink*?

"Many sink," he said. "Many die. The waves break the glass. The boat go down." He paused and smiled slyly. "I didn't tell you that."

Indeed. Later, when we would return to Phnom Penh and meet Hunter Weiler, he would tell us that the ferries between Kampong Som and Koh Kong are Malaysian-made riverboats. "Those boats are designed for river travel," he said. "If they hit a wave the wrong way, they go down like a stone."

A few hours after our arrival in Koh Kong came a knock at the door. When I opened it, there stood Sun Hean, holding his shirt open like a bat spreading its wings. All over his chest and back were dozens of long, half-inch-wide red stripes, filled with subcutaneous blood.

"Sun Hean! What has happened?"

He gave me a radiant smile.

"*Kos khsall*," he said. He and Kimchhay had visited a traditional healer. She had oiled his skin, then created these bruises by vigorously rubbing a coin-sized metal disk at a forty-five-degree angle against his skin. Like cupping—the application of heated cups to the skin, which produces similar, though round, bruises, a procedure called *chup khsall*—the treatment is supposed to draw out "bad air" and thus cure ailments and remove pain.

Sun Hean now felt fully restored to vigorous health, and ready for another meal. In front of the restaurant where we ate that night, two beautiful yearling male moon bears were confined to a seven by two-foot cage. They had already removed most of the fur from their bellies by rubbing against the wire, trying to get out.

*   *   *

Ten of us set out the next morning: Sun Hean, Kimchhay, Gary, and I were now joined by the five soldiers with their three AKs, and Sorn Piseth, of the Forestry and Wildlife office of Koh Kong, with his radio. Gary and I learned, to Gary's private horror, that for the next ten hours, we would be traveling together by motorcycle.

Gary knew that the bumpy ride wasn't going to do him any good. Shortly after earning his Ph.D., he had permanently injured his back lifting a box of fossils; he had later exacerbated it in a car crash. But the stoic professor kept his concerns to himself. After all, there was nothing to be done—motorcycles were the only way into the forest of Koh Kong and the eleven thousand-square-kilometer Mount Samkos Wildlife Sanctuary, the largest in Cambodia. We roared off in the rain, two to a seat. I sat in back of Sun Hean and clutched his middle like a life raft. Gary rode in back of Kimchhay, but to maintain his professorial demeanor, he instead held on to a metal loop in back of the seat.

Shortly the paved road of the city gave way to a red, rutted, muddy gash bulldozed through the forest for loggers. Three years ago this road wasn't here, Sun Hean yelled to me over the roar of the motorcycle; it was just a track. But now the road rips all the way to Pursat, a distance of 175 kilometers to the northeast. "As you know," Gary said to us when we first dismounted, "this is the way forest gets destroyed. Roads are the worst thing in the world."

For Gary's spine, this one certainly was. Our motorcycles were usually pitched at a thirty-degree angle, traveling over mud as slippery as grease, and we often dropped half a foot or more over rocks. Of course we had no helmets. For an alarming percentage of the trip, only one part of the body—the ball of one foot, usually—seemed to be actually in contact with some part of the motorcycle. One could not help but wonder whether the motorcycle and the airborne body were traveling at the same speed. Therefore, each time my butt rejoined the motorcycle seat I rejoiced. Gary did not. With each bump came a jolt that compressed the entire length of his injured spine. Although I could see he was in terrible pain, not once did he complain—not even when he and Kimchhay were pitched off after crossing a small rivulet. I fell off twice: once on top of Sun Hean, who had made a rough landing on red gravel, another time sinking into sucking gray mud. At one point Sun Hean and I found Kimchhay and Gary dismounted ahead of us. Gary was serenely surveying the forest, while Kimchhay was fishing in a shallow stream with a stick. "What are you looking for?" I asked. Kimchhay replied, "My shoe."

Each time we stopped, the view around us took our breath away. To either side of the road rose a seemingly impenetrable wall of bamboo, vines, and great spreading trees, green stretching to infinity. We were in the midst of what E. J. H. Corner, emeritus professor of Tropical Botany at Cambridge, called "the most luxurious forest on earth," and Oxfordshire botanist J. Wyatt-Smith considered "the richest and oldest forests of the world."

The Indo-Malayan rain forest, of which the Cardamoms are a part, extends from Burma to New Guinea, and owes its sumptuous floristic diversity to the recent marriage of broken continents. Thrice—fifteen, five, and three million years ago—pieces of the northward-drifting southern continent of Gondwanaland collided with the southeast extremity of the northern continent of Laurasia. The joining mingled the non-pine conebearers of the southern continent with uniquely Laurasian plants such as the rattan palms and the towering, large-leafed Diptocarps. The marriage gave birth to a forest unlike any other, hosting the most startling wonders of the vegetable world: the monstrous, leafless Rafflesia, discovered in Sumatra, grows a flower that stretches a yard in diameter and can weigh as much as fifteen pounds. Its warty, maroon petals form a vast cup, floored with bristles and spikes, which can hold a gallon of water. The Poison Tree, first reported from Indonesia's Celebes by seventeenth century soldier-naturalist Georg Everard Rumph, was mistakenly believed so toxic that "everything perishes that its wind touches." Its shade, he wrote, was littered with the corpses of birds.

The forests of this region hold beauties to burst the heart: the blazing crimson blossoms of the Poinciana tree, "a mass of flaming glory," wrote H. W. Ponder, "almost too blinding for human eyes to bear." The brilliant yellow Cassia, whose blossoms are called "golden rain" by the Javans. The Carmine cherry, "a frozen fountain of precious stones," as F. Kingdon Ward described it. On his travels in Burma, Ward felt "drunk with the glory of it."

In the canopy of these strange and lofty forests, rhododendrons grow on branches; galaxies of orchids bloom. Flowers, seeking the feathery tongues of moths, bats, bees, and birds, exhale their desire in scent like cucumber, fox musk, sour milk. One, the "Midnight Horror," earned its name because at 10 P.M., as Corner described, "the tumid, wrinkled lips part and the harsh odor escapes from them. By midnight, the lurid mouth gapes widely and is filled with stink."

The plant species of the Cardamoms have never been fully cataloged. We caught but the briefest glimpse of their riches: bamboos towering a hundred feet high. Burrowing gingers, fragrant and furtive. A host of palms, the oldest of flowering plants, originating 120 million years ago. To step behind their green curtain would be to enter the "furious embraces of envy and jealousy; phrenzies of egotism in the vegetable kingdom . . . strange expressions of formidable hate and love, of aggression and vengeance," as wrote Captain C. Cerrunti, an Italian ethnographer visiting Southeast Asia in 1906. Figs, the tyrants of the vegetable world, slowly strangle their mothers. They arrive by seed in the canopy and drop their great latticed roots downward to not only encircle but actively crush the bark of their hosts. The deadly embrace takes a hundred years to complete. Rattans scramble over the ground, turning, twisting, and climbing as if endowed with the muscle and will of a thinking being. They grow rapidly—one species grows a stem thirty feet long in five years from seed, and by age fifteen can stretch a hundred feet. The longest stem recorded, by botanist Corner in Malaysia in 1940, was 556 feet long, but one far longer was trampled by elephants before it was retrieved from the forest for measurement. The sword of this viney palm's crown becomes a fine and tenacious whip, barbed with hooks, which attach to any convenient object, and the angle at which the thorns are set makes them penetrate farther with additional movement.

This we soon discovered. Dismounting our motorcycles, we fought our way through the rattan into what had once been a little clearing, perhaps a hundred yards off the logging road. The army captain of our small group of soldiers, Sun Yee, wished to show us where he had trapped and killed two tigers, ten days and ten feet apart from one another. Tall and slender, the twenty-nine-year-old captain wore one gold tooth and two long, manicured thumbnails to testify to his station. "They call him 'Famous Forest Man,'" Sun Hean told us. Part of his fame sprung from the tigers he had killed in 1997.

Tigers are more common here than anywhere else in Cambodia. A National Tiger Survey was conducted by Sun Hean's Wildlife Protection Office and one of the conservation charities with which Hunter Weiler works, Cat Action Treasury, from January to March 1998. It estimated the Koh Kong tiger population at over two hundred. In interviews with hunters, every man reported seeing tiger tracks almost every time he entered the forest. Tigers not uncommonly raid hunter's traps, the hunters said, eating the wild pig, deer, and other animals caught in their snares. People run into tigers fairly often. One hunter reported seeing a tiger killed before his eyes as it stepped on a land mine. Another described watching a fight between a tiger and a moon bear—a battle the tiger eventually won, dragging the dead moon bear into a streambed and abandoning it there.

"A walk in the woods in Koh Kong-Pursat can be a dangerous proposition," reads the interim report on animal distribution compiled by the tiger survey team. Ten of fifteen hunters interviewed in Koh Kong province knew of people who had been killed by tigers here. One area of the province was plagued by a tiger who had killed more than twenty people, and in another, supposedly fifty people had died in a tiger's jaws.

Because all the man-eating happened at night, Hunter Weiler wondered if the killers were really leopards instead. But it is the tiger to whom these deaths are attributed, because the tiger is feared and revered like no other animal.

At one time, reverence protected the tiger. In Battambang Province, an interviewee said that in one village, a tiger could be seen walking across the road every month; but no one would shoot it "because the tiger had the magic." In the province of Stung Treng, villagers regularly saw a tiger in their village after they conducted a certain religious ceremony. They called it "God's tiger" and no one would harm it. But Asia's new wealth has now created a burgeoning market for tiger parts, just as it has for bears. In the 1998 CAT survey, Koh Kong hunters told interviewers that tiger-part buyers were willing to pay hunters three times the price they got three years before. Tigers are now slaughtered for parts previous poachers left behind. Whiskers, sinew, penis, blood, and especially bone are all sold to supply a seemingly bottomless market for so-called elixirs. Tiger wines, balms, soups, and pills are believed to ease rheumatism, restore energy, cure fever, combat dysentery—and the bones and organs are far more difficult to track than skins on their way to illegal markets in Hong Kong, China, and Taiwan, and in Chinatowns in Europe and North America.

Sun Yee told us he sets snares in the forest for deer and wild pig. But as he noted, "Any animal that passes will be captured." And of course, should a bear or a tiger be captured, it is too dangerous to release it, he said. Besides, who could pass up a chance to make a thousand dollars? So when he found a snarling tiger in a snare in 1997, he shot it. Ten days later his snare caught another one, and he made a tidy little fortune from the two.

People were glad he killed those tigers, he told us. About ten people in the nearest settlement—folks who earned their living collecting rattan and lianas for making furniture—had been killed by tigers earlier that year. At the time, Prince Norodom Ranariddh, the elected leader of the country, had forces near the Thai border that were fighting current leader Hun Sen's army. The fighting, he said, had driven an unusual number of tigers into this area. He had seen about a hundred tigers in the past ten years. He had also seen many bears—though never a golden one. But these days, he said, tigers and bears are far less common. "Before, there were many animals," he told us through Sun Hean, "but now, not so many. Now, the animals are afraid."

And with good reason. A 1998 World Wildlife Fund review of the status of tiger, Asian elephant, gaur, and banteng in Indochina reports that although surveys are few, tiger numbers seem to be rapidly plummeting throughout the region because of poaching. "If I were a tiger," Josh Ginsberg, Wildlife Conservation Society's director for Asia programs, recently told a Harvard audience, "I would not want to live in Indochina. Poaching is wiping them out." Comparing the plight of Cambodia's tigers with those in Laos, Yunnan, and Vietnam, the WWF report concludes, "The limited law enforcement in Cambodia may mean that numbers are dropping faster there than elsewhere."

The logging road on which we traveled would only make matters worse, Gary noted. The logging itself—fairly selective, we were to learn later—was relatively benign compared to the road that made it possible. "The access road is the bigger impact," Gary said, "because the road provides easy access for hunters."

But I was, by then, only half listening to our Khmer/English conversation. Movement on a tall shrub had caught my eye. To my dismay, I discovered that the shrub we were standing next to was covered with one-and-a-half-inch-long ants.

A physician with the French navy, Dr. A. Maurice, had written vividly of what he called "the plagues of Cochin-China": "It is impossible," he warned in a book detailing his voyages through what are now Cambodia and Vietnam in 1872–73, "to even sniff a flower without first freeing it from a crowd of ants." Each kind he described was more horrible than the one before. One species was black with two castes: most were minuscule, but others were so large that they might be seen carrying ten companions on their antennae. Their immense heads, armed with great, pinching mandibles, could deliver a painful bite—but this was the species least feared. Less common but far more terrible were the long, slender black ants, who flow over the ground like black rivers and sometimes head into houses. "Sometimes one meets them in unending columns in the forest and one better not disturb them," he had reported. The sting is worse than a wasp's. When he was staying at the Cambodian-Vietnamese border during the wet season, these ants invaded the hut where the doctor lived with his adored pet macaque, a golden furred creature of whom a houseboy said, "He knows everything." The ants devoured him alive in his cage. There were also big red ants that lived in trees and on bushes, attacking and biting anything that disturbed their home. "I believe that a man who is persecuted by a ferocious beast and who had to find refuge in a tree inhabited by these animals," Maurice wrote, "would prefer to re-descend and try to fight the last battle with the brute that was waiting below." The pain from their bite "takes a long time to fade."

Individuals of a third species were small and red and unfortunately, he reported, "rather often penetrate into beds." (Worse, these ants often reduced to dust the precious animal specimens in his collection, and to protect his scientific booty he resorted to smearing the legs of all the furniture with tar or setting them in shallow vases filled with water and phenic acid or absinthe.) Maurice called this the fire ant of the Annamites, and described its bite as yet more cruel than the others.

Alas, the good doctor had not even begun to catalog the ants of the region. More than a hundred years later, scientists had discovered well over seventy species of army ants *alone* in tropical Asia. Some of the army ants have camp followers: a swarm of raiding *Aenictus* may be followed by flocks of birds that try to eat the bugs flushed out by the ants, and butterflies that eat the birds' droppings. There are ants with mandibles longer than their heads; ants who hunt in groups of over a hundred thousand; ants who form fan-shaped raids twenty-nine feet wide. And those are just the army ants. Some of the more formidable ants hunt alone. Each worker of the large-eyed species *Harpegnathos salator*, for instance, is a solitary huntress: she captures cockroaches and spiders, injecting each with a para-lyzing poison, then brings it back to the nest. The prey will remain alive but will be unable to move for up to two weeks.

There are also harmless ants, who eat only vegetation and do not at-tack. But the ants on our bush were not among them. Sorn Piseth began to slap his neck, and soon I felt a stinging bite behind my ear. Gary saw my distress and began to explain that the shrub was surely an ant-pro-tected plant. Many species of ants take up residence in a certain tree or shrub and defend their home bravely against all comers. We had encoun-tered some of these in the Amazon, he reminded me, defending the tan-garanga tree, which as a result of their attentions is never plagued by browsing animals or—

"Ants!" I shrieked—and we retreated to the red scar of the logging concession road.

* * *

As we raced along in the rain, we passed a number of other people trav-eling as we were. The first group we saw, five people on three motorcy-cles, had a shotgun in their party, and were clearly hunting. The second group we saw were soldiers, armed with AKs with collapsible stocks. We stopped to ask them if they knew about golden bears—they did not—and saw that they had just shot a foot-and-a-half-long, black, white, and reddish-brown creature Gary identified as *Callosciurus prevostii*, or Pre-vost's squirrel. It belongs to a genus that means "Beautiful Squirrels." It was a huge male, spectacularly colored: the top of the head, the back, the luxuriant tail, and the sides were shining jet black. The cheeks and inside of the arms were pure white, and the underbelly was a gorgeous reddish brown. His intestines protruded from the bullet's exit wound in his back. Otherwise he was perfect, his eyes just closing and his paws not yet clenched in death.

This was the second death we had witnessed in our first two hours on the road. The first had died at the hands of our own soldiers. Shortly after we had begun the journey, a bluish-green snake, delicate and beautiful, thin as a child's pinkie, had attempted to cross the road. By the time Sun

Hean and I arrived at the scene, the soldiers were throwing rocks at its head. It writhed in pain as Sun Hean had two nights before. "Stop! Stop!" I cried, and I looked at Sun Hean to do something. But he only said quietly, "Poisonous," and the men ran over the little snake again and again with their motorcycles. Finally the creature turned its white belly up, surrendering to death.

In fact, every animal we would see that day was dead.

We met a Vietnamese man walking along the road. He had nothing but thongs for shoes, no socks, and his ankles were a solid mass of feeding leeches. But he had a gun. He had been hired, he told us, by one of the logging concessions as a security guard. Had he ever seen or heard of a golden bear? we asked. He replied that he had recently killed an animal with a golden coat, explaining it had paws like a bear and a snout like a pig, and that its paws, penis, and gallbladder could be used for medicine.

We asked to see the remains of the animal, so he led us to his wall-less camp, surrounded with a midden of discarded cloth, plastic, and fish guts strewn everywhere. Here the three-foot-long skin of the creature was laid out to dry. Shiny bluebottle flies buzzed around the golden fur, and their maggots squirmed in bits of the remaining flesh. Gary, undeterred by the smell, picked some of the bones out of the sodden earth and plucked some hairs from the rotting skin and put them in his breast pocket. Only a small bit of cartilage remained of the nose, which did not look like a bear's. Unfortunately the paws, which would have provided a positive identification of the animal's species, were gone, too. Someone had stolen them, the Vietnamese told us sullenly. Gary noted the skin seemed to have a four-inch tail—much longer than any bear's. He tentatively identified the slain creature as a hog badger, *Arctonyx collaris*. A large, squat member of the weasel family, the hog badger's back fur is often yellowish. Like the moon bear, the animal eats mainly roots, shoots, and other plants as well as small animals it excavates with its dexterous, digging paws and piglike snout. Much later we would learn from a colleague that these badgers are often so tame they come into villages and sleep among the people's pigs. One hog badger, he said, had once followed the editor of the *Natural History Bulletin of the Siam Society,* Warren Brockelman, along a forest path in eastern Thailand. The badger trailed a few steps behind the scientist for several hours—presumably just for the company.

We motored on. As the rain began to clear, we stopped at a little camp in the forest where workers were reconstructing a log bridge that had washed away in a flood. The men lived in collegial squalor in a wooden house on waist-high stilts topped by a blue tarp for a roof. Pumpkin seeds mildewed on a woven reed platter and the recent remains of a fish dinner were scattered on the ground. The scales glittered like diamonds, and the guts had drawn crowds of four-inch black, blue, and cream-colored butterflies, sucking salt and fluid with their long, rolling tongues—death covered in blessing.

No, no one had seen or heard of a golden moon bear here, either. The men spoke nervously. They knew we were eyeing the drying pelts of seven muntjacks, the corpse of a rare Asian wild dog, the skull of a turtle (another item sold for medicine, ground and used in tea to ease difficult childbirth, Sun Hean told us), and the figlike gallbladders of wild pigs—and possibly bears. Here Sun Hean confiscated a gun whose make and model eluded even Gary. At first it looked to him to be a Chinese copy of an American M1 automatic rifle, but then he'd decided he'd never seen anything like it before. Sun Hean did not arrest its owner or issue a fine. Later we saw one of our soldiers carry the gun happily off to his home.

Pressured by Sun Hean's Wildlife Protection Office, in early 1999, Cambodia's government had announced a complete ban on logging and declared all guns and all hunting illegal. But only one in five of the hunters interviewed in the CAT survey knew about the new laws. And no wonder: at the time of our visit, there was no staff, management, or any other kind of official presence in the Mount Samkos Wildlife Sanctuary, the largest in the country.

Laws alone can't protect the wildlife in Cambodia. "You need the laws, education at all levels—police, border patrol, shopkeepers, subsistence hunters—all these need to be in place for conservation to work," David Smith had said when I had spoken to him about his student. "Everybody needs to know what's coming. And that's exactly what Sun Hean is doing, with compassion for the hunters as well as the animals. He really sees the importance of getting the whole community involved."

Sun Hean, and some of his colleagues in wildlife charities, have wisely harnessed the hunters as a resource: because hunters trust and like them and their staff, hunters' honest answers to interviews have provided conservationists with an important preliminary picture of the ubiquity, methods, and importance of hunting. In the Cardamom region, for instance, 90 percent of hunters use guns while 80 percent use snares and traps; 85 percent of hunters say hunting is "somewhat important" to self and family; 80 percent use some wildlife and sell some; but only 5 percent sell most of it. And most important, all the hunters who had been interviewed in the CAT survey in the Cardamoms knew wildlife had decreased there in the last five years—and 90 percent, like Sun Yee, were worried about it. Most of them agreed with the concept of conservation once it was explained to them. The Wildlife Protection Office has even hired ex-poachers as rangers. For conservation, this is an achievement as profound and symbolic as beating swords into plowshares, as Cambodia emerges from three decades of foreign invasions, genocidal atrocity, and civil war.

"Before, we had Khmer Rouge," Sun Hean would later explain to us, "we can say an expression: Khmer Rouge help us to safeguard the animal, because when we have Khmer Rouge in the forest, then the local people, the hunters, cannot go to hunt the animal. That's the positive thing that we had war. But now, war is finished, so the people have a lot of freedom to come into the forest, and they do anything like hunting, trapping— any job they can do in the forest, they do."

Ironically, war once preserved this hidden Eden. Now peace and prosperity pose worse threats to Cambodia's wildlife and wilderness than ever before in its long and tumultuous history. Sun Hean and his conservation colleagues face at once an unparalleled challenge, and a historic opportunity.

"The country is essentially at Year Zero in terms of a conservation infrastructure and knowledge base," wrote CAT's Kristin Nowell in a 1999 paper co-authored with Sun Hean, Hunter Weiler, and David Smith.

A struggle against all odds—or a chance at a new beginning.

* * *

We rode on . . . and on. It seemed that the bumpy, torturous logging road was endless. But daylight was not. After six punishing hours on motorcycles, it was clear we should turn back lest we be caught by the darkness.

Back at the hotel, Gary slowly dismounted Kimchhay's motorcycle as if his back had aged ten years in ten hours. "Never again!" he pronounced. Clutching the metal loop in back of his seat had rubbed enormous, oozing blisters on both his hands. Before he hobbled off to take a shower, he confided to me that his back was so sore that he wasn't sure if he could even get into a cyclo.

An hour later, when we all met to travel to the restaurant in town for dinner, Sun Hean had everything ready. There, in front of our hotel, were the motorcycles again, waiting to carry us away.

CHAPTER FIVE

Refugees

Standing on his hind legs, Stripe, a 250-pound moon bear with yellowish eyes, is looking Gary in the face through the partially closed window of the Jeep's passenger seat—a window that Gary discovers with some dismay is not easily rolled up. Meanwhile, another bear, having chewed for some time on one of our tires, is attempting to remove the hubcap of a rear wheel with his claws.

"No, no, no," chides Johan Lindsjo, the Swedish veterinarian in the driver's seat. Speaking very gently and slowly, as if to a small child, he tells the enormous beast, "No, no. You're destroying the car."

Inside our parked vehicle, we are adrift among a sea of bears. Besides the two who are chewing and probing the Jeep, there are another five moon bears within twenty feet of us, and perhaps another ten within sight. Some lounge in shallow pools. Sitting upright with arms spread out, they look like fat old men in the whirlpool bath at a health club. A few relax beneath trees, leaning their backs against the trunks, their stumpy legs akimbo, showing the smooth, moist soles of their feet. Some stand, watching us with benign, almost avuncular interest, while others lunch on rice mixed with dog biscuits, just delivered, still steaming, by the workers manning the green food truck in front of us.

I have never been to a Club Med, but this is what I imagine it might look like—if all the guests were big, fat, black, and hairy.

But this is no resort. Nor is it a zoo. For these animals, as well as an-other forty-five moon bears and fourteen sun bears, fifty macaques, thirty gibbons, ten crocodiles, four binturongs, and two hundred dogs, Thailand's Banglamung Wildlife Breeding Center is essentially a well-appointed refugee center.

Gary and I had heard about Banglamung shortly before we had left the United States for Cambodia. Located just outside the popular Thai resort city of Pattaya, 140 kilometers southeast of Bangkok, the center hosts some sixty moon bears—surely one of the largest concentrations of moon bears in the world. It would be a good place, we figured, to check for golden bears on our way back from our travels with Sun Hean.

Despite the name of the facility, none of the animals were bred here, Johan explains. Except for the dogs—strays who were dropped off at a nearby temple—all these animals were once wild, captured by poachers, and then confiscated by the Thai Royal Forest Department. These bears are like war refugees, but they are refugees from the illegal trade in wild animals, the war on Asia's wilderness. Some were once pets; many had been destined for the dinner plate or the pharmacy.

"A few years ago, eighteen bears came in one load from a restaurant," Johan tells us, shaking his blond head. The soft-spoken veterinarian removes his wire-rimmed glasses and pinches the spot above the bridge of his nose, as if the memory physically hurts him to recall. Although far fewer bears are coming into the facility these days, Johan says, in the years after Thailand declared the trade in wildlife illegal in 1992 and began to actually enforce the law, it was hard to keep up with the flow of animals.

Two years ago, a bear even came to them via a Bangkok brothel. When a man had stopped at this "massage parlor" for directions, its staff couldn't help but notice the female moon bear cub in his pickup. They asked what he was going to do with her. He was going to sell her to a Korean restaurant. At this, the ladies were so distressed that they pooled their money and bought the bear for twenty thousand bhat—the equivalent of over five hundred dollars—and then turned her over to the

Forest Department. When she arrived at Banglamung, the volunteers named her Harem in honor of her saviors.

Banglamung wasn't originally set up to accommodate bears at all. When it opened two decades before, the place was, as its name implies, part of a network of Wildlife Breeding Centers run by the Thai Royal Forest Department for native pheasants, monkeys, and deer. Their progeny, it was hoped, would restock Thailand's overhunted forests. But when confiscated animals started pouring in, needing a place to live, a private charity stepped in to help. The Thai Society for the Conservation of Wild Animals (TSCWA), founded in 1996 by an expat Australian and two Thai, procured the funding to build spacious cages and outdoor pens and amassed volunteers to care for the animals. The World Society for the Protection of Animals donated sixty thousand dollars for the ten-acre bear enclosure, and then provided money for another thirty-five thousand-square-foot pen for nine more moon bears. Johan, who leaves his lucrative practice in Malmö, Sweden, for three months each year to volunteer at Banglamung, personally raised much of the funding for another large, outdoor enclosure to house an additional twenty confiscated moon bears, who will be transferred from another facility when this one is built.

"Considering they spent most of their life in a small cage before they came here, or their mothers were killed in the forest, it's so much, much better here," Johan says, surveying the scene before us. Giant black moon bears are everywhere, free to loll and snuff in peace and comfort. Some dig and sniff in holes in the earth; some paw at coconut husks; several more step from behind bushes to stare dimly at our car with mahogany eyes and quest after our scent with wet, pink-lined nostrils. One bear is enjoying a good scratch. With half-closed eyes, he leans his back against a tree trunk. The scrape of his great claws against the itch on his belly sounds as delicious as biting into a juicy papaya.

"I've never seen so many moon bears in my life!" Gary exclaims with delight. "And frankly, I've never seen such large moon bears. Some of them are surely more than two hundred kilograms. These are very impressive animals—just wonderful!"

Another bear, with a huge, thick mane and a wide white V on the chest, approaches the Jeep, rises on two feet, and peers at us through the windshield. The other bear continues to paw at our hubcap. "No, no," Johan repeats gently. "I wouldn't say he would destroy the car just to have a go at us," Johan says to reassure us. "He just wants to chew everything and examine everything—"

"He is taking off the hubcap," I announce from the back of the sauna-hot Jeep. "Can he puncture the tire with his claws?"

Johan casts another glance behind us. "Oops. Yes, I see this," he says. "Okay, I think we have to leave now." He starts up the engine, and we move on to survey another group of bears.

* * *

Bears with pointy faces, bears with huge bushy manes, bears with almost no manes at all; bears with stumpy legs, bears with long black fur, bears with woolly undercoats. We saw muddy bears, dusty bears, wet bears, pudgy bears, fat bears, and some, weighing over four hundred pounds, really, *really* fat bears (one of whom we later discovered was named Lardy). Timid bears peered at us cautiously from behind the protection of trees. Occasionally, we saw quarrelsome bears—when bears argue, they stand on their hind feet and with hunched postures, make hideous wrinkled faces at one another, showing their huge yellow teeth and snarling.

Although we were baking in the Jeep, it was lovely to be in their presence. The sorrow was that all of these bears should have been wild. For every one rescued, probably dozens, if not hundreds, more had been killed—murdered so their cubs could be stolen, or butchered for delicacies or elixirs for which substitutes were cheaply available.

Gary scrutinized each bear with the exacting eye of a taxonomist. Several years ago he was in charge of cataloging the Field Museum's collection of forty thousand mammal fossils, a job that sometimes demanded he be able to classify species on the basis of the cusp shape of a single tooth. "Now, the nose of that bear looks slightly undercut, like the bear we saw at Prey Veng," he would say to me—a feature that even with binoculars I couldn't detect. "This bear's forehead seems slightly less sloping than the others," he would note. And then, "The rear claws on this bear seem to have an ivory tinge. . . ."

But of course, the feature of greatest interest was coat color. "There's a greater range of coloration in these bears than what I anticipated," he told Johan and me. "These bears range all the way from coal black to black with brownish tinges to bears with blondish hairs on different parts on the body, to bears that seem to have black hairs that are almost silver tipped, or perhaps blond tipped."

We saw a number of bears with unusual pale markings. One of them was Stripe, who had been trying to get into Gary's window. Stripe is also called Farang, a rather impolite Thai word for "foreigner." He had acquired both names because of the light fur on his face. Parts of his legs and back were blondish, too, and his claws were ivory. Like our Cambodian golden bears, his eyes were ringed in black, and the black mane framing the distinctive face made him especially handsome. We also met a similarly colored bear named Louis, with a notch in his left ear. He, too, sported large black eye rings set against a pale face, as well as pale inner ears, front legs, and hind paws.

These animals seemed a sort of "intermediate" between the golden bears we'd seen in Cambodia and the black moon bears that were commonly known. This gradation, from black bears to blond ones, was a disappointment for Gary. "I don't think we're dealing with a new species," he said with a sigh.

Gary was disappointed, but not dejected. "We could still have a subspecies if the paler bears are all concentrated in a geographic area," he pointed out. The criteria for naming a new subspecies, set forth, along with those for new species, in the International Code of Zoological Nomenclature, boil down to two basic requirements: to qualify as a subspecies, its members must not interbreed with another population. (Usually this is because the populations are separated by a geographic barrier, like a river or mountain range.) And the majority (75 percent, according to the great taxonomist Ernst Mayr) of the adult specimens must be physically distinguishable from those in other populations by at least one measurable, physical characteristic. When "The Code" was first adopted in 1901, the characteristics separating subspecies were visually identifiable—features like color, the shape of a bone of the skull, general size. But in subsequent revisions (which are issued every few years by the International Congresses of Zoology, London) "The Code" increasingly recognizes genetic differences as physical characteristics. Not all the bears in one population would have to be golden, or even light-faced, to constitute a new subspecies. Depending on what the lab work showed, Gary might still be able to name a new subspecies. He already had a name in mind, one that would honor his parents, Don and Ruth: *Ursus thibetanus donruthi.*

* * *

We saw no golden bears; but then, we could not see all the bears in the main enclosure. Some had climbed into trees; others were resting in the shade of concrete dens; still others were hidden in the grass. And there were yet more bears to see elsewhere. After our drive with Johan, as gibbons whooped and dogs barked, we walked around the 190-acre compound, peering over fences and into cages—searching, like shoppers in a mall full of clothing stores, for coats that caught our eye.

One of them was Romeo's. A sizable sub-adult male, he had a pallid, grizzled face, light front legs, and black rings around the eyes. Romeo proved to be Gary's favorite bear. Romeo clearly liked Gary, too. In fact, it seemed the professor and the bear were engaged in a perfectly cogent conversation.

"I'd like you to show me your chest," Gary would announce to the bear. "Would you do that?" Almost immediately, Romeo rose to his hind legs, placed his paws on the green bars of the cage, displayed to Gary a narrow, V-shaped white chest mark, and held the pose for several photographs.

"Every bear I've looked at in Southeast Asia seems to have a white chin," Gary then noted. "Is your chin white?" Romeo tilted his head up. "Yes," said the professor, recording this on his memo pad, "yes, it is."

"Now I would like to look at your belly," Gary said. Romeo rolled over.

"Are you the Bear Whisperer?" I asked, only half-joking.

"No, but if you were asking him to pose and show every part of his anatomy bit by bit we could hardly do better," the professor replied matter-of-factly. We both knew that Romeo, if he understood human language, probably knew Thai, not English. But it was possible that this very active and alert animal may have been reading Gary's subtle, inadvertent posture or scent cues to determine that he had struck a pose that pleased his visitor.

Whether or not he was a genius, Romeo was certainly a very friendly bear. So was Somsri, the large, black female who shared his spacious, cement-floored enclosure and its piles of tree trunks for climbing. Both allowed us to scratch the backs of their tall, round ears and touch their wet noses through the bars of the cage. When we mentioned we would like to pull hairs for DNA sampling, Johan simply reached in and plucked out some of Romeo's hair with his hands. Romeo's hairs were particularly valuable not only because he was an "intermediate" but also because he was one of the few bears here whose capture location was known. If all unusually colored bears were genetically distinct, and if they came from one, clearly defined geographic area, it could mean a new subspecies. If not, they were probably color phases that cropped up throughout Southeast Asia's moon bear populations. That would still be an important discovery; but *donruthi* would have to wait for a new animal.

Romeo, we had learned, had come from the Thai side of the Thai-Cambodia border, just north of the Cardamom ranges. The story was that Thai police heard a shot—probably his mother being killed—and followed the sound to arrest a Cambodian poacher with the cub in his possession.

Romeo had been about three months old when he arrived at Banglamung in October 1998. He had first lived in a different wildlife breeding center in central Thailand, and by the time he came to Banglamung he had become quite aggressive. In fact, we learned, he had taken off part of a British veterinarian's lip with his claws.

"That vet was just plain *stupid!*" said Gary van Zuylen, in Romeo's defense. "Forty stitches later, we figured out we never should have let him volunteer."

The trim, thirty-eight-year-old director of the Thai Society for the Conservation of Wild Animals, Gary van Zuylen, an Australian with a close-cropped mustache and lively green eyes beneath arched eyebrows, did not appreciate stupidity. Nor was he fond of ignorance, inefficiency, or incompetence. But he had numerous stories of his encounters with the same—even from well-meaning, Western donors. ("One donor was upset that the animals' dishes looked unclean at one of our facilities," he told us. "So they had an automatic dishwasher sent—from Sweden! But guess what we don't have? Running water!") He often pulled faces, mimicking the slack-jawed response of a slow-witted person, usually an idiotic official, hanging his head like one of those head-bobbing dashboard toys. One wondered how he had survived so long working alongside the numbing bureaucracy of a Third World government agency.

He was alarmingly forthright. Hours after we had first met him, which was only that morning, we mentioned to him the name of a mutual acquaintance. "She's a horrible, fat, ugly, screaming, crazy old woman!" he responded. She could have been my beloved auntie for all he knew.

Gary van Zuylen was smart and tough and fit—he runs three hours a day—as sharp-witted as he was sharp-tongued. He had a sort of hyperalertness to him, and he both listened and spoke with great intensity, his green eyes darting and dancing. He knew what he was talking about, too: often, in his sharp-edged Australian accent, he would rattle off figures—the number of national parks in Thailand (sixty), the date of the country's Wildlife Protection Act (1992), the percentage of an acre that constitutes the Thai unit of land measurement, the rai (.395)—and I would write them down. When I got back to the States and could check, I found each time he was right on the money.

And he was very kind to us. He had generously picked us up that morning from our hotel in Jomtien Beach. We were staying, to our delight, at the astonishingly cheap Mermaid's Beach Resort hotel, whose bright blue swimming pool and sumptuous breakfast buffet were favored by huge, pink Germans and Swedes. Jomtien Beach is a more wholesome suburb of Pattaya, a seaside resort first developed for American GIs during the Vietnam War, now renowned less for its beach, littered and polluted, than for its lively sex trade. ("Beautiful educated ladies, handsome gentlemen, and pretty ladyboy," promised one ad in a tourist flyer.) Jomtien Beach offers some of these services—as we noticed from the goings-on at the neighboring Do-Do Beer Bar and the Pupay Beer Bar. But mainly the town is an enchanting if incongruous picture of what the East thinks the West wants. Most store signs are in English, from the suitably obsequious "Yes Boss Custom Tailors" to the reassuringly tame "Slo-Bunny Horse Riding Training Center" to the ring of antiquity at "Ancient Coffee." Several storefronts combine services for Westerners on-the-go, like the Restaurant/Sauna (presumably not air conditioned) and the Shower-Toilet-Laundry (suggesting a thrifty, if unhygienic, water recycling effort).

Restaurant menus offer items geared to Western tastes, such as "Grilld Chicken Species Crumed and Fried Goden"; "Super Surrem Pepperoni Ham Grounp Beef Pork"; and, as a nod to American cuisine, "Fried Spegetti" and "American Fried Rice in Tomato Sauce."

Yet for all its Western influence, Jomtien Beach is still possessed of graces unquestionably Thai. At the cafés, beautiful young women with tiny, delicate hands set down each teacup and spoon soundlessly and with great tenderness, as if to make any noise or sudden movement might shatter the customer's Buddha-like meditation. And at the edge of each shopping center, outside each gas station, beside every restaurant, hotel, and Internet café, there is a spirit house.

In Thailand, as in Cambodia, spirits are everywhere. The old animist beliefs coexist graciously along with Buddhism. There are river spirits and mountain spirits, spirits of deceased people, spirits of caves and of rocks. (I had even read of a Hmong village in northern Thailand where there is a spirit who presides over the cooking of tofu; if the spirit is not honored, the tofu won't set properly. Cooks create a sort of doll made from soybean paste with two red chiles sticking out from the top, and with this, they persuade the spirit to help them.)

The spirit houses outside most urban buildings are erected to house the spirits of the place—the spirit who might have inhabited the tree that was cut down to make room for the store, or the spirit who inhabited the soil now paved for the parking lot. A large complex such as a shopping center or hotel necessitates a particularly spacious and attractive spirit house, so that the spirits will voluntarily move there rather than haunt the new structure built for humans. The spirit house outside our hotel was exceptionally well appointed: flanked by two tiers of flower boxes, a herd of carved teak and stone elephants massed outside the house proper, along with crowds of horses, cows, and human servants for its spirit occupants. The whole structure was piled daily with offerings of fresh flowers, fruits, sweets, and incense.

To some, this ancient practice thriving in a busy, modern city might seem odd. But to me, it seemed to reflect a rather sophisticated environmental ethic. To be sure, of late, the Thai have been no better stewards of their environment than Americans. Bangkok remains one of the major markets for illegal wildlife trade. Since the turn of the century, loggers have destroyed more than 60 percent of Thailand's natural forests. Illegal logging was, until recently, so flagrant that in 1988 the director of the Forest Department himself was arrested for his illegal timber deals. The next year, so many trees had been cut that a flood that normally would have caused little damage resulted in landslides that killed hundreds of people in southern Thailand.

But the spirit houses remind the Thai daily of truths Americans have made a national credo of forgetting: that resources are finite. That space is finite. And that in our hunger for more houses, more hotels, more shops, more gas stations, we continually disrupt and displace other beings—beings perhaps as varied and complex and needful as we are.

* * *

Thailand's Buddhist heritage, too, was immediately evident to us at Jomtien Beach—as soon as we saw all the dogs. Each block had a stray dog or two, sometimes three or five or ten, roaming free on various canine errands. Unlike many African and South American countries, where people stone or hit dogs for no reason, or Cambodia, where people eat them, or America, where strays are rounded up and euthanized, the Thai don't persecute stray dogs. A tenet of Buddhist teaching is compassion for animals.

I am often lost in cities because I do not seem to take in landmarks like buildings; but in Jomtien Beach I was often able to navigate by recognizing which dogs held territories on which streets. Getting to Banglamung, though, was another matter. Even though the center was only ten kilometers away, it is located on unmarked roads amidst a 950-acre forested sanctuary. Without Gary van Zuylen, we would never have found it.

Shortly after we passed the edge of town, we saw the tall white spire of the central pagoda of Wat Yansangwararam—mercifully called Wat Yan for short. Reportedly the most spacious of Thailand's more than thirty thousand Buddhist temple complexes, its construction began in 1979 to honor the current and much beloved monarch, His Majesty King Bhumibol Adulyadej. Wat Yan is a country monastery whose buildings spread over 118 acres. More important to our host, it is the source of most of Banglamung's dogs.

"People dump unwanted dogs and puppies at the temple," the Australian explained. Although the notion of so many homeless dogs distressed us, at least, we offered, this was better than killing a healthy animal, as is too often done in our culture.

"There is no euthanization here," our host told us. "It's not against the law per se—at least no one knows it to be—but . . . well, it's like stepping on money. You're in pretty hot water if you do it." To pin a flying bill with the toe of the shoe or to trap a rolling coin beneath the foot is considered a grave offense in Thailand. All coins and bills are emblazoned with the image of the king, and to place the foot—the lowliest part of the body—

atop his image is considered an insult to His Majesty and to all of his subjects.

The Thai proscription against euthanasia sometimes conflicts with Western notions of humane treatment. Once, when the monks brought in a dying stray covered with bleeding tumors, one of Gary's vets put it out of its misery. Word of the forbidden act spread through the monastery. Some of the younger monks approved, but most of the elders were deeply upset. The rift took weeks to mend. "This was so important to us, to establish a strong relationship with the people around us," Gary said. "That's why we got involved heavily with dogs. And our vets look after the odd buffalo or goat for free."

They also minister to the health of the local elephants. As Gary drove us out of town, we noted "No Elephant" signs along the road—a drawing of a pachyderm within a slashed red circle, like a "No Smoking" sign on an airplane. Elephants were no longer allowed on Pattaya's congested streets, but half a dozen thatched-roofed elephant camps still dot the countryside within view of skyscraping hotels. Elephants and their mahouts, formerly employed in the logging industry that Thailand officially outlawed in 1988, now earn their living giving rides to tourists. Almost none of the mahouts can afford to pay for veterinary care.

The work of Gary's organization, we learned, was not confined to the Pattaya area. In northern Thailand, TSCWA had funded, designed, and built an enclosure for eight confiscated moon bears and offered veterinary care for rescued monkeys and gibbons at Om Koi Wildlife Breeding Center. Further north, in Mae Hong Song's Surin National Park, the organization had constructed a large electric-fenced enclosure for eight moon bears, formerly confined to tiny cages. And at Krabok Koo Wildlife Breeding Center, it had stationed four veterinarians and two wild animal keepers to care for its more than four hundred rescued primates and twenty bears.

All this work is done with volunteer labor. Gary amasses volunteers from Thailand, Canada, New Zealand, the Netherlands, Sweden, the United Kingdom, Australia, Germany, and the United States. Each volunteer comes for a minimum three-month stay, and pays for the round-trip airfare to Bangkok as well as for all food and toiletry items. We were deeply impressed with the volunteers' commitment—and with Gary's.

"You must have a deep and abiding love of animals," I said to him, admiringly.

"No," he answered to my surprise. "Not particularly."

How could that be?

"Surely you must have had a beloved dog when you were growing up, or something," I said.

"No, not really." His mother was wild for Alsatians, and growing up in the suburbs of Sydney, his family had owned a Labrador retriever. "But it was a *dog*," he said. "Like, 'Catch the ball.' Come on!"

I was flummoxed.

"So, what was your background?"

He'd been trained as a construction engineer—which was why he was so good at building escape-proof outdoor enclosures for the animals. That this is no easy feat is often the reason that animals are confined to tiny cages. We had heard of one outdoor enclosure (one Gary had not built or supervised) that had to be closed the first day it opened, because a moon bear had immediately escaped from it. The fact that this particular moon bear was a cripple with only three legs made the engineering failure even more ignominious.

But at age twenty-eight, Gary had given up on building professionally and had come to Thailand. He was actually on his way to London, but stopped off to help a Thai girl with her luggage. At check-in at the Sydney airport, he had claimed her overweight luggage as his own to save her the charges, and so when the flight stopped in Bangkok he stopped off to visit her. He liked Bangkok. After earning a journalism certificate at the London School of Journalism in a record three weeks, he chose Bangkok as his base. He began covering corporate issues in the music industry for English-language newspapers.

That, I pointed out, did not begin to explain how he came to work with animals.

Well, meanwhile, he said, two friends, in an effort to improve conditions for a number of gibbons rescued from the wildlife trade, asked him to design and build some cages for the rescued apes. Out of their efforts, the three inaugurated a new wildlife charity, the Thai Society for the Conservation of Wild Animals.

But while the new organization was being set up—a legal process that took over a year—one of the friends, a Scottish zookeeper, left to work in Kenya. The other went home to America. Running the new society—which he founded with the help of two other friends, who were Thai—fell to him. As Gary put it, "I ended up with the organization by default."

That still didn't seem to explain why, a decade later, he was still working for free, in appalling heat and often confounded by infamous bureaucracy, to run a Thai fund for animals.

Gary van Zuylen arched one eyebrow and looked at me from beneath the bill of his baseball cap as if he thought, as he might put it, I had lost the plot.

"It was a job that needed to be done." And then he pointedly changed the subject.

Though Gary himself was an enigma, his organization was an open book—quite literally. At the end of the day, we asked him if it were possible to find more information on where his bears were originally captured. He offered us complete access to his records.

Over the years, volunteers have compiled voluminous data on each bear, and this is kept in three large looseleaf binders stored among the bookshelves in the little cinderblock house where the volunteers stay, next to the dog compound. Each bear is represented by a photograph as well as a verbal description, and further identified by a microchip implanted just under the skin, whose number is duly recorded. The number can be read (at close range, requiring the bear be sedated) with a hand-held device like those at American supermarket checkout counters.

The written records, we found, were mostly concerned with each bear's medical history. Volunteers noted the date and details of each health check and the bear's dental condition. Skin and gut parasites were noted and treated, and vaccines were recorded, complete with dates and batch numbers. There was a space on each form to note behavior: when he first arrived at Banglamung in 1998, Stripe, the yellow-eyed bear who had peered into Gary's window, was so shy, a volunteer wrote, that he "would rather sleep outdoors in the pouring rain than to try sneak inside the dens" with the other bears.

But we were disappointed to find almost no data on where most of the bears had been captured. Perhaps no one ever knew; or perhaps, as information with little bearing on the animals' health or welfare, it had been deemed superfluous. "Their focus was obviously not on genetic variation," noted Gary. There was not even a spot for recording this data on the forms.

However, we noted a number of animals described as having lighter coats, or portions thereof. To these we paid particular attention. Besides Louis, Stripe, and Romeo, two bears stood out: Harem, the bear rescued by the good ladies of the massage parlor, had a "blondish" face. Another female, Babe, had a "raccoon effect" around the eyes—brown eye rings set against darker fur. There was no information on where either came from. A few others were listed as having minor coat variations—light speckles on the forehead, a pale streak between the eyes—and we noted these bears and their microchip numbers. But most surprising was what someone (the entries were unsigned) had written in the behavior profiles of Stripe, Louis, and Harem: "Laos subspecies markings" and "possibly Laos subspecies."

"There *is* no Laos subspecies!" Gary said. Of this there was no doubt. Gary had scoured the records. Some fourteen species or subspecies of the moon bear have been named or proposed, and he knew all of them. The brownish-furred moon bears from southern Pakistan were designated *Ursus thibetanus gedrosianus;* some very small moon bears of Japan were named *japonicus;* the large ones living in Siberia and Manchuria, *ussuricus* . . . But there were no subspecies of moon bears anywhere in Southeast Asia. There was almost nothing published in the scientific literature on bears from Laos. Further, there was no reason to think that

Stripe, Louis, or Harem had come from Laos, as there was no information on their profiles about their origins.

We were nonetheless intrigued. Of course, the idea of a lighter race of
moon bears centered in Laos may merely have been the wild speculation
of an untrained Western volunteer. But possibly, this entry reflected gen-
uine local knowledge that the mystery volunteer had somehow picked
up. After all, local people had known for many years about the Sao la, the
Vietnamese warty hog, and the other new species that scientists only discovered in the 1990s. No scientist had ever reported golden or light-
haired moon bears—but perhaps they were already well known to the
Laotians who live among them. And if local people distinguish these
bears from the common, black moon bears, perhaps the difference was
sufficient for them to constitute a new species after all.

*   *   *

Although there were no golden bears at Banglamung, we had heard of
another place in Thailand that reportedly had one: a zoo, 150 kilometers
north of Bangkok, in the town of Lop Buri. Still sore from the motorcycle
ride, Gary had rented an air-conditioned Mercedes and a driver to take
us there. But we faced an awkward dilemma. We had written to the zoo
director, whose name we'd obtained from a friend, but received no response—probably because he could not read English, and we couldn't
write in Thai. Though Lop Buri was once a capital—from there, the
Khmers had administered to their empire's Tai population from the
ninth through thirteenth centuries—today its main attraction is an ancient temple overrun with seven hundred pink-faced, long-tailed monkeys known as rhesus macaques. (The monkeys are considered sacred in
the town, and the people, crediting them for bringing happiness and
prosperity, freely allow the macaques to steal belongings, ransack shops,
tease school children, assault temple worshipers, and stop traffic.) The
place receives few foreign visitors. Almost none of its citizens speak English. We were worried about the kind of welcome we would receive
when two Farangs showed up and inexplicably began to pull hair out of
the zoo animals.

"No worries!" exclaimed our Australian host. He knew the facility; it was run, he told us, by the Thai military, and was one of the oldest zoos in the country. In fact, one of his current volunteers had previously worked there. He generously offered to free her from her duties at Banglamung so she could accompany us there.

"You can't imagine how many monkeys escaped during the month I was here, just because someone left the door open!" said Corina Sutel, the twenty-four-year-old veterinary nurse whom Gary deposited at our hotel the next morning. "There's not one trained zoo worker—just soldiers going into tiger cages with nothing but a broom!"

When she'd first appeared at Lop Buri, Corina had caused quite a stir. A rail-thin woman with beautiful blue eyes and large, gentle, slow-moving hands, Corina sported a silver stud in her lower lip, another just like it in her left nostril, a third shaped like a kangaroo in her right nostril, and buzz-cut blond hair framing ears sequined with pierced earrings. She also had three tattoos and was considering a fourth, provided she could find an artist to create a credible binturong. When she'd come to Banglamung, Gary van Zuylen had eventually banned her from visiting Wat Yan, because the monks would drop everything to stare at her.

She'd come to Lop Buri as part of a volunteer program to help train the soldiers in the task of caring for their charges, and to find ways to make the animals' lives more interesting inside their sometimes tiny cages. Corina lives for opportunities like these. Trained just outside Hamburg as a veterinary nurse, she had spent a year working for an animal clinic before volunteering on an eleven-week sea turtle conservation project in Greece. She was hooked—not just on the travel, she explained, but on using her skills to do more than give Fifi her annual rabies shot; as a volunteer on projects like these, she could help animals who were in desperate need. Returning to Germany, she had worked at a bakery, and then for two months at a McDonald's (the ultimate sacrifice for her, a strict vegan) to earn the money to go back to Greece to volunteer again during the summer of 1997. Since then, she has spent all her winters working at a printing office close enough to home that she can ride her bike there—working shifts, nights, weekends and overtime—just to earn the money to work as a volunteer at jobs that desperately need doing but for which no one will pay.

Lop Buri Zoo, she explained, did not begin as a zoo, but "as a bin to dump animals." When people no longer wanted their pet bear, or found an orphaned monkey, they brought it to the local authorities; in this case, this was the military. Locals still bring unwanted animals here. Just during the month Corina worked at Lop Buri, the zoo acquired an unwanted pet oriental small-clawed otter and took in two crab-eating macaques (whose cage bore an English label reading "crap-eating macaque") as well as a cast-off moon bear.

The soldiers at this "Special Warfare Center" do their best as zoo-keepers—but this is a zoo unlike any Gary or I had seen before.

When we first arrived, the place seemed much like an American zoo of perhaps forty years ago. Cartoonish sculptures of animals adorn the paths to the exhibits. Treats to hand-feed the animals are sold at booths. And people can—and do—easily pass their hands through the bars of all the cages to touch the animals, including the tigers. But the two Indochinese tigers, we quickly noticed, weren't the only species in their exhibit. Along with the two huge adult cats lived a family of dogs—five black and one yellow—prey items who, to our amazement, the tigers were not eating. The tigers were brother and sister orphans, Corina explained. Both were suckled by the mother dog along with her own litter, and today they all lived together peacefully as a family.

Dogs, in fact, roamed all over the zoo. While working elephants merged with motorcycle and auto traffic on the highway outside its gates, dogs lived inside the zoo. They waited by the food concessions. They guarded the exhibits. Some of them had visible mange. They entered the exotic animals' cages with impunity, eating their food, defecating in the enclosures, and sometimes harassing the inmates. Although the strays were known to spread disease (one of the zoo's four binturongs, Corina told us, had recently died of canine distemper) nothing was done to dissuade them. Dogs followed us everywhere from the moment we entered the zoo. Each seemed to have staked out a territory, and would bark at you when you entered it, accompany you as you walked through it, and then, at some boundary known only to them, pass your company on, like a baton, to the next dog down the line.

Stray cats were fewer, but they also turned up in strange places. One enclosure held a cassowary, a tall, flightless, vicious bush bird native to Australia and New Guinea, and a number of large, handsome, greenish monitor lizards. These meat-eating lizards are second only to Komodo dragons in size and ferocity. Fleet and strong-jawed, they can take down a deer and slash its throat. To our dismay, we saw a small tabby kitten inside their enclosure. Had some cruel tourist tossed it in, over the moat where the predatory lizards now swam? One of the reptiles emerged from the water and, flicking its long, black, forked tongue, headed directly toward the kitten. We began to shout to try to warn her, but the kitten ignored us. When the four-foot lizard finally reached her, we braced for the worst. She simply rubbed her lips and chin against its scaly flesh—like a house cat greeting her owners come home from work at the end of the day.

The bear enclosure was heralded by a large billboard announcing in English that this was "Mary's Bear Home." The exhibit—which besides the indoor cages includes a large outdoor yard with two bathing pools and plenty of climbing trees—was donated by Mary Hutton, we read, an Australian with her own organization, Free the Bears Fund. Nine bears lived here: seven moon bears and two sun bears. From one of the sun bears arose the sound of a swarm of bees. Although he seemed to be nearly adult, he was sucking his paw, emitting the same strange, almost mechanical noise that baby bears make when suckling from their mothers. At close range it sounds like a cross between the nickering of a goat and the hum of a sump pump. I had heard this before; Ben's orphaned cubs made it when they sucked on his ears, and they continued to do so even when they were more than a year old. Bear cubs taken too early from their mother's breasts suck their paws for comfort like a child sucks its thumb.

That was surely the case with the bears here. All of them, we read, were rescued from the illegal wildlife trade. One of the moon bears had only three feet. Corina told us he was named Stumpy, and that he had been rescued from a poacher who was caught in the act of amputating his left rear paw for soup.

Then I saw at a glance that there was a lion living in the bear exhibit.

A tawny, fat, male lion with a huge, fluffy, light brown mane, was placidly chewing what looked like a bit of bok choy held between its giant paws, in among the big black ursines in the cages. This was odd for a lion, I thought. And then I saw, surrounded by the lion's mane, the face of a bear.

"This is the largest, blondest bear we've ever seen!" said Gary.

She was the first blond adult we had seen—proof that the blond color was not merely a growth phase. Another large moon bear in the enclosure looked like a more dramatic version of Stripe: a big, pale-faced, eye-ringed male, with a head, forelegs, and mane even darker than Stripe's but a much lighter back.

But the most important data was still lacking. We needed to know where these bears came from, and if that could be determined, to pull some hairs.

* * *

This, with Corina's kind help, we arranged the next day. One of the keepers she knew, a young soldier she called Tam (but whose real name was Sangphet Unkeaw), spoke some English. Tam agreed to ask Lieutenant Colonel Wirat Phupiangjai, the zoo's director, about the bears' origins, and to act as our translator as we interviewed him.

Tam also agreed to help us pull hairs. It proved remarkably easy. The bears' indoor enclosure was, we were thrilled to learn, equipped with what is known in the zoo trade as a squeeze or crush cage: a portion of the cage is fitted with three walls that can be moved from the outside to confine the animal in a tight space, for administering shots and other treatments without tranquilizing the animal. Most of the bears were easily persuaded to enter the squeeze cage for a food reward.

With no danger to either us or the bears, we plucked to our hearts' content. As well as the blond bear, Bertha, and the intermediate, Dave, we harvested the black moon bears, too. "Why not?" suggested Gary. Though we didn't really need their hairs, they could come in handy, especially if something happened to the other black bear hairs we were using for comparison with the gold ones. So into the squeeze cage, and into our test tube, went, respectively, each bear and its DNA: the enormous Daisy, who had been held in a small cage for so long that when she did venture outside she stayed near the door; the towering male Linz, whom Tam had to coax into the crush cage, after the huge bear stood up and snarled spectacularly at him, by brandishing a metal bar; the smaller Luke, still impressive with a big mane; and the smallest moon bear, Baby, with a bald patch on his side that Tam told us was produced when his previous owner dropped on him a pot of scalding water. Baby cried in fear in the squeeze cage. I plucked him as quickly as I could. We took hairs from all the moon bears except Stumpy. We figured he'd been through enough already.

By the time we appeared in the director's octagonal, fan-cooled office for our interview, Colonel Wirat, a dapper, cheerful man of fifty-two, had scoured the zoo's records. He had great news: while there was no information on any of the black bears but Stumpy —who had been rescued in Nakhon Sawan Province—he knew where both Bertha and Dave had been captured.

Bertha—who was now quite elderly—had been found as a cub on the slopes of a highland bamboo forest while farmers were clearing it by burning. "The people living in the mountain catch lots of bears," Tam translated, "sometimes for food. But sometimes the bears are special, and this family, they were eager to have it. Someone wanted to buy it but the family wanted to keep it because she is pretty." The same family, some years later, had similarly captured Dave as a cub. Both bears, Colonel Wirat assured us, had come from the same place: in the Louang Phabang Mountains, on the Thai side of the border with northern Laos, near a village that the colonel identified as Ban Pang Kae.

Gary hauled out one of his maps, and began to plot the locations of all the known golden and light-colored bears we had found. Remarkably— from Sun Hean's bears in southwestern Cambodia, to Romeo's rescue site in Thailand, to Bertha and Dave's original home at the edge of Laos, to Gary's first bear in Yunnan—all the points strung out in an arc that ran right through northern Laos.

We would return to America in a few days. But we had already begun to plan our next expedition.

PART TWO

The Magic Ingredient

LEARNING HER husband is soon to return from a long war, a woman prepares for his arrival with great joy. She works hard to cook all his favorite dishes. She cleans the house again and again. But when the couple is finally reunited, the husband is too sullen and withdrawn to even speak with his wife.

So the woman consults the village shaman for help. Does she know a potion or medicine to restore the husband's war-torn soul?

Ah, yes, says the healer, but there is one ingredient missing. She sends the wife on a quest to find it: a hair from the coat of a moon bear.

The woman embarks on a dangerous journey. To find the moon bear, she travels through stony deserts. She climbs tall mountains. Wild animals of all kinds swoop down upon her—but she wishes them well, they let her pass unhurt. She endures hunger, exhaustion, heat, and cold. Finally, she meets the moon bear in its mountain den. The bear looks like a frightening monster, and she is terrified by its earth-shattering roars. But she makes it an offering—some of the food she had brought to eat herself—and so she persuades the animal to allow her to pluck from its coat a single hair.

She returns from her long journey with the prized hair. But to her horror, the healer throws the hair into the fire! Why? "Remember each step you took to climb the mountain?" asks the healer. "Remember how you captured the trust of the moon bear?" This—and not the hair—was the point, says the shaman: to accomplish the healing, the woman will need to draw upon all she had learned and discovered on the arduous journey.

*　*　*

Shortly after we returned to the States, I read this tale in Clarissa Pinkola Estes's wonderful book *Women Who Run with the Wolves*. The story had been told to her by a Japanese soldier. And it was no wonder the woman in the story was sent to search for a moon bear, Estes noted. It is said in some parts of Japan that the moon bear can speak directly to the gods. In ancient Japanese legends, the moon bear is the emissary of the Buddhist Goddess of Deep Compassion, Kwan-Yin. It is she, they say, who gave the animal its white chest crescent, an emblem of the power of her healing love. In many other cultures, too, the bear is the totem animal of a deity. Bears are associated with the Greek and Roman goddesses Artemis and Diana, and with the Latina deities Huerte and Hecoteptl. These goddesses bestow upon their followers the ursine powers of tracking, knowing, and digging out deeply embedded truths.

At the time I read the story, Gary and I were awaiting the results of the DNA testing—the truth embedded in the bears' genetic code. The hairs we had plucked were being analyzed by a laboratory in Idaho. We were anxious. The genetic material in the bulbs of the hairs is somewhat fragile, and is particularly vulnerable to fungus—a constant threat in Cambodia and Thailand during the monsoon season. We'd been very careful to store each set of hairs in clean, dry, stoppered vials. These we had packed carefully in Gary's camera bag, and around the tubes, on advice of a colleague who had done DNA studies on American black bears, we had packed small bags of silica, a desiccant to remove any moisture that might be inside the camera bag. But to our horror, when we arrived back in the states, Gary found a message from the colleague waiting for him on his answering machine: "Oh, I hope you haven't left yet," she said.

"I meant to tell you to make sure you put the desiccant *inside* the vials *with the hairs.*"

We had desperately hoped that the genetic information in the hairs would prove the golden bear was a new species. But now we faced the prospect that they would give us no information at all.

As we anxiously awaited the results, I was grateful for the story. Perhaps, as the tale had promised, the value of our trip extended beyond what we had expected. Perhaps the moon bear would guide our work in a direction we could never have imagined.

CHAPTER SIX

Essence of Bear

Our answer was to come from halfway around the world, from a land very different from the jungles our moon bears had known. But here, too, nearby mountain forests had once harbored bears—until the land had been irrevocably altered.

Grizzly bears once roamed the pine-covered Bitterroot Mountains of central Idaho. Looking like great mountains themselves, their eight hundred-pound bulk surmounted by the peak of a great shoulder hump, some one hundred thousand grizzlies inhabited the lower forty-eight states in the 1820s. Today, only nine hundred American grizzlies are left outside of Alaska. Those from the Bitterroots are gone.

Just west of the Bitterroots, much of Idaho's northern panhandle is composed of rich, rolling farmland known as the Palouse—former prairie where Nez Perce Indians raised spotted ponies that became known as Appaloosas. Today the hills are clad in lentil and wheat. White farmers began staking homesteads here in the 1870s. They eradicated the Bitterroot's grizzlies; they seized the Indians' prairies; they replaced the ponies with pigs. The roots of the wild camas lily made perfect food for swine. The biggest town was known as Hog Heaven. In the Chamber of Commerce spirit, town fathers quickly switched to calling it Paradise Valley. But in 1877, when a farmer named Samuel Neff filed for a postal permit, he formally gave the community the name it has today, in honor of his hometown in Pennsylvania—Moscow. It was here that state leaders chose to build the state's land grant educational institution, the

University of Idaho, in 1889. And it was here, more than a century later, where we sent the hair from the moon bears.

In their heavily padded Federal Express box, our test tubes passed beneath the glass eyes of the two mounted elk heads that guard the foyer of the university's College of Natural Resources. Through a door, down a corridor, and through another door, our samples entered the reception area of the Department of Fish and Wildlife Resources, where visitors are greeted by a stuffed cougar playing with a grouse, a stuffed fox dismembering a partridge, and two living secretaries. The samples were delivered to a tiny corner room, decorated with photos and cartoons of bears and the artwork of children, and occupied by a slender, thirty-year-old brunette—the office of Dr. Lisette Waits, mother of two young sons, long-distance runner, and one of the world's top experts on the molecular genetics of bears. At her lab, the hairs we had collected would be utterly transformed: their cells burst, their subcellular parts purified, their DNA chemically parsed into submolecular units—analyses so different from our work in Southeast Asia it seemed impossible to believe that both were aspects of the same science.

We'd learned of Lisette through a colleague we'd met at the University of Minnesota, black bear researcher Kristina Timmerman. Kristina collects hairs from her study animals by placing low strings of barbed wire around baits. When the bears slink beneath the fence, they leave follicle-bearing hairs on the wire; from their DNA, the lab can estimate how many individuals inhabit the northern Minnesota study area, their sex, and how they are related. The lab also analyzes DNA from hair and scat to determine the population sizes of grizzly and black bears in Glacier National Park. Yellowstone researchers send hair samples from grizzly and black bears collected at sites along cutthroat trout streams to see how many and what kind of bears use that food resource (which is now threatened due to the introduction of competing lake trout). The lab has analyzed hairs from brown bears in the Gobi Desert to determine gene exchange between oases; extracted DNA from the skulls of extinct cave bears to chart ancient lineages; and obtained DNA from fecal samples to determine species identity and population sizes of pronghorn antelopes and wolves, pygmy rabbits from Washington State and spectacled bears from South America.

There are fewer than ten U.S. laboratories capable of analyzing genetic information from animal feces, bone, and hair—and this is the only one in the nation that handles this volume of DNA from bears. "In the bear community," Lisette later told us with justified pride, "this is considered *the* DNA lab."

She hadn't planned on working on bear genetics when she'd begun her thesis work at the University of Utah in 1991. At the time, she was working on a case study of high blood pressure in humans, looking at which genes might predispose certain ethnic groups to the disease. Lisette had always loved animals—growing up in Georgia, she had planned a career in marine biology since fifth grade. But after she began a biology major at the University of Georgia, she was transfixed by biochemistry and genetics classes. "I became amazed by the specificity and promise of what you might be able to do with these new molecular methods," she later told us, widening her large brown eyes for emphasis. "Always my grounding had been in biology and ecology and natural history, but when I hit biochemistry and genetics, I thought: whoa! This seems like we can get such specific and definitive answers to questions that in field research would take years and years and years collecting data and still not be quite sure." For instance, a biologist might have to watch groups of animals for years, even decades, to determine which animals were brothers and sisters, half-siblings or grandchildren, and who is breeding with whom. A molecular geneticist can tell within hours. Using this powerful new tool, said Lisette, "we might answer questions we hadn't even started to work on, but now we might be able to address."

It was a time of thrilling new discoveries in molecular techniques. Only in 1986 had Kary Mullis, a biochemist with the biotechnology giant Perkin Elmer Cetus, developed a process by which DNA could be copied. The idea for the method came to him in a daydream while driving his car. The new process won him the Nobel Prize. Prior to this, molecular

Prevost's Squirrel

Lesser
Mouse-Deer

Simao
Bear

Bertha & Dave

C.H.I.N.A

Hainan

V.I.E.T.N.A.M

L.A.O.S

B.U.R.M.A

T.H.A.I.L.A.N.D

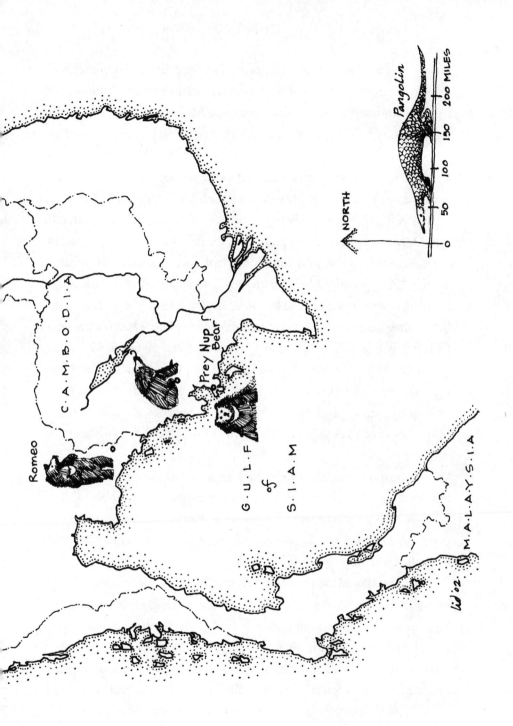

Golden Moon Bear Locations

genetic analysis was expensive, technically laborious, and sometimes dangerous and inaccurate. Researchers required very large amounts of tissue to study the genetics of an organism. Mullis's development of the Polymerase Chain Reaction meant that researchers could, at least in theory, generate an almost unlimited amount of DNA from a small sample—even the bulb of a hair. It allowed geneticists to examine and manipulate the essence of life with unprecedented precision and ease.

As a graduate student, Lisette found herself at the forefront of developments in molecular techniques just as the field was exploding. Though there seemed to be no jobs combining molecular genetics with wildlife biology, the applications for human medicine shone with promise: drugs could be engineered molecule by molecule. Diseases could be diagnosed before they happened. A project to sequence the entire human genome had already begun. Lisette had won a coveted National Science Foundation grant to pay for her graduate school, supplies, and travel, and was making important progress on her hypertension study. She was expecting to spend her life researching human genetics. And then something happened to change her life: "I fell in love," she said, "with bears."

*   *   *

When our moon bear hairs arrived, Lisette pulled the tubes from their box and logged them in with laboratory identification numbers in her computer. But no one would open them before passing through the doors of the Waits lab downstairs, where technicians extract the DNA from the samples.

This large basement room is known as the lab's "clean zone" ("even though there are fecal samples in there," notes Lisette). Fecal samples, bone, and hair have such low quantities of DNA that they are more vulnerable to contamination than are samples of blood or skin. Grad students who work upstairs with these tissues, or with the products of the Polymerase Chain Reaction, aren't allowed to work downstairs on the same day—unless they go home, change clothes, and shower first. No keys or notebooks, no equipment or supplies that have ever been in the upstairs lab are allowed downstairs.

Wearing surgical gloves and sitting at a long table beneath a bright halogen light and magnifying scope, Chris Cegelski, one of Lisette's graduate students, unstoppered the first of our vials and poured its contents onto a piece of white paper. Carefully she selected the hairs with the best bulbs. Each sample typically takes fifteen minutes to prepare. With surgical scissors, she clipped a one-centimeter piece of bulb from the choicest ones available from each sample and transferred them with tweezers into a 1.7-milliliter Eppendorf tube. The tiny tube contained an extraction solution, to which she then added a chemical buffer. The chemicals would lyse, or burst the cells, and cause them to release their DNA.

Next the DNA must be separated from other products of the cell—such as proteins and salts, or contaminants that might have been on the hair. After adding more buffers and water, the solution is repeatedly spun in a centrifuge at 13,500 revolutions per minute—essentially a two- or three-minute laundry cycle to wash out the contaminants, while binding the DNA to a fine membrane of silica near the bottom of the tube. One tube for each set of samples contains no hair. It holds only the washing and purification chemicals, to act as a control to test for contamination.

At the end of this process, the DNA—if in fact there ever was any in the sample—is presumably purified and stable enough to be stored in a refrigerator for a month or two. For longer storage, even into eternity, there is a negative-eighty-degrees-Centigrade freezer. Sitting at one end of the long room, this ordinary-looking refrigerator-freezer is a library of the genetic blueprints of thousands of individual animals. It is probably the largest repository for bear DNA in the world. And our samples—clipped, lysed, spun, washed, and purified—would represent the first and only moon bears in it.

Or so we hoped. So far, our many weeks in the field, and the technician's hours of work in the laboratory, had produced only colorless liquid held in fewer than a dozen test tubes, each smaller than a newborn's fingernail.

Still, no one knew whether they contained any DNA at all.

* * *

When Lisette began her graduate work in molecular genetics, her adviser was approached with an unusual request. Yellowstone's wildlife managers were developing a recovery plan for its endangered grizzlies. The U.S. Fish and Wildlife Service had just been sued by an environmental group claiming, correctly, that the recovery plan did not address concerns about the genetic health of this isolated population. In fact, virtually nothing was known about it. Could the new molecular techniques be applied to investigate the genetics of grizzly bears?

At the University of Utah, Lisette's adviser, Ryk Ward, worked mainly in the medical field, but had also begun a project tracking the lineages of the native people of North and South America. Theoretically, he agreed, there was no reason this could not be done for bears. Lisette was invited to sit in on the meetings, and soon found herself drawn into the intellectual challenge of the project. "When we started to work on the genetics of the Yellowstone grizzly bears," she recalled, "we realized we didn't even know the relationship of the brown bear to the other species. We decided to step back and look at the question of how unique is a brown bear? How does the Yellowstone brown bear relate to other brown bears? How does the brown bear relate to other bear species? How old is it evolutionarily? Because the amount of genetic variation you'd expect to see in a species is dependent upon different life history traits and depends on how long the evolution of that species has been occurring. If a species is very young there's not much time for differences to accumulate. So you can make wrong conclusions about very specific questions if you don't have the broader picture of how it fits into the evolutionary history of the species."

The managers invited the young Ph.D. candidate to visit the bears of Yellowstone. She vividly recalls the moment she saw her first grizzly. Early in the morning, the team set up their spotting scope on a hill. For some time, of course, no bears appeared. But then, she saw a mother grizzly, and then her cub, come lumbering and gamboling across the hill. "It gave me goose bumps," she said.

What is it about bears that so thrilled her? "Power," she answers instantly, "and their wildness." Everything about a bear speaks to her of wilderness: "Even their gait. Even the way they move. It's very beautiful. No animal moves the way they do through the landscape." She remembers watching a male grizzly one evening in Yellowstone. He was hunting for elk calves. For most bears, meat is a rare delicacy. Only during the first three weeks after elk calves are born, when the babies are still hiding in the grass, can a grizzly hope to catch one; after this period, the calves can outrun them. She remembers watching this male through a spotting scope, mesmerized by his movements: "His gait was sliding, stiff-legged, meandering—almost nonchalant. You know they are moving with great purpose, but they look like they are just meandering along. Then an elk calf pops up! He caught one after another." That evening she watched him catch and kill five elk calves. "That's an incredible predatory ability. That predatory level"—and there is a catch in her voice—"it's just really spectacular."

For a year, Lisette worked on both the bear project and the human hypertension study, shuttling from wilderness to laboratory. She presented data at professional meetings on both projects. Her heart lay with the bears. But the Yellowstone managers had never paid her for her work. They didn't have to: her National Science Foundation grant allowed her the freedom to work on any project she wished, including a generous budget for supplies and travel. Once her doctoral degree was completed, though, that money would disappear. Could she even make a living working on bear genetics?

Meanwhile, jobs in human genetics were booming. Her parents, accountants and entrepreneurs who had urged her to go to medical school (as long as she was going to get a Ph.D., they argued, why not be a doctor and make some money?) were unenthusiastic about a career in wildlife conservation. But her adviser told her this: "Do what you love. Be very, very good at it. And everything will be okay."

She believed him. And she believed in the bears. Theirs were the mysteries she pursued in her Ph.D. thesis, and the kinds of mysteries she explores today: are these bears genetically distinct from others of their kind who inhabit different areas? How old a species are they? How much genetic variability is necessary to sustain an isolated population?

Her work in the laboratory was more than just intellectually exciting; it was morally and emotionally compelling. The questions she was asking were among the most basic and essential for understanding these endangered creatures' biology and evolution. Bears, to her, are the essence of places of unspeakable beauty and wildness, places like Yellowstone and Glacier national parks, like the Cardamom and Elephant mountains. And in the test tubes in her university laboratory, in the blueprints for life called DNA, she is exploring the very essence of bear.

* * *

The recipe for life is written in an alphabet of only four letters: A, C, G, and T.

Each of these letters stands for a nucleotide: adenine, cytosine, guanine, thymine, nitrogenous bases. Each adenine reaches to its partner, thymine, and each cytosine to its guanine, across the DNA molecule's dual backbone of phosphate and sugar, like rungs on a twisting ladder. The order in which these neucleotides appear codes for the production of amino acids. Amino acids, of which there are twenty, in turn string into polypeptide chains. A gene is the set of nucleotides that codes for one polypeptide chain. Polypeptide chains make up proteins. And proteins make up us.

Each mammalian cell offers two sources of genetic material. The comparatively weighty nucleus of the cell contains nuclear DNA, with about thirty thousand genes. DNA from the tiny mitochondria contain fewer than forty.

That mammalian cells contain two types of DNA reflects an extraordinary event that occurred perhaps two billion years ago. The modern cell arose from the fusion of two different cell types, when big cells swallowed little cells and for some reason did not digest them. The little cells that ended up living inside the big ones are known as mitochondria. Mitochondria resemble bacteria. A billion of them would fit into a grain of sand. But they produce all of a cell's energy, consuming the oxygen we breathe to help us burn the food we eat. Their genes contain the recipe for cellular energy production.

Mitochondrial DNA divides, evolves, and is inherited separately from nuclear DNA. Nuclear DNA is inherited from both parents; mitochondrial DNA is inherited only from the mother; there is no recombination from mating as there is from nuclear DNA. (The tiny sperm cell has only fifty to a hundred mitochondria, and those few are usually destroyed by the huge egg, containing tens of thousands of mitochondria.) Gary had earlier explained to me why mitochondrial DNA is particularly useful for tracing lineages—and thus identifying species and subspecies—backward through evolutionary time:

"Both sorts of DNA mutate occasionally," the professor explained, "in that a particular nucleotide changes identity spontaneously and randomly. Nuclear DNA has repair mechanisms that reverse many such mutations, but mitochondrial DNA does not. And mitochondria reproduce very rapidly. As a result, mitochondrial DNA evolves much more rapidly, on average, than does nuclear DNA—something like ten times the rate of nuclear DNA, and at a rather regular rate. So it is somewhat like a ticking clock."

The idea of the molecular clock is based on this set of simple and reasonable hypotheses: as species diverge from a common ancestor, they accumulate mutations on DNA in a random and thus fairly steady manner. The longer two species or lineages have been separated, the greater the amount of divergence. The amount of difference—called the genetic distance—between the two would be roughly proportionate to time elapsed since their ancestors diverged from one another. Working backward with a matrix of genetic differences between species, mathematical methods can be used to construct an evolutionary tree—similar to the trees genealogists construct to trace their ancestry.

And in fact, analysis of mitochondrial DNA has led to some of the most astonishing breakthroughs in the study of human ancestry. In the mid-1980s, geneticist Douglas Wallace of Emory University in Atlanta, with the late Allan Wilson of the University of California, announced they had found the African Eve: by tracing distinct changes in mitochondrial DNA in blood samples taken from humans around the world, they found all modern humans are descendants of one woman who lived in Africa two hundred thousand years ago.

In the years that followed this discovery, other studies of mitochondrial DNA provided evidence to help solve a number of enigmas about different mammals. One of them was the riddle of the panda. Ever since its discovery, for more than a hundred years, scientists argued over whether this strange, bamboo-eating carnivore was a bear, or a kind of raccoon, or whether it should be classified with the small, tree-dwelling red panda in a new family, the Ailuropodidae. Mitochondrial data, along with that gathered with other molecular techniques, has now identified the panda with relative certainty as the earliest branch of the known living bears—a discovery that was new at the time Lisette began working on the grizzlies of Yellowstone.

One of the components of Lisette's Ph.D. thesis entailed mapping sections of bear mitochondrial DNA, to discover which regions of the molecule contain the most useful information for comparative studies. How different were the grizzlies' sets of nucleotides from those of other bear species? And were there significant differences in the sequence of nucleotides within the species? She found one area on the mitochondrial molecule that was particularly diagnostic: a string of 520 base pairs, including part of a gene known as Cytochrome B, which codes for the critical pigment-like molecule that controls reactions within the cell, and part of a neighboring area known as the control region, which has the highest mutation rate of the entire DNA molecule.

Using single-stranded pieces of DNA called primers, the geneticist can selectively target the specific area of DNA of interest. Adding the protein, DNA polymerase, allows Lisette to copy it for study. And this was the next step in the labyrinthine process our samples were to undergo.

To set up the reaction, using a multichannel pipette—a device that looks like the tiny fingers of the hand of a sophisticated robot—Lisette's technician squirted into yet another set of tiny test tubes a master mix of primers, polymerase, and cofactors including salts and magnesium. To this the technician added the colorless liquid that comprised our samples. Finally the DNA was ready to begin the trip upstairs to the Laboratory of Ecological and Conservation Genetics.

Our samples would now embark on a voyage of transformation so strange it sounds like a child's clumsy first attempt at writing science fiction: the hairs we had removed from live bears with my eyebrow tweezers had become colorless liquid, and next they would turn into blue Jell-O. The blue Jell-O would be converted to glowing points of light. Pink juice would change the light into pictures of stacks of multicolored chips. And with a computer, the chips would be transformed into volumes of history, written in the ancient alphabet of G and C, A and T.

* * *

The Laboratory of Ecological and Conservation Genetics houses three PCR machines, nicknamed Bonnie, Clyde, and Wattana. They're named less out of affection than for clarity: if one isn't working, it's easier to explain which machine to avoid, or to sign up for them in a busy lab.

The size of an old-fashioned cash register, a PCR machine is basically an exquisitely calibrated heating and cooling device controlled by a computer. First the samples are heated to ninety-four degrees Centigrade. This breaks the bonds holding together its double helix structure, essentially unzipping the double-stranded molecule to a single strand. Then the PCR cools down to the annealing temperature, at which the specific primers you have chosen will stick to a precise area on the DNA—there and nowhere else on the genome. In our case, that temperature was sixty degrees, held for thirty seconds. Then the samples are heated again, to seventy-two degrees—the temperature at which the polymerase works to copy the DNA. Most proteins, including the polymerase, would denature at such high temperatures, but Perkin Elmer Cetus scientists circumvented the problem: they discovered a bacterium, *Thermus aquaticus*, living in the hot springs of Yellowstone National Park, and cloned their polymerase from that. So the cycle can proceed without interruption, expanding logarithmically. After forty cycles—about three hours—the genetic material can be copied thousands of times.

The copied DNA—known as "the PCR product"—next travels to another room in the upstairs lab. Here the technician mixes the product with an agarose gel, to create a kind of DNA Jell-O. Once the agar gels, it is pierced with small holes, into each of which the technician drops a sample of the PCR product, mixed with blue dye. The whole gelatinous mass is subjected to ninety volts of electricity for an hour. Because the nucleotides in the DNA are arranged on a sugar and phosphate backbone, and phosphate is negatively charged, the electric current will cause its nucleotides to separate out, from a positive to a negative pole, in a string. And a compound in the gel, ethidium bromide, causes the DNA to fluoresce under ultraviolet light. A camera transfers the image of the fluorescing sample to a computer, where it can be viewed, hugely magnified, on the screen. At this point, for the first time, the technician could see if any of our samples contained enough DNA to work.

In another laboratory across the hall, the Brunsfeld plant lab, more chemical reactions and more expensive machines would reveal the actual sequence of the nucleotides of our samples. Another set of gels is prepared and placed between two plates of glass. This time the gels contain a new ingredient: "pink juice," a fluorescent cocktail that glows a different color for each of the four nucleotide bases. The Sequencer looks like a tan-colored cabinet the size of a refrigerator and makes the sound of an air conditioner. A laser at the bottom scans the gel and excites the fluorescence, which is read by a computer: green for adenine, yellow for guanine, blue for cytosine, red for thymine.

A series of mathematical computer programs then compares the nucleotide sequences from the samples to generate a series of phylogenetic trees. The simplest model of evolution suggests, of course, that the individuals with the smallest number of nucleotide changes are most closely related. Were the golden moon bears different enough from the normal black moon bears to comprise a new species? Was there even enough DNA in our samples to tell?

* * *

Lisette sent the results to Gary by e-mail in October. He shared it with Sun Hean and me at a meeting at a Chinese restaurant in Chicago. Sun Hean was back in grad school by now, apparently cured of his stomach ailment. Now, he was accompanied by his beloved Lina, the couple having married that summer.

Gary, thoughtful host and gifted storyteller, waited until we had dispensed with small talk and settled into our seats. He cleared his throat, as he does before a lecture. "The results are very exciting," he said, "but they are exciting in a way I didn't at all expect." He paused. "Shall I?" he asked me ceremoniously. I nodded assent, and he began, as fine teachers always do, at the beginning.

"We had considerable reason to be worried about whether the hairs would in fact yield viable DNA results," he told Sun Hean for the first time. "However, in fact, almost all of the Cambodian and Thai samples gave very good results, I'm happy to say." All of our samples had turned out, except two: Luke, whose hairs we had pulled at Lop Buri; and more disappointingly, the pathetic little female cub we had taken such risks to find in the Elephant Mountains.

"And all the golden bears—from the thin female from Mong Rethy's plantation, to the elderly Bertha from Lop Buri—were identical on all base pairs examined," Gary said. Such a sequence of base pairs in nuclear DNA is called a genotype; on mitochondrial DNA, it is called a haplotype. Interestingly, he explained, the pandalike bears we had sampled—Romeo, whose hairs Johan had harvested with his bare hands at Banglamung, and Dave, from Lop Buri—shared the golden bears' haplotype, too.

"Do we have a new species then?" Sun Hean asked anxiously.

It certainly would have appeared so—except, said Gary, for one of the black moon bears: the male at the senator's zoo at Prey Veng.

"He has the exact same haplotype," he told us. "The genes are the same. So this, together with the fact that we've seen every possible intermediate between nearly completely blond and completely black in the bears, suggests to me strongly that we're looking at two color phases of the same sort of bear."

Sun Hean looked disappointed.

"Wouldn't this be comparable to, say, discovering the first white tigers in India?" I interjected. "They are actually a color phase of the Bengal tiger—the same species. And there are other examples of color phases, aren't there?"

Sun Hean brightened. "I think one is the black leopard. And also I have heard information about the white elephant."

"Yes," Gary agreed. Our golden bears were not, he stressed, extremely rare genetic accidents like five-legged cows: they appeared to be a normal, though previously unknown, color variation in the wild. "It's still a matter of great biological interest to know that there are multiple color phases within any species," he told us. "Variation is what biology is all about. We've discovered something that's new. We're describing something that's new. That no one has documented this before is amazing."

He paused to let us consider this. Of course we were disappointed that the golden moon bear wasn't a new species. Nonetheless, this discovery was important. But this news was not what had gotten Gary so excited.

"Now the other interesting fact, though," Gary continued, "is that among the bears that we got haplotypes for in Thailand—and not all of them necessarily caught in Thailand either—there are, in all, three distinct genetic haplotypes. And they are so different that there must have been hundreds of thousands of years of geographic separation between them! And this means that at least within Southeast Asia, we're looking at very distinct groupings that perhaps became separated during an earlier time when there was less forest available in Southeast Asia, and bears became isolated."

This was the part that had so fascinated the professor.

Having collected a very small number of samples, we were already seeing evidence of three deeply separated moon bear evolutionary lineages—one of which, the lineage which included the golden bears, we could already correlate with geography. "Even if animals *look* alike, if we can show they are genetically different, and if we can show they are predictably different in different parts of Southeast Asia, we may be able to name different subspecies in different parts of Southeast Asia," Gary pointed out. We might not have a new species, but we might still discover the next best thing: a new subspecies.

And that was not even the most exciting part. What intrigued the professor was that we had quite unexpectedly stumbled on a way to solve a mystery even deeper than discovering the identity of golden bears: "How and when and where did these bizarre shaggy things get to be in this strange tropical place?" he had always wondered. "They are as out of place as an Eskimo in the tropics."

Now we had a way to find out. We had found, in the lineages revealed by the DNA, a way to see back into time.

Changes in the nucleotides, as they occur over time, record the bears' ancient histories. By comparing their similarities and differences, we could sort them into groups within groups, creating lineages that, like those wooden Russian dolls, nest one within another within another. The relationships between the ever-larger groupings could be shown as a branching tree. And—if we could expand our sample size and match each group with a geographical location—the tree's branches, limbs, and roots could be plotted against a map to suggest to us the routes the pioneering bears had taken as they colonized the strange, new tropical world of Southeast Asia.

We would need to return to Southeast Asia, of course. We needed to collect many more samples. We needed to cover as wide a geographical area as possible. And it was essential that we get hairs from bears whose capture sites were known. But if we could do so, the rewards could be rich: a mitochondrial map could reveal to us the barriers that might have, in the distant past, cut off the different lineages of bears from each other, forcing them to evolve for millennia in isolation. It could show us vanished refuges where such evolution had taken place.

"It's incredible," said Gary. "After yanking these hairs out of the moon bears we've met, we can find out where these big shaggy bears actually bumbled around a hundred thousand years ago. It's even more incredible than looking at fossils!"

And the importance of our work was not just academic. Once we could match each lineage with a geographical location, our mitochondrial map could become an important conservation tool. "If one were to reintroduce captured animals in the wild," Gary told us, "one would probably want to try to reintroduce them in an area where they are the same haplotype." Once we had developed a lineage map of Southeast Asia's moon bears, a handful of hair from any captive animal could tell us the area to which it could be returned.

Our work could fuel the first project in the world to use molecular genetics to return formerly wild bears to their homelands.

The three of us gleefully launched into a series of toasts: "To the golden moon bear!" Gary offered. "To Sun Hean and Lina's marriage!" I added. "To His Excellency Chhun Sarreth!" Sun Hean cried. "And to our future expeditions!"

We might have toasted, too, the blessings of chance—and faith. The message in the Japanese story of the woman's quest for the hair of a moon bear was true for us, too: the bear hairs had proven invaluable, but not for the reasons we had expected. And we had acquired our greatest treasures not by our own carefully laid plans, but by chance along the journey. Unwittingly, we now found ourselves on a path to discoveries with profound implications both for science and for conservation.

"This project has more plot twists than one of your whodunits!" I said to Gary.

"That's why I love science," he replied.

Sun Hean urged us to return to Cambodia to continue the research. He was also eager to mount an expedition to search for the mysterious Khting vor, known from its horns alone. "No one's written any paper on that yet!" Maybe next, he suggested, we could combine the search for more moon bears with an expedition to northern Cambodia, where his surveys found hunters reported these buffalo-like animals with some frequency. Also, Gary and I hoped to further map the golden moon bears' range into Laos. And Gary van Zuylen had generously invited us to sample hairs from any of the TSCWA's projects in Thailand . . .

As we floated ideas for our next expedition that evening, we couldn't imagine that the next twist in the plot awaited us far closer to home.

CHAPTER SEVEN

The Hmong of Skokie, Illinois

In the Thai refugee camps, rumors abounded: America was a frightening place. It was full of ogres, giants, dinosaurs, gangs, and ghosts. The police were terrible: they would even arrest your grandfather just for smoking opium. The doctors were worse: they would draw out your blood with needles. Instead of healing patients like the village shaman, American doctors killed their charges, and packed the dead bodies into tins for food.

That's what the refugees heard. But, bravely, they came anyway. Along with other desperate Hmong neighbors and strangers, Ko Vang, her husband, Xia Lee Xiong, and her uncle, Shuttong Vang swam the Mekong from Laos to Thailand at midnight. The people swam all night long. The husbands tied their wives to them with ropes. The wives strapped their babies to their backs. Mothers drugged their infants with opium so they would not cry and alert the soldiers. Many drowned trying to escape; others were eaten by crocodiles. But Ko and her family made it to Thailand, and from the refugee camps there to America.

In this way, they came to live in Illinois, where Ko worked in an antique oriental rug store down the street from Gary's apartment.

The Hmong are a brave people. Their courage, wrote Father François Savina, a French apostolic missionary in Laos in the 1920s, is "inferior to that of no other people." Never have they had a homeland, he wrote; but "neither have they known servitude and slavery."

The Hmong originated in the valleys of the Yangtze and Yellow rivers, say accounts that claim to stretch back to 2700 B.C. Their full history was once recorded in a book, Hmong legends tell, but, alas, it was eaten by cows and rats. Everywhere they have lived they have been considered outsiders. Even in their native China, they were known as *Meo*—Chinese for barbarian. As late as the nineteenth century, the Chinese reported the Hmong had tails. Earlier accounts claimed they had arms like normal people, but beneath those arms, small wings—with which they, unfortunately, could not fly. But they had no need for wings. They were fierce warriors. For five hundred years, from A.D. 400 to 900, the Hmong say they had their own kingdom in Henan, Hubei, and Hunan provinces, which they defended dressed in copper and buffalo hide armor, shooting poisoned arrows and firing crossbows so huge it took three men to carry one. In the sixteenth century, the Chinese so feared them that they built a wall, like the Great Wall of China, a hundred miles long and ten feet high, to keep out the Hmong. It was said the Hmong were such savage fighters that in 1730, hundreds of warriors killed their own wives and children, believing they could fight more fiercely unencumbered by family.

But the Hmong have always been outnumbered. Persecuted for three millennia, they have migrated through China, then to Laos, Vietnam, Thailand, and finally, with the greatest of reticence, to the terrifying land known as America.

Ko's family, like all the Hmong who came to the New World in the 1970s and 1980s, were part of the refugee remnant of the three hundred thousand who lived in prewar Laos. Shuttong Vang had been recruited and trained in the "secret Army" supported by the American CIA to fight the Communist Vietnamese and Pathet Lao insurgents in northern Laos. Thirty thousand strong, the Hmong Armée Clandestine was the biggest CIA operation in the world, financed in part by the Hmong's traditional opium crop, which was ferried from the mountains of northern Laos to markets in Vientiane by American aircraft.

In the secret war, Hmong soldiers died at ten times the rate of American soldiers in Vietnam. About a third of the prewar Hmong population perished—killed in battle, massacred in raids on their villages, victims of cannon and mortar fire, land mine and grenade explosions, poisoned by the defoliant "yellow rain," or blown apart by cluster bombs left unexploded until struck by a farmer's hoe.

Three days after the North Vietnamese occupied Saigon, some one to three thousand Hmong were airlifted by American planes to Thai refugee camps, from which they would be resettled in America. After the planes left, 150,000 Hmong, like Ko and her family, followed them, swimming the dangerous river. But that crossing was not nearly as treacherous as the perils they feared they might face in the New World.

When they arrived, they found no ogres, no giants, no dinosaurs. But they faced other monsters: the police *would* arrest your grandfather for smoking opium. And though they didn't pack corpses into tins, doctors *did* suck your blood out with needles. If all Americans were not monsters, at the very least, most Hmong considered them shockingly ignorant. American mothers, for instance, just throw away their babies' placentas! The placenta, to the Hmong, is the soul-jacket. It must be buried under the dirt floor of the house—for without it, the soul, upon death, could never make it past the gauntlet of evil spirits, venomous caterpillars, jagged rocks, and boiling waters to the place of the ancestors, beyond the sky.

Americans often found their new Hmong neighbors equally shocking. In many American cities, Hmong have held fiercely to traditional ways. In her wonderful book *The Spirit Catches You and You Fall Down,* Anne Fadiman describes how at hospitals, Hmong would sometimes bring live animals to be slaughtered at bedside healing ceremonies. Some raised rats for food in their apartments. Occasionally, they sacrificed shrieking pigs and yowling dogs in parking lots and suburban yards. They planted and harvested crops in public parks. In Philadelphia, one Hmong family was cited repeatedly for shooting pigeons with crossbows in the streets, and in Fresno, California, Hmong persist in shooting endangered eagles and hawks out of the skies, where they also hunt and eat hummingbirds, skunks, squirrels, possums, and raccoons.

Few animals are safe from Hmong hunters. In their mountainous homelands, the Hmong are renowned as among the best hunters—not only because of their fearlessness. The eight-toned Hmong languages include a plethora of poetic words describing the sounds different animals make under specific circumstances: *mig mog,* the sound of tigers playing; *ig awg,* the sound of wild pigs fighting. Their observations of the natural world are extensive and penetrating.

Gary knew little about the Hmong, but he understood this: even after living in America for twenty years, they would likely remember the ways of the old country. And as former hunters, they would know the animals they had pursued in Laos extremely well. That is why, when he learned from the owner of the rug store that Hmong were among the workers restoring his elegant antiques, Gary was eager to talk with them about moon bears.

Their first, short chat took place shortly after we had gotten our DNA results. It was tough going, Gary told me. Ko Vang spoke very little English, but more than her companions did. And Gary, of course, spoke no Hmong. He did, however, understand one important point: they knew about bears, and knew they were not always black. In fact, one of Ko's coworkers had seen one with a light brown coat. The women confirmed the color of the bear by pointing to one of the hues on a rug they were restoring: it was tan.

Generously, Ko invited Gary to visit her at home in Skokie. Her uncle, Shuttong Vang, spoke better English than she, she explained, and would be there, too. Gary invited me along for the interview.

So, on an evening in April, in the name of science, Gary and I found ourselves in a traditionally Jewish suburb of Chicago, knocking at the door of a neat, one-story house, to interview Hmong tribespeople about bears they had hunted in Laos.

* * *

"In our country, we got both kinds of bear," Shuttong Vang said.

He was looking at photos of a sun bear and a moon bear in what Gary called his "Rogues' Gallery" of bears: a series of pictures the scientist had carefully mounted on sheets of paper, held in a purple folder. In one photo, a sun bear climbed on a branch, clearly showing the small ears, short coat, and long claws. In another, a moon bear sat up on his rear legs, showing the tall, round ears, long fur, and large, white crescent on the chest. There were other pictures of moon bears, too. Gary had included one of an unusually colored, two-year-old brown-backed moon bear we had photographed at Banglamung; a photo of Dave, with his panda-like markings; one of Bertha, the golden bear at Lop Buri; and one of the golden subadult Sun Hean had shown us on the palm plantation near Kampong Som. For good measure, Gary also threw in a photo of a grizzly, showing the distinctive shoulder hump, as a "control." Then again, he reasoned, perhaps there were grizzlies in Laos: he had always wondered about the supposed subspecies *Ursus arctos shanorum* rumored to have come from the Shan States of upper Burma.

As the family had done, Gary and I had slipped off our shoes when we entered the house—a traditional courtesy throughout Southeast Asia. Except for small details, the house looked like any other in Midwestern suburbia. Ko's husband, who spoke no English, was sitting on the couch, watching a boxing match on TV. An unseen child burbled from somewhere. The carpet beneath our stocking feet was bright red—the auspicious color of the Lao New Year—and the walls were covered with family photos, many of which featured the traditional Hmong dress: black pants and black jacket adorned with bright strips of color.

Now, though, Ko was wearing a white T-shirt emblazoned with an American flag, perhaps to welcome us. She led us through the living room, past her silent husband, and into the dining room.

As it turned out, Ko told us, Gary's conclusions from their earlier interview had been in error. Her coworker had not seen the tan bear after all. It had been her uncle, Shuttong Vang, who had seen it. A small, strong man of forty-eight, missing the tip of his right index finger, he was waiting for us at the dining room table, wearing a black leather jacket. Ko went into the kitchen, from which soon arose the tingling scents of garlic, lemongrass, and ginger. Many of these ingredients were growing in pots in an indoor garden in the downstairs bathroom.

Shuttong Vang examined Gary's photographs. Most of them, he said, he did not recognize. "I saw only three kinds," the former soldier told us.

We asked him to point to those he knew.

"Like that one," he said, pointing to the sun bear picture.

"Um-hmm," said Gary.

"And," he said, "not too many, not very black—a little light, light black," he said.

"Okay," said Gary.

"Third kind, very, very, very dark black," Shuttong Vang continued.

"Dark black," Gary confirmed.

"And we got some light, light bear they call white bear. White one."

"White," echoed Gary. "White."

White?

"Yeah," continued the solider, "but bear can very dangerous. When you saw it you had to—you don't like him saw you or her saw you. They come over and bite you right away—kill you right away!"

"Have you seen them in the forest?" I asked.

"I saw one before. When I was in country."

"And did one run after you? Did it bite you?" I asked.

"Yeah!" he said, "but we've got the gun! We shoot in back!"

Ko Vang's slender twenty-year-old daughter, Shua Xiong, joined us. She had lived in America since she was four months old and her English was perfect; her nineteen-year-old cousin, Chumpit Chang, also helped us with translation. We soon learned that the bear Shuttong Vang called "white" was really golden—just like Bertha.

Shuttong Vang's hunting party had shot the golden bear near a village not far from Xam Nua in Houaphan Province, in extreme northeastern Laos, a mountainous area of big trees, deep caves, and waterfalls. He had no doubt of the location; later, he even showed Gary on one of the professor's maps. "Now we have a location for the pale bear, way, way off our line," Gary had said to me, "on the other side of the Mekong!" More important, Gary pointed out, this suggested that though rare, the golden bears were fairly widespread. "I think we're going to find blond bears occur nearly everywhere in Southeast Asia," he predicted. "It makes it even more remarkable they've never been described."

Shuttong Vang had lived in different villages in two Laotian provinces—moving, as Hmong do, when the soil is exhausted from growing opium and they have hunted all the game out of an area. Since he was a little boy, Shuttong Vang had hunted with a gun. He described it for us fondly: "Long, and fires one shot, like cowboy—like in 'Gunsmoke'!" ("A flintlock," Gary explained. "The hunter has to be really close to make a kill." This feature, he noted, surely accounts for the survival of many of Southeast Asia's edible species—and the early demise of all but the most skilled Hmong hunters.)

Once a month or so, all the men and boys would go hunting—looking for squirrel, birds, deer, anything. They hunted bears whenever they could, even though they do not eat the meat; it decays too rapidly, within three days. But the gallbladder, Shuttong Vang explained, is a valuable medicine. He said that decocted into homemade wine, it cures an aching back and helps bones to heal as well. They could also sell it for much money.

They saw bears often; every time they hunted, they would see bears in the forest. Often they would see bears near the village, too, where they raided cornfields and were shot as a nuisance.

But the golden bear had been encountered in the forest. Shuttong Vang was hunting with his brother-in-law, and they saw it in a tree. Unfortunately, it saw them, too. "You cannot let them see you," he stressed. "They saw you, they got to bite you right away." The bear raced down from the tree and charged at them. They shot it dead at twenty yards— the distance, he said, between the front door of this house and the sidewalk.

We still didn't understand, though, what he meant by three kinds of bears. We only knew of two, the sun bear and the moon bear. Perhaps the Hmong, as we once had, considered the golden bear a different species.

Such errors are common. For many years, for instance, Western ornithologists classified the male and female ecclectus parrot of South

America as separate species, because one is bright green and the other, bright red. Explorers at the South Pole made the same mistake with sleek adult king penguins and their fat, brown, fluffy young—classifying the latter as a separate species, the "woolly penguin." But more often than not, at least the idea of a species is universally understood, even if in different cultures it goes by different names. It is not merely a useful concept scientists made up. The late classical geneticist John Maynard Smith, a leading theorist in evolutionary biology, remembers instantly recognizing different birds as separate species even as a child growing up in western Britain. "The experience has persuaded me ever since," he told an interviewer, "species are real things. It's not something that we impose upon nature, it is something that is there to be recognized."

With the help of our young interpreters, Shuttong Vang explained how the Hmong classify bears. The girls carefully wrote out the names for us, in both Hmong and English.

One bear is called *Dais npuas,* which Ko's daughter translated as "pig bear." Shuttong Vang again pointed to the picture of the sun bear, confirming this was what he meant.

The largest bear, he said, is *Dais neng,* or "horse bear." It has a chest mark, which is either yellow or white. He recognized it in our gallery: he pointed to a standing moon bear and said, "We saw them. We call it horse bear."

As for the "white" or golden bear—which they call *Dais dawb*—he pointed to the photo of Bertha.

But there was another bear—a small bear—which he called *Dais dev,* or "dog bear." The body and hair, he explained, are like a dog's, the size of, perhaps, a German shepherd or a golden retriever. It does not have a marking on the chest. It has a pointier face than the other bears. He did not see its picture in Gary's gallery.

What was it? Gary wondered whether it was a bear at all. Might it be a binturong? Did the dog bear have a long tail? Gary asked. No, answered Shuttong Vang. That ruled out the binturong. Did it dig a hole and sleep in it? Yes, he answered, and the baby was born in a hole. The creature was certainly sounding bearlike. But perhaps it was actually a giant hog badger. What did the dog bear eat? Did it eat mainly insects? No, Shuttong Vang answered: like the horse bear, it ate mainly fruits and corn.

Our heads were spinning. Gary had heard of dog, pig and horse bears before. In Khmer, we remembered, the sun bear is called *kla khmum chruk,* the pig bear, and in Prey Veng, Sun Hean had told us, the moon bear is known as *kla khmum chkai,* the dog bear. In Vietnamese, too, the sun bear is known as the pig bear, *con gau heo,* and the moon bear is called the horse bear, *con gau ngua.* But the sun bear was sometimes called a dog bear, *con gau cho.* Gary recalled from his extensive reading, when he was researching his first golden moon bear eleven years before, that the Han Chinese had described five kinds of bears: their "white bear" was *bai xiong,* the giant panda, also sometimes called *hua xiong,* the banded bear. Their horse bear, *ma xiong,* was the grizzly. Their dog bear, *gou xiong,* at least in Sichuan and northern China, was our moon bear. Gary wasn't sure from the literature and dictionaries he had consulted whether their pig bear, *zhu xiong,* was a hog badger or a sun bear. And then there was the Man Bear, *ren xiong,* which sources admitted was "seldom seen."

* * *

The family told us many stories that night. With the girls translating, with that odd lilting question mark in their voices characteristic of so many American teenage girls ("The spirits cry really loud? That's what everyone believes?"), they told us how the Hmong people arose: After a huge flood had drowned everyone but a brother and sister, the pair produced an egg-shaped baby whom they cut into pieces, and the pieces gave rise to the different Hmong families. They told us about the spirits in the thickest forests. They cry out at night, and you have to build a bonfire and make an offering of roasted meat to appease them.

They related how a soothsayer in Laos had told their uncle's fortune: that he would marry and have five children, but one of his children would be killed. Sure enough, on a snowy day in America, their truck slid off the road, and the youngest son was killed. They showed us stories told in Ko's embroidery. Besides embroidering the family's clothes, she also made elaborate panels, which she sometimes sold as wall hangings in America. One told the story of a tiger who killed a hunter, and then put on his clothes and went back to his village to live like a man with his wife and family. A bird came to the family's rescue, and the wife scared away the tiger by throwing sand and pepper in his eyes.

But what stuck with us most that night was the mysterious dog bear. Gary examined the possibilities from all sides. "These names have come down from the Chinese literature"—pig bear, dog bear, horse bear—"and they may see the need to find these things in the new country, even if they are different things."

This seemed likely. But, importantly, Shuttong Vang did not seem to be applying names randomly, just to use up old words. He did not claim to recognize pictures of bears that did not live in Laos. He told us he had never seen anything like the picture of the grizzly. Neither had he seen anything like the pandalike moon bears, which also seemed reasonable given their apparent rarity. But he had insisted that we did not have a picture of his dog bear.

Perhaps he was confused. After twenty years of living in America, maybe his memory had faded. Maybe the language barrier, even with the girls' help, was just too much to surmount. Or maybe he was just wrong. The family had just finished telling us tales of people arising from egg-shaped babies, of soothsayers, of spirits that cried out in the night. Perhaps the dog bear was rarer than the other bears for the same reason the Chinese Man Bear was "seldom seen": perhaps it never existed at all.

If the truths in folklore are distorted by culture, such is also the case with science. Over the years I had known him, Gary had often complained to me that science was becoming so specialized that the big picture was lost. Molecular journals trumpet "new" findings about the relationships among organisms, when in fact taxonomists had pieced together the same picture from fossil or anatomical evidence decades before. (Such was the case with the panda. In a monograph published in 1964, Field Museum anatomist Dwight Davis, having dissected and scrutinized every detail of the panda's anatomy, had firmly concluded it was a bear, based on a host of similarities throughout the anatomy—a fact almost never mentioned in molecular journals.) Likewise, the leading paleontologist of ancient whales continues to publish his fossil evidence that they are descended from extinct carnivores called mesonychids—never mentioning that data from molecular labs firmly places whales in the same lineage as the hippo. And taxonomists routinely publish "new findings," ignoring historical evidence that non-scientists knew about it all along. The paper announcing the discovery of the giant Laotian muntjack, for instance, does not mention it was described (though not named) in a hunting book in 1930. And when Gary was a postgrad, he recalls an adviser often pointed out articles in the latest scientific journals reporting "new findings" that had already been published before—by Charles Darwin.

"Each field of science pretends that the others don't exist!" Gary had complained. It was as if each scientific specialty had become a xenophobic culture unto itself, so suspicious of its barbaric neighbors' beliefs that any evidence coming from outside their own little world was instantly dismissed as superstition and ignored.

But a broader way of doing science is gaining acceptance, he told me, in which clues from all fields are carefully considered before offering a conclusion. This is the kind of science he has always done—his broad curiosity allowed him no less. But now, Gary explained, the old way of doing science was billed as something new. It was called the Total Evidence Approach, he said, "as if you need a name for just thinking about everything!"

Would our total evidence—in addition to Lisette's careful laboratory analysis of moon bear DNA—now include the stories of a Hmong hunter, trying to communicate with us in a language he did not speak, about things he had seen twenty years ago, half a world away? We could not take Shuttong Vang's word as gospel. But neither could we ignore it.

Except for the existence of the dog bear, everything he had told us about bears we knew to be true. He knew what bears ate, that they gave birth in dens, and even the time the mothers emerged with their young in the spring. We had been impressed with his knowledge.

And that gave credence to another possibility: that there really was a third species of bear in Southeast Asia, unknown to science, waiting for us in the misty, forested mountains of Laos.

CHAPTER EIGHT

Dog Bear

In the months that followed, it seemed everything was in flux: we were pursuing an unexpected line of inquiry—through their lineages, trying to chart the moon bears' travels back in time. Instead of seeking out golden bears, our quarry was now far more elusive: we were searching for evidence of refuges that had vanished a hundred thousand years ago. And now it also seemed there might, just possibly, be a new species of bear here after all—but not the one we had thought.

And it seemed that everything was going wrong.

We began to plan to work in Laos. Forget it, colleagues told us. Everyone we contacted told us working in this cloistered, Communist country was impossible. Permits, like those we would need to keep us from being arrested for taking hairs we needed for the DNA study, took months or years to obtain, and were often revoked without notice. Even respected scientific organizations like the New York Zoo's Wildlife Conservation Society and the International Union for the Conservation of Nature were considering closing their small offices there.

We considered returning to Cambodia. But we hadn't heard from Sun Hean since Christmas. His plans for combining more bear work with an expedition to search for Khting vor seemed to have dissolved. He was trying to run his Cambodian office from Minnesota via e-mail, while trying to finish his master's thesis on Cambodia's Indochinese tigers. He couldn't think about bears now.

Just as we were despairing, in the spring, we learned from Gary van

Zuylen, via e-mail, that his organization had begun working in Laos. How that had happened was another one of his tales of chilling organizational incompetence.

Nearly two years before, at a tourist attraction billed as a "Cultural Park," near the Friendship Bridge between Thailand and Laos, a reporter from an Australian TV station noticed thirteen underfed moon bears languishing in tiny, dirty cages. The situation was so pathetic she mounted a drive to save them. Within months she had raised twelve thousand dollars. A number of animal welfare agencies from abroad got involved. Expat experts from England and Cambodia were consulted about new cage designs. Money was raised to fly them to Laos. Squabbles broke out among the charities as different designs were submitted and potential sites for the new enclosures discussed. Many meetings were held.

As the months went by, the bears were starving. One by one, they began to die. By the time Gary van Zuylen got word of the crisis, it was February of the following year. Only five of the thirteen were still alive. From Swedish and American donors, the Australian secured the promise of money to build outdoor enclosures for them at Laos's biggest zoo, just outside the capital, Vientiane. Gary was ready to begin building in March. The money came through in April, and two days later, a keeper from the zoo and one of TSCWA's staff arrived at the Cultural Park to pick up their charges. Only three bears were left. And one of them quickly died.

But now that the enclosures were nearing completion, the Tulakhom Zoo, like Banglamung, was becoming a refugee center for bears. The place was stocked with rescued bears captured from all over the country. There, with Gary van Zuylen's assistance, we could greatly expand our lineage map—as well as look for the mysterious dog bear.

So, late that spring, our plans sprang together. Our Thai-based friend would arrange for our permits to collect hairs from the bears in Vientiane. Then we would return to Thailand and visit the towns of Mae Sariang, Om Koi, and Mae Hong Song. At Royal Forest facilities with which he worked in the north, Gary van Zuylen thought at least some of the rescued bears' original capture sites would be known. Finally, we would travel together to the jungle along the Salaween River, a waterway as mighty as the Mekong, to view a sanctuary on the border with Burma. Once overrun with poachers, the site was now secure, he said, and—given government approval and backed up with data from our mitochondrial studies—a possible area to which he might begin to return captured bears to their forest homes.

Our picture, now, was as clear as the map of our travels ahead. But before we would reach these destinations, we would see the picture again transform. With outlines ablur, the new, shimmering vision would reveal what before was concealed: the mutability of fate and of time, of species and of souls.

*   *   *

On the rainy, midnight drive from Bangkok, where he picked us up at the airport the following June, the sardonic Gary van Zuylen, to our astonishment, began telling us about a miracle.

He didn't put it in those terms. A hardheaded businessman, always suspicious of others' motives, he doesn't believe in miracles. But how else to describe what had happened? Actually it was a suite of miracles, each more astounding than the one before.

It had happened just a few months ago, while the professor and I had been Stateside trying to plan the next steps in our study. We'd gotten the news by e-mail from Corina: our Australian friend was in a terrible car accident. It was feared he might not survive.

The day of the accident, Gary van Zuylen had just flown back to Bangkok from Chiang Mai, where he was visiting one of TSCWA's projects. He'd hailed a cab at the airport. They took the expressway, where everyone drives at breakneck speed.

"No one knows how the crash happened," Gary van Zuylen told us as he drove us along that same expressway in the dark. "It was a head-on collision at high speed—but with what? I'll never know. I was unconscious and can't remember anything, and the driver was killed." The force of the impact threw the driver from the cab. He died instantly. And Gary would have, too, except for one thing: in the backseat, he was wearing a seat belt.

That was nearly a miracle in itself. We were incredulous. In most American cities, you can hardly find seat belts in a cab if you want to; they are all swallowed up by the backseat upholstery. Who wears a seat belt in a cab? In Bangkok?

Gary van Zuylen was not the cautious type. This was well illustrated by a story he had told us earlier: when he was working as a construction manager in Australia, a rich man had hired him to build a two-story extension to a Sydney mansion overlooking the harbor. When it was complete, the owner wouldn't pay. "I had half a dozen guys working for me, and the courts wouldn't do anything. But," Gary told us, slyly arching an eyebrow, "I was entitled to reclaim my materials." So he demolished the top two floors of the house.

That incident was one reason he'd left his country and profession. "By the time I was twenty-five, I had lots of money and fancy cars and had traveled around the world—but in a couple of years, I'd had enough," he told us. "I'd had enough of building, and enough of Australia, and I had lost all interest in money."

When the former contractor arrived in Thailand, he courted more risks. As a freelance journalist, although he had started out covering the music industry, he soon began to cover breaking news, including hostage situations and border skirmishes with Burma. (Covering one such story, he was shot at—not by any means for the first time—less than a week after he was discharged from the hospital after his taxi accident.) But perhaps he faced the greatest dangers while running his humane organization. "If you're going to do something, do it right," he often likes to say. This attitude has won him powerful enemies running TSCWA in a country where the illegal trade in wildlife is rampant, and even other humane organizations can be dangerous rivals. They've paid off police to have him arrested and sent soldiers to threaten him at gunpoint. His views of this? "Doesn't worry *me*."

So what possessed him to buckle up a seat belt while riding to his apartment from the airport in a cab?

Simple, he explained. It was habit. He used to be a race car driver.

The seat belt may have saved his life, but it was hanging by a thread. Bleeding buckets from multiple wounds, knocked comatose by head trauma, and trapped in the crumpled cab, he desperately needed an ambulance fast. "But there are no ambulances in Bangkok," he told us. Instead, there are the Body Snatchers.

"There are these two charity groups," he explained, "both based at temples. They're volunteers. They're called the Body Snatchers because they race each other in their pickups and come and get the injured and dead people from the highways. They take the dead people to the temple and the live people to the hospitals. They almost fight over the bodies. And they loot you."

A few years back, he said, the Body Snatchers arrived at the scene of an airplane crash north of Bangkok. They stole all the dead people's luggage, hauling it away in their trucks. When the grieving relatives later came to the site, they found the Body Snatchers had set up a market to sell the possessions back to the relatives.

"After that, the Army got involved," Gary said. The resolution? "They insisted that the Body Snatchers only loot what they could carry— money out of the wallets, the credit cards. But also," he told us, "going through your wallet, they can find a contact to call, to see what to do with you."

Bangkok has several fine hospitals, as sophisticated as any in the West—but few Thai can afford to pay. Most accident victims, without evidence that they can afford these facilities, are refused admission, and end up at hospitals that are little more than poorhouses.

Gary continued: "So I, a foreigner coming from the airport, have only one thing written in Thai in my wallet. And guess what it is? It's Preecha's name and his cell phone number in Bangkok."

Preecha Rattanaporn is a powerful—and scrupulous—official in the

Thai Royal Forest Department. At the moment, he was chief of the Salaween Wildlife Sanctuary, the same one we would later visit at the border with Burma, where, of course, he spends most of his time. The Body Snatchers gave the number to the police to phone.

He happened to be in Bangkok, and his cell phone was on.

"Preecha says to them: 'Take him to the top hospital. He can pay for it.' The police have them throw me in their pickup and take me to Vipawadee Hospital—the best in Bangkok—and the Body Snatchers didn't take a single thing from me!"

Miracle Number Two gave way to Miracle Number Three: "So the nurses next look in my wallet before they admit me, and what do they see? My insurance card and credit card. I get admitted, and who is working at the hospital at that moment? An American-trained brain surgeon and an American-trained plastic surgeon!"

Twenty-two minutes after the accident, they were operating on him. Had they not, he would not have survived. His right eye had popped out of its socket. His skull was so smashed they had to rebuild part of his cheek with a metal plate. Everyone was sure he would die. He did not regain consciousness for days, and when he did, was amnesiac. It was feared the brain damage was permanent.

Friends lit into action. An American acquaintance called his parents—first phoning two doctor friends in the States to learn how to break the news to them. And then the man called every Forest official Gary knew, asking them to call the hospital to put in a good word for him. A Thai girlfriend handled police and insurance matters. A German volunteer came down from Chiang Mai to sit by his bedside.

Of all the marvels he recounts, this is what leaves him dumbstruck. His friends' outpouring of care caught him by surprise. But so did his feelings about working with animals, the task that fell to him by default. When I had pressed him about this, he finally admitted, "You do get a buzz"—using the second person, as if to distance himself from anything that might be construed as sentiment.

"How much fun do you think it is to build a thirty-story building? 'Oh, great, the crane's not working. And where's the concrete pump?' Oh, that's a whole lot of fun," he said with characteristic sarcasm. "And what sort of motivation is there? After the tenth one, do you think I'm getting thrilled doing my hundred and first? So what else can I do? Well, I work as a journalist for money. But," and he pauses. "When you see an animal moving from this shocking-condition cage and all of a sudden, it's climbing up a tree—there's a benefit here. And it has nothing to do with money at all. It doesn't take a genius, or an environmentalist, or a bunny-hugger to see."

We were approaching Banglamung, where we would stay for several days before heading to Laos. What had the staff there made of his miraculous recovery? we asked.

"When I returned to Banglamung, the first three people I spoke with all asked me exactly the same thing," he told us: "'What amulet were you wearing?'" In Southeast Asia, amulets are believed to exert strong influence; some are specially blessed by monks at powerful temples. Of course, he wasn't wearing any—he doesn't believe in such things. Like my scientist-companion, Gary van Zuylen doesn't believe in charms, or in gods, or in miraculous transformations.

But he was struck by what each person he encountered said after learning that no amulet had protected him. "All three, again, said exactly the same thing: 'But of course you'd be all right—because you are taking care of the animals.'"

* * *

While Gary van Zuylen and his staff negotiated permits for us, the professor and I spent our days among the bears.

A large outdoor enclosure was new since we last visited. After it had been built, in January, nine bears had been tranquilized for the transfer, and at that time, Johan, before returning to Sweden, had plucked hair for us. Analyzed at Lisette's laboratory, this second set of samples revealed that five bears—Mo, Pot, Flower, Harem, and Curly—had shared the same haplotype as the Cardamom bears, which Lisette was calling Haplotype II. "The fact that all these bears are of one haplotype suggests there was a refuge, and that their spread was relatively recent," the scientist said.

Two dark black bears had grouped differently, however: the haplotype for Banglamung's Gem was only slightly different from Lop Buri's Linz; but Pammy, almost certainly the sibling of the giant Tommy Lee, revealed a unique haplotype. She represented a lineage that Lisette estimated had separated from the others perhaps as long as one to two hundred thousand years ago.

How did these populations of bears diverge from one another? Why were they forced to disperse? What routes may they have taken? We don't know the geology of Southeast Asia a hundred thousand years ago. Three hundred thousand to about fifty thousand years ago was a time of erosion in much of Southeast Asia, a Thai geologist had told us; "the geological record," she said, "has been erased." But we do know this about the world at the time: for long periods, Europe and North America were glaciated. So much of the ocean was locked up in ice that most of the Philippine Islands were joined in a single landmass. Indonesia's islands were joined with the rest of Southeast Asia. Northern Asia, North America, and Europe were covered with herds of giant grazers—the woolly mammoths, woolly rhinos, and giant camels. Bamboo forests were hugely widespread in China—not just patches as today—and pandas, the professor said, "were all over the place."

"There never were ice sheets in southern Asia," he explained. "If Africa is a good analogy, montane rain forest spread down, but the lowland forest became savanna in what is now the Congo Basin. It makes sense the same thing happened in Southeast Asia. Perhaps most of Southeast Asia at this time was dry thorn scrub—and the forest refuges for the bears were restricted to the mountains." There is, Gary noted, a steady run of hills suggesting a geologic folding from the Cardamoms north to Nan, near where Colonel Wirat told us the golden Bertha and the panda-like Dave had been captured. Perhaps this was the refuge in which the golden bears' haplotype had evolved.

But what about the other haplotypes? And what to make of our Hmong informant's third species of bear?

"It is just conceivable that the Pammy haplotype could be a new species," said the professor, "or Haplotype II could. Is one the horse bear and the other the pig or dog bear? To prove a new species, we'd need to show morphological correlation with haplotype and that the two live at the same place at the same time."

We could see some of the nine bears in the new enclosure just twenty yards from the fence. They began moving out of the vegetation toward us, like big, slow-moving, friendly, nonbarking dogs. We wondered if they remembered us from last year. (We were surprised to discover that the staff at Mermaid's Beach Resort had remembered us—and after all, they see far more visitors than these bears do.) "Hello, bears!" the professor said, as if greeting old friends. And in a sense, he was: since we had returned from Southeast Asia last year, he had continued to live with them in his mind. There had not been a single day that the busy professor had not looked at their pictures, rerun the video, or searched the scientific literature for some new knowledge about moon bears.

"If we have more than one kind of bear here, it won't be arbitrary," Gary continued. "You will *not* be able to consider them two races. You can have two haplotypes locally and only one species. But we would need two different haplotypes, one of which correlates with a distinct appearance.

"Maybe it's just a pipe dream on my part," he said, "but it's every biologist's dream—to name a new species of mammal."

So the scientist scrutinized each bear for unusual features, no matter how subtle, attempting to match them to haplotype. He had little trouble recognizing some of the bears. Gem, an average-sized female, was distinctive because of her remarkably lush mane, which stood up straight at the crown of her head like a crew cut. Mo, he noted, last year had a dark cinnamon tinge, but now his coat, except for his chest crescent, was utterly black. Pammy was easy to pick out, too. She was almost always in the company of her enormous brother, the nearly five hundred-pound

Tommy Lee. We found the pair lying, with heads touching, on the cool cement in the open cage fronting the outdoor enclosure. Pammy's arms and legs were stretched akimbo, opening her loins to any potential stirring of the still air, her paw over her forehead, palm out, like a lady aswoon in the heat.

How like us bears are, we remarked again and again. So often, we share the same comforts, the same fears, and the same ways of coping. Pammy and Tommy Lee had arrived at Banglamung in a tiny crate, in back of an open-topped truck, having traveled for eight to ten hours without food or water. Both were thought to have malformed hindquarters from confinement. "Both are extremely nervous and attempt to hide when their cage is approached," a volunteer had written in their behavior profiles. "They seek confidence with each other and should not be separated if possible." When Pammy was separated from her big brother, we noted she would often suck on her own abdomen, emitting the vacuum-pump sound of a nursing cub—like a traumatized child who sucks its thumb into adolescence.

But now, the bears have nothing to fear. Their glossy black coats glisten like polished onyx after a dip in one of the enclosure's many pools. In the distance, we watch one of the giants climb a tree. Bears are the original tree huggers: they climb embracing a trunk with their great arms, steadied by their front claws, and anchored by their inward-turning back feet, whose soles look like they are on backward. We are astonished to watch a more than three hundred-pound bear ascend to twenty-five feet in ten seconds.

Next to the new enclosure is the larger one we had driven through the year before, with even more bears. We walk the periphery of the fence, careful of the red, biting ants who live in the hollows of the plants and crawl on the mesh fence, and watch for shivers in the grass that could signal a cobra. These snakes are said to be highly intelligent. They can climb trees, but they can also stand up as tall as a man, and may chase you. They can shoot venom two yards. The previous year, Gary van Zuylen had mentioned, quite casually and after we had spent an afternoon walking through knee-high vegetation, that the grass is crawling with them, and that he had once seen one here who grew 10 feet long. ("Oh, great," the professor had remarked under his breath at this news. He'd developed a healthy fear of poisonous snakes when, as a grad student, peering into an armadillo burrow brought him nose-to-nose with a rattlesnake coiled to strike. The young scientist, not normally given to feats of acrobatics, performed a backflip to escape. But that snake still visits Gary in his nightmares.)

We soon forgot about the snakes, though, and the biting ants; we were completely absorbed by the bears. My partner was busy noting the minutae of their physical characteristics as I documented them with camera and video. But something older and deeper than science was at work between us as well, something we had not felt when we drove among them in the Jeep a year earlier, separated by metal and glass.

Once, when I had left the scene to get a drink of water, Stripe ambled slowly over to the fence toward the professor. "He seemed genuinely focused on me," Gary told me when I returned. "I was down, kneeling or bending over, and he moved his head very close to the wire. He just stayed there—my head just by the electric wire, and his head as close to the wire as he could get. Here's this partly gold, lovely animal—it felt like something special was happening. It was as if he wanted to check me out. It was kind of a beautiful thing.

"This is as close as I have ever gotten to a bear," he said. "And then he slowly ambled away. Without two sets of wires and bars we could have touched noses. There wasn't any aggression. I'm sure of that. He was helping me out there. After driving through and straining to get photos in the hot car last year, this was really lovely. It was a quiet moment with a magnificent, big bear."

Like their black fur absorbs light, like their size dwarfs our own, each movement of one of these shaggy, more-than-human bodies seemed to draw us into the presence of a gigantic, enveloping power. Barry Saunders, author and scholar of English and history, writes that we have probably felt this since the dawn of our kind. "As he peered into the bear's eyes, the Neanderthal may have found a reflection of his own conscious-ness," he writes, "but one that seemed somehow deeper."

* * *

When the heat got too bad, we would retreat to the two-bedroom cin-derblock house where Gary van Zuylen's volunteers stay. On one side of the house live the bears; on the other, the dogs. The hot air reverberates with their barking. Nearly two hundred dogs share the one-and-a-half-acre outdoor enclosure, just fifty yards from the dorm's door: shaggy dogs with square faces, short-hairs with pointy noses, dogs with wiry hair and floppy ears. Most have curly tails, and clean white teeth, and voices as rich as scent.

The bears are refugees from the forest; the dogs are refugees from the streets. When most of the dogs arrived here from Wat Yan, they were mangy and covered with sores. In the shade where we sit sipping water just outside the dorm, there is a terrible, fleshy, decaying smell. It is coming from Pretty Pup. A gray mid-sized mongrel, he is entirely bald from mange, and bleeding from a festering sore on the side of one ear. He smiles and wags his scraggly tail whenever he sees a person approach. His testicles have shrunken to a single empty-looking sac; he looks utterly naked and vulnerable. His toes are swollen from infection. When he was picked up a few days ago from the temple streets, he was given a shot of Ivermectin, which is already killing the mites, but the volunteer vet tech, Phil, tells us it will be months before his hair grows back.

A small pack of the sickest dogs—one with a bloody eye, another with a chewed ear—stays by the house. Twitch, a sweet black female with short hair, bounces when she walks because of neurological damage to her hindquarters. Both legs twitch constantly when she lies down, as if she is having a dream. Brains is a spotted puppy so named because half her skull was exposed from a wound when she was picked up from the temple. When the other dogs pick on her, she yelps piteously, and Gill Basnett, 23, a volunteer with a degree in resource and environmental management from Australia's National University in Canberra, rushes to comfort her. No one here hesitates to cuddle even the sickest, smelliest, mangiest dog. One volunteer got mange herself, we were told, which I had not thought possible. The staff doesn't name any dog until it has survived a week, because otherwise their hearts would be broken again and again. And unlike the supply of dogs, the supply of good names isn't limitless.

The volunteers who work here are the Mother Teresas of animals. Caring for the poorest of the poor, nursing the sick, they live for three or six months in this tiny house, cooled only by two electric fans, washing at two sinks, using a bath they call The Swamp, and cooking food stored in a half-sized refrigerator on a hot plate. Reading material in the volunteers' library consists of volumes with names like *Langur Behavior and Husbandry Notes, Mazuri Zoo Foods, Evaluation of Traditional Herbal Remedies for Thai Elephants.* On the Things to Do blackboard today: castrate two pups; catch mange dog x 3; vaccine and deworm binturong; deworm macaques; deworm deer.

With the worms and the mange and the homeless dogs, quite a number of the volunteers quickly turn around and go back home, Gary van Zuylen told us. "I can understand them wanting something for themselves," he said, "but that's not the sort of person we need here. You have to be in this for the animals—not the people who benefit from them." In fact, two of the new volunteers we meet here, having pledged three months, will be gone within a week.

Those who stay, though, come to see the world differently. "It's amazing," says Gill, blond and sturdy and competent, her T-shirt smeared with muddy pawprints. We wait to hear of some exotic marvel. "In the afternoons," she says, "I like to sit and watch the dogs when they have settled down and are playing together." Watching the dogs, she feels the same sense of wonder we feel among the bears.

"Growing up in Canberra, I always wanted a dog," she muses. "Though two hundred is a bit much. But back home, most of these dogs would be put down." In the pen holding the healed dogs, where most of them will now live out their lives, the formerly doomed animals all seem likable, healthy, whole. One has a twisted, broken tail, but the rest seem as clean and friendly as from any breeder's kennel, and far happier. They dig dens in the earth, sing, and even though they are neutered, mate. The other dogs seem excited and happy about the coupling and one female joins in mounting one of a tied pair. Occasionally one of these dogs is adopted. Four have found homes since Gill first came to volunteer six months ago.

Panit Sanpote, the Royal Forest Department official who is head of the Banglamung Wildlife Breeding Center, wishes the dogs could be taken away from the bears and the other native species in the pens here. The dogs are a source of some strain between the Forest Department and the TSCWA. The dogs in the pens are technically housed on property owned by Wat Yan, so the Forest Department can't evict them. But dogs also run freely through the compound, squeezing through the spaces in the metal mesh sliding fences. One dog, a yellow curly-tailed female named Weasel, actually lives in one of the outdoor bear enclosures, and eats dog food and rice right among the ursine giants. Forest Department staff have tried to remove her, but they can't catch her. She seems eerily immune to dart guns. Half of the dogs running loose belong to the Forest Department workers on site, and Mr. Panit, who prides himself on being the pioneer of the breeding center twenty-three years ago, doesn't want to make his workers unhappy.

He is a friendly man with a wide smile, big white teeth, and gold-rimmed glasses, who smokes using a long black cigarette holder and wears a thick gold chain around his neck. He was trained in Thai forestry school to draw hard and fast lines between "good" and "bad" species. The bears—magnificent, powerful, endangered natives—are valuable and should be protected, like useful lumber trees in a forest. The dogs—diseased, pathetic, and as common as weeds—should be removed.

Who could blame him for making this distinction? "The human mind has to think of separate kinds of things," the scientist noted. In fact, investigating the separateness of things—of species and lineages—is what we are doing here. "Before biologists can talk intelligently about the world around them," the professor pointed out, "we need to be able to talk about how many different kinds of things there are."

Naming the animals was Adam's first task, and we, his progeny, have been doing this ever since. But for many native peoples, the bear's name, like Yahweh's, remains too sacred to utter. The Hairy Ainu of Japan call the bear "Divine One Who Rules the Mountains." Siberians speak of him as "Owner of the Earth." The Laps call the bear "Master of the Forest" as well as "Sacred Man" and "Sacred Virgin."

Other names go unspoken as well. "If we applied the same standards to humans as we do to other species, the Navajos and the Zunis would be separate species," the scientist ventured. The Navajos are Athabascan-speaking people whose ancestors came from East Asia over the Bering Strait eight thousand years ago. The Apaches are another member of this same group. But the Zunis are part of the ancient Paleo-Indian lineage who inhabited North America long before Columbus, twelve to thirteen thousand years ago or even earlier. They look and behave very differently: the Navajos are tall, slender people; the Zunis, short and powerfully built. Zunis and their relatives built the cliff dwellings of Mesa Verde; Navajos live in hogans, built of wood or hide, and they are spooked by the stone ruins of the Zunis, believing them haunted. The two Indian groups have lived side by side for centuries or millennia—but they do not intermarry, and have not exchanged genes for thousands of years.

"Two populations not exchanging genes whose ranges overlap are considered separate species—in fact, in nonhuman animals, the best evidence of separate species is living in the same space without breeding," the professor said. Yet he is well aware that to suggest that Zunis and Navajos are separate species would be morally offensive. To do so would suggest a separation with which modern humans are not comfortable. It was our God-given task to name the animals, we like to believe. But we—the People—inhabit a separate and privileged sphere. In the modern world, we draw a line in the sand between us and the animals. Because we are the namers of species, we use the excuse of our separateness to exempt animals from our moral universe, and to measure other animals' worth by their value to us.

But as man clings insistently to separateness and stability, larger forces whirl and wheel, driving the universe toward change.

*   *   *

Perhaps because of so many canines nearby, every time I looked into the face of a bear, I would see a dog. To my immense frustration, every bear began to look like it could be Shuttong Vang's dog-bear. But to Gary, the biologist, this was no wonder. "It is impossible to look into the face of a bear and *not* see a dog," Gary explained, "because bears and dogs are such close relatives."

They are members of a group of animals who arose in the Eocene, the Dawn Epoch, fifty-five to thirty-four million years ago, when new families and orders of mammals evolved with breathtaking rapidity. It was during this epoch that the ancestors of the rodents arose. The ancestors of the swift runners appeared, their toes slated to grow together and harden into the hooves of deer, tapirs, pigs, horses, antelopes, camels, and oxen. The predators who would become the cats arose, to chase them. And, too, on the northern landmass that was already breaking into Europe, North America, and Asia, the ancestors of another group of carnivores appeared: they are called the Arctoids, who eventually gave rise to the bears, dogs, weasels, raccoons, skunks, seals, and sea lions. The name is derived from the Latin word for North, honoring the constellation that rules the Northern sky. The Arctoids are all children of the Great Bear.

"Bears are, in a sense, giant dogs," Gary explained. "And seals and sea lions are, in a sense, swimming bears." (In fact, early sealers called sea lions "sea bears" because of the rolling, powerful, ursine way they heave their bulk over rocks.)

The original Arctoids all looked like civets. But soon, their progeny would change again, transforming into a bewildering plethora of creatures—some of them related but looking quite different from one another, others unrelated but looking quite the same. Before the end of the

Eocene, long before the first true dogs and the first true bears, there were creatures called bear dogs, or Amphicyonids; and before they became extinct, there were dog bears.

Who were these first bear dogs? I asked Gary. "They don't look like bears," he replied. He speaks of them in the present tense—and from the distant look in his green eyes I can tell the professor sees them before him. "They don't look like dogs. They have long tails and relatively long legs, and they're the size of American black bears—like really big wolverines."

Gary often dwells in the prehistoric past, as he has since his childhood—a time he spent divided equally between the oak swamps and backyard willows of Kentucky, and the fern-shaded landscapes of the Triassic and Jurassic. For him, time is permeable. His popular Diversity of Life course at Northwestern is dominated by nautilus-like ammonites of extinct oceans, giant club mosses six feet high, twenty-five-ton sauropods, eel-like sharks, dog bears, woolly mammoths—creatures who vanished long ago. But the professor can see them still. "They are no less real," the professor explains, "simply because they don't happen to occupy the Earth at this particular moment in time." Life is larger than that, he teaches his students: it stretches back, its vibrancy undiminished, more than three billion years.

Perhaps, as he conjures the bear dogs, he can even smell their breath. It might have smelled like those of hyenas, for like them, the bear dogs were bone-crunching scavengers as well as sometime predators.

The bear dogs were a successful group, persisting and diversifying for twenty-five million years, before becoming extinct in the final third of the Miocene Epoch. But before they had died out, animals of a different lineage had arisen: the dog bears.

They appeared early in the Miocene, as the world became cooler, drier, and more seasonal. The mastodons, which had evolved in Africa, had already spread to Europe and Asia. Gibbons and large apes were thriving in subtropical Spain. Living in an age of spreading savannas, ten to twelve million years in the past, the bear dogs and the dog bears would have inhabited a northern landscape of grasslands dotted with conifers, birch, juniper, oak, elm, and willow. Their world teemed with prey. Gary conjures them, like a magician, by speaking their names: megatylopus, a giant camel; aphelops, a hornless rhino; amebelodon, a shovel-jawed elephant. Huge herds of three- and one-toed horses, ranging in size from zebras to Shetland ponies, thundered over the greening plains: pliohippus, protohippus, cormohipparion, nannipus, calippus, hypohippus. The bear dogs and dog bears may have hunted aepycamelus, a camel with a giraffe-like neck, as well as antelopes and musk deer. Hunting in packs, they might even have brought down zygolophodon, a kind of mastodon, or teleoceras, a hippo-like rhino. They would have competed for this prey with other predators, including nimravidis, a cat built like a leopard; and at least one kind of saber-tooth, barbourofelis, the size of a modern jaguar.

Paleontologists class the dog bears in the bear subfamily Hemicyoninae, whose Latin name means "half-dogs." "They look like dogs," said Gary—they had long tails and long legs—"but the skull says bear." In minute dental characteristics, the shape of the protective covering of the ear at the base of the skull, the configuration of the tiny holes in the bone through which nerves and veins would run—in these ways, the dog bears were more bear than dog.

Other doglike creatures—leptocyon, for instance, which may have looked like a modern jackal—were hunting, too, beneath the Great Bear constellation of the Northern Hemisphere. These were true dogs. Their kind would race onward, running on their toes, to cross the continents chasing meat. They would transform into the wolves that howl in snowy nights, the giggling jackals of Africa, the whistling dholes of Asia, and the domestic dogs we coddle in our homes and despise on our streets.

But it was neither bear dogs nor dog bears that gave rise to the modern bears. Rather, it was another Miocene group, the Ursavine bears. These probably had legs of moderate length and a shortened tail. They varied greatly in size. Their descendants would develop massive bulk, modify their jaws and teeth, and on flat soles like ours, plod ponderously across the globe. They would reach rain forest and tundra, desert and mountain, and become the eight species of bears that today people around the world worship and massacre, fear and revere.

Though the shared ancestors of bears and dogs diverged toward very different destinies, the two species' connection with each other, and with us, is fixed forever, embedded in the permeable past. Their story comes to us across the millennia from the fossils paleontologists excavate from their earthen graves. Scientists like Gary call them to life from the earth. And other peoples say their stories still live in the sky.

The Inuit tell us that long ago, a woman once chanced upon a house filled with bears who could take on human form. She lived among them until one day she longed to return to her village. The bears asked her never to tell of their existence. But being human, she betrayed them. A bear broke into her human household and bit her, to punish her for what she had done. The people's dogs attacked and chased the bear, the story goes—but by magic, the dogs and the bear rose to the skies, burned with blinding brilliance, and turned into stars. Which is why, in heaven, the Great Bear is always accompanied by dogs, whirling together in conjoined constellations.

*   *   *

Gary and I looked forward to the bears' feeding time, perhaps as much as the bears themselves did. This was the time of day we could count on seeing almost every bear. Each afternoon, Mr. Panit's sinewy, smiling assistants, Suchart and Darunee, would bring steaming rice and dog biscuits into the pens, and the bears would emerge from their hiding places among the trees and grass to meet them. It was a good time to take note of the bears' different markings, size, and conformation. But it was also wonderful to simply lose ourselves in their pleasure as they ate.

On our second day, I ask the men if I could go in with them. Though surprised, they agree to take me. Why, they must have wondered, would this foreign woman want to walk into an enclosure full of bears? I was not going to attempt to pull hairs. I simply wanted to be with them, to share their enjoyment, to watch at closer range as they took in the scent and the savor of the steaming, fragrant food. Or perhaps it was something more: like the woman in the Japanese soldier's tale, I wanted to make them an offering, to be part of an exchange of food for blessing.

As we pass through the gate with our steaming buckets, the bears emerge like spirits from the forest. My friend Ben believes that because their senses are dominated by scent, they cast glances only to verify what their noses tell them. But they do look at me and seem surprised. One raises his head and gives a quizzical look, then opens his doglike nostrils wide to inhale my scent. I huff to them, sending forth my breath, warm and alive, from my lungs and nose and mouth. In a number of tribal languages, from India, Burma, and Borneo, the word for kiss is the same as the word for smell—for to kiss is to inhale the other's scent. I imagine my scent in their nostrils is like their image in my mind's eye. It is a sensuous and thrilling moment, being inhaled by a bear only four body-lengths away. I feel as if I could reach out and touch his fur as easily as I could touch one of the dogs. But bears, unlike dogs, do not like to be petted. Ben's bears would moan in irritation when he would instinctively reach out to stroke them and swipe his hands away with their paws. So I keep my hands to myself, and stay by the man with the stick, watching the bears closely, enveloped in the thrill of their proximity. Parting supple black lips, opening cavernous mouths spiked with yellow teeth, they pick up the food with their front teeth, and bring their heads up to chew, like dogs. Then they sniff the ground for any last morsel, which they seize with flexible, ribbonlike tongues.

The men didn't consider it safe to take me farther from the gate. Gary, watching from the other side of the fence, was visibly nervous. Though I would have loved to stay, all too soon I passed through the gate and returned to the side of the fence that separated our two species. But when the bears finished eating, I, too, felt sated, full.

Later, as I walked the perimeter of the fence with Gary in the thick, bright sun, again I smelled their breath. It smelled like dog food, rice, and life-heat.

* * *

Shortly after the bears were fed, at about 3 P.M., a commotion arose near the entrance gate. We heard a dog cry out in distress, and people rushing to help. We stayed with the bears, not wishing to get in the way.

When we returned to the little cinderblock house, we learned what had happened. Em, a mid-sized orange dog who tended to hang out by the bear gate, had eaten poison. She had returned to her usual post, in extremis, asking her human friends for help. But it was too late. Gill, the vet-tech Phil, and Catherine, a newly graduated vet who had arrived from England just the day before, tried to make her vomit. This would have worked with Waferin, the slow-acting anticoagulant most often used to poison rats. But this poison was strychnine, a faster-acting and more lethal toxin. Despite their efforts, she died within minutes, pleading for help.

When we saw her, she was lying on the table, already stiff-legged. Her body would serve as practice for Catherine's first solo spay.

Gill was terribly distraught. She had seen many deaths here. Animals they had valiantly tried to save. Animals they had come to love. But this one, she said, was more terrible—because she had been poisoned by Forest Department staff.

The strychnine had been laid out beside the Forest Department's deer pens, half a mile away. Banglamung, after all, had been founded as a breeding facility for these imperiled native deer, and three dogs had been harassing them, getting inside their enclosure and chasing the inmates. Mr. Panit knew who the culprits were. Little Em was not among them. The Forest Department had issued Mr. Panit a gun, and he could have shot the problem dogs; but Mr. Panit was a devout Buddhist, and his faith forbade him from killing them. He found a way around it, though. He set out poison instead.

In all religions, as in all legal systems, people find ways to skirt the rules. We obey the letter of the law without honoring its spirit, and then reassure ourselves of our righteousness, like the Crusading Christians who murdered thousands in the name of the Prince of Peace. Some Buddhists, not wishing to kill fellow creatures but still hungry for flesh, catch and eat fish without guilt: they explain that they are not actually killing the fish, but simply removing them from the water. One is reminded of a 1980 case in Brooklyn, in which defense lawyers argued that their client, who had shot the victim in the head and rendered him brain-dead, was not guilty of murder. Because the victim's heart, in accordance with the wishes of his family, was allowed to continue beating until his organs could be removed for transplant, the lawyer argued it was the doctors, not the shooter, who had caused his death. The wildlife researcher Alan Rabinowitz tells in his book about his work in Thailand, *Chasing the Dragon's Tail,* of watching in horror as Buddhist vendors skinned frogs alive for sale at a market. Why did they not at least kill the animals first, instead of dooming them to suffer lingering deaths? Because, he was told, the Buddha admonished us not to kill fellow creatures. Surely the owners of the Lao Cultural Park who allowed ten of the thirteen moon bears to starve would have bristled at the suggestion that they killed those bears. Like so many guilty clients of American defense lawyers, the vendor, the fishermen, and the Cultural Park were freed from guilt on a technicality.

And this was how Mr. Panit squared poisoning the dogs with his religion: it was not he who killed the dogs who took the poison. For, to his thinking, it was the dog's choice—in choosing to take the poisoned bait.

Two days later, a second dog died before our eyes. Again, it happened toward the end of the day, when everyone was hot and sweaty and the sun's glare had become as wearing as a constant scowl. A volunteer found the dog lying by the side of the road with ants and flies crawling into her eyes and ears. She was still breathing when we first saw her, lying on the table where Em lay two days before. When she took her last breath, it was filled with pain. A fly settled on her open eye. The last thing she had seen were people whom she expected to help her. But we could not.

* * *

We felt our time at Banglamung should be coming to a close. The professor had decided upon three bears whose appearance might be distinctive enough to constitute subspecies: besides Pammy and her brother, he was also very interested in another bear named Babe, who lived in the main enclosure. Although adult, she was an exceptionally small bear, which also made her a possible candidate for Shuttong Vang's dog bear. Unfortunately, where she came from was unknown. And we would have to wait for the next time she needed to be tranquilized to get hair from her; it was too dangerous to try to pluck her surrounded by thirty other bears, and we couldn't ask anyone to tranq her just for our study, as anesthesia always carries the risk of killing the patient. Until we expanded our mitochondrial map with more DNA samples, we could learn no more by staying here.

We decided to go ahead to Laos, where we expected our permits to pluck hairs from the zoo animals there to come through any day. But before we left, I was plagued by a question. To answer it, I asked to visit Wat Yan.

* * *

Gary van Zuylen's graceful young Thai assistant, Pranee Thongnoppakun, who we called Nee, drove the professor and me to the temple. She led us to the cool, shady, plant-filled sanctuary of a monk's cell. Suthep Janthavawong would answer my question:

"What is the difference," I wanted to know, "between a bear and a dog and an elephant and a person?"

* * *

The monk, 36, is handsome, with an open, wide face, high cheekbones, and dark, alert, searching eyes. He smiles easily as he gesticulates with his free right arm, the other draped in the brownish cloth of his robe. His head and eyebrows are shaved—a way of renouncing the cravings of the world.

"Actually," he answers, "humans and animals are not different at all."

His words come through Nee, translating his Thai into English. "Although," he concedes, "some person, just only the body looks like a person, but it is the same as animals. Every animal, every person is the same."

Nee's translation is halting, her English strained by the vocabulary of metaphysics. But I find myself listening for more than just information.

The Thai language is musical, and the tones of the two voices curve like a song. Each syllable seems struck by the wand of a xylophone, as precise as the intricately carved fruits at Thai banquets, or the pleats of satin that surround the banquet tables. Nee offers a musical "hmmm" of her own after each answer, then lets silence swallow the last sound, like a stone dropping into a still pool.

I ask how the monk came by his knowledge.

"Every man must become a monk," he answers. In many Asian countries, a man who does not spend time as a monk is considered *dip,* or "unripe." Most men spend three months as monks, usually before marriage, for in doing so they can accumulate blessings that benefit the entire family in their next lives. During this time, the monk must uphold 227 precepts, or laws, which are recited at the full moon. He must not touch a woman—not even her hand as she fills his begging bowl at dawn. He must not handle money. He must take no food or drink after noon. He must eschew comfortable beds, and must rise before dawn. He must never kill, not even swat a biting mosquito. And there are many other, more obscure rules as well, including abstinence from urinating upright (as this might soil their robes). Most men are happy to be relieved of their monkhood after their three months. But Suthep decided to stay on. Monks are welcome to stay monks as long as they like, and unlike the Catholic priesthood, there is no shame in returning to the world, nor in reentering the monk's life again and again. "I love this way," he explains, "and I stay longer and longer."

"You learn to take neutrality around yourself," Nee translates. "Life, people—everything in this world, like a small tree, gets older and dies and everything changes—a cycle."

"Humans and animals," Suthep says, "are not different at all. Because just only the body looks like a person. It is the same as animals. And the cycle doesn't stop because you die. Your spirit you have still."

The monk has seen souls who come back as dogs, he told us. Nee says when her husband was a monk, he could see spirits all the time, as could other monks. Now he no longer sees them. But he knows they are there.

The monk's eyes dart around the room like butterflies, searching the ether, the past, the future, the worlds of people and animals and spirits, as he contemplates each answer.

"The animal can know if a person is peaceful. The animal can know if the person is angry. Sometimes the animal can be more advanced than a person," he says. "Within one species, an elephant can have a high spirit, which another might not."

Many Thai believe that people of great merit are reborn as white elephants, to live among humankind and help them in times of trouble. (Unless you were a criminal in Khmer times, when a white elephant might be called upon to crush you with his head.) The Buddha, Suthep says, was a white elephant in one of his five hundred reincarnations. A Cambodian folktale tells that the incarnation of the Buddha entered his mother, Maha Maya, as a white elephant who appeared to her in a dream—it walked three times around her, then entered her body through the right side. She felt neither pain nor heaviness through her pregnancy, and at the birth, the prince leaped out of her side like a roebuck as she stretched forth her hand to pick a flower while she walked amid shady trees.

"How can you see an advanced spirit?" I ask Suthep.

Now the monk speaks directly to me—in English, bypassing Nee. "Pur-i-tee!" he cries out emphatically. "You know: pur-i-tee!"

Purity. He can see the purity in his teacher, he tells me. He can see it also in some of the dogs around the temple. It is something far more real to him than species distinctions.

There is one monk, he says, who adopted a dog who is extremely devoted to him, and very helpful. If he drops his towel on the floor, the dog picks it up for him. In a past life, he explained, the dog was a person and the monk was her husband. At the moment, he is a monk and she is a dog, but little else has changed.

He has three dogs himself—all of whom have been treated by the vets and volunteers at Banglamung. One is nearby—a sheep-doggish gray, fluffy female, whom he adopted from the compound. "He knew them before," Nee tells me about these dogs. But the monk does not wish to elaborate. Instead, he wants to tell me about the forest.

He belongs to a class of the monkhood called *Thammayut,* or forest monk. "Forest monks cannot cut trees. Trees do not have a spirit, but they have life. To live in the forest," he said, "is to learn easy life. If you can stay like that, you can think about the life—not about the house, not the new car."

Monks are taught to live lightly on the earth—light as bees. The Buddha's life revolved around forests. Born a prince beneath a sala tree, he had attained enlightenment beneath a ficus, whose beauty and majesty so absorbed him he did not notice when it rained, and seven cobras spread their hoods to spare him from the downpour. He delivered his first sermon at a deer park, a sanctuary for animals, and when he died, passing into Nirvana, it was again beneath a ficus. Trees bestow wonders: the nearest Buddhist heaven is Daovaduengsa, where divine trees, the Parichart, bloom with flowers so fragrant those who smell them can recall former births. Trees give birth to angels: the Kontans are mystical singers and musicians born from the sweet, fragrant trees.

"To live in the forest is to learn easy life," he says again.

But to live in the forest is not easy. It is difficult, even for wild animals. Even for a bear, who is wildness incarnate, hazards abound in the forest, even without human hunters: from lightning strikes and falling trees to prowling tigers and rival bears to drought and starvation. And to live in the forest is far more difficult for a human. "There is no greater challenge to the cultivated serenity of a Buddhist monk than the requirement that he spend a period of solitary meditation alone in the wild woodland," wrote the Southeast Asian historians Ian Mabbett and David Chandler.

But in the forest, the monk finds a different kind of ease. This, I know, is what Suthep is trying to say. "Actually it is not different from the wild animal," he continues. "If we can live like that, you think about life—not the house. Not the new car. One thing the human has—the human thinks he need things, and tries everything to have them." In the forest, one is freed from the prison of human greed.

And here, one can pursue true freedom, the freedom the Buddha exhorted the faithful to contemplate. Among the blessings of the sweet, fragrant trees, one can discover what wild animals know: in awareness of the moment lies the wholeness of life—an always-open doorway to eternity.

There is a Buddhist koan, or riddle, about the permeable nature of time: "Firewood becomes ash, and it does not become firewood again," the Buddha taught. "Yet, do not suppose that the ash is future and the firewood past. You should understand that firewood is firewood, which fully includes future and past."

* * *

The monk, of course, had no idea of our scientific quest. He could not have known that we were using hairs of living moon bears to trace their ancestry back in time—nor that we sought to use that knowledge to help secure the bears' future. He surely could not have shared the professor's command of the broad sweep of evolution's transforming power. Nor could he have guessed at the depth of my disorientation: I was traveling with a paleontologist back into time, through a world populated with recycling ancient souls, where a dog could be a bear and a bear could be a dog, and an elephant and a dog and a human and a bear were all the same.

And yet, the monk spoke to us in riddles whose truth the scientist had already grasped, and which I desperately needed to learn.

"If we understand the nature of the immediate present," the monk said, "we understand the nature of all things."

CHAPTER NINE

The Kingdom of a Million Elephants

"Perhaps in the Pleistocene, the Cardamoms were an upland refuge when the lowlands were too dry," Gary mused. "It's hard to believe that before people got here there was anywhere that bears couldn't live."

The great sociobiologist E. O. Wilson once said that a successful scientist thinks like a poet but works like a bookkeeper. In pursuit of the lyrical vision of a vanished refuge for bears during the Pleistocene drought, Gary was as meticulous as any bean-counter. At every available moment, from every available angle, he thought and rethought his hypotheses. "Or perhaps the gradations between the separate lineages were wiped out by people," he continued. "Or possibly, have sun bears confined moon bears to the mountains? Maybe in the Pleistocene we should think of lowland tropical rain forest sun bears competing with the moon bears, and restricting the moon bears to these refuges . . ."

We discussed these ideas endlessly. In the minivan taking us to Bangkok's airport, we passed fruit markets under tin roofs, herds of blue pickups, stores selling spirit houses and lawn furniture, junkyards, Kentucky Fried Chicken outlets, and forested hills where bears should be living but they have all been kidnapped or killed. But, in the same way that the monk saw multiple incarnations—the dog who was once a wife, an elephant who was once a king—Gary saw, outside our windows, the landscapes of multiple pasts: dry scrub, lowland rain forest, mountain refuge.

Now we were going to widen the scope of that lost geography. "We're going to Laos today!" I announced to our fellow passengers as we neared the airport.

"We are if the plane ever takes off, and ever descends in anything other than a vertical dive," Gary muttered under his breath.

Investigating the best way to get to Laos, we had considered several forms of transportation. "Slow boats," known as *heua sa,* we had read in our travel guide, "are hammered together with ill-fitting pieces of wood, the gerry-rigged engine coaxed along by an on-board mechanic . . . do not have any seats . . . landing involves ramming the boat into the river-bank . . . a process that can be very wet and muddy." Speedboats were faster. Powered by Toyota engines, they jet along at fifty miles per hour. We discarded that option when we learned that crash helmets were handed out before journeys. Train, often the best way to travel in Europe, was also out: very little was left of the tracks, installed early in the previous century, and none of them led to or from Thailand. We could enter Laos by plane, of course, but airfare was expensive—except for the national airline, Lao Aviation. Several Western embassies, including our own, had issued travel advisories against it. We had asked Gary van Zuylen what he thought:

His answer: "They crash."

How often?

"One crashed last week."

Is this a regular event?

"They crash a lot," he replied. He added, "They're very cheap."

Would *you* take it?

"It wouldn't worry *me.*"

So we had purchased our tickets on the national airline to Vientiane.

In the previous week, we had read in the *Bangkok Post,* there had been two armed raids in Laos and a spate of bomb explosions in the capital. Although Lao authorities insisted they had no idea who might do such a thing, diplomats agreed it was almost certainly the work of Khmer and Hmong minority rebels. Their two-decades-long insurgency had intensi-fied since March, when the first of seven bomb explosions had wounded ten tourists in a crowded outdoor restaurant (named *Chock Jai Mak* or "Thank You Very Much") in Vientiane. Besides those that had exploded, several other bombs had been defused, including at the capital's airport, at the main morning market, and outside the Vietnamese embassy. The day before we left, a gang of sixty anti-Communist insurgents, dressed in the stolen uniforms of high-ranking officers, had briefly captured the state offices at the border checkpoint between the southernmost province of Laos and Thailand's Ubon Ratchathani Province. The rebels had fled with more than a hundred automatic weapons.

We flew off in the dark.

* * *

"Soon after, they reached Laos, whose putrid exhalations had proved fatal to all the missionaries who had encountered them." Count de Carne wrote these words in 1872, in a preface to the book written by his son, Louis, *Travels on the Mekong*, about his explorations of the Mekong as a trade route between 1866–68. The book was published posthumously; De Carne died at the age of twenty-seven of ailments he contracted during his voyage. The author described Laos as "a region of evil name, protected by the rock with which its river bristles, and still more by the miasma exhaled by the sun's heat."

Laos has suffered bad press ever since. "It's the worst place in the world!" a family friend, a retired army colonel who had ventured there in the 1960s, told me. "There is nothing you could give me to go back there!" Like most Americans, he pronounced the name of the country as "Louse" (it is actually pronounced "Lao" as in "ow")—an error that has done nothing to lend glamour to this little, landlocked, mountainous country.

Today, Laos is one of the ten poorest countries in the world. Its currency is nearly worthless. Upon landing, in exchange for a hundred dollars, we were handed a three-inch stack of no fewer than 779,000 kip. "My eyes tell me I am either the world's richest man, or using the world's most inflated currency," Gary commented as he tried to figure out where to stash the wad.

Per capita income here is about $250. One child in five dies before its first birthday. The cars often live longer than the people. The opium addiction rate is twice the literacy rate. "Laos is not a country," Gary van Zuylen had told us. "It's a village." Until 1990 (when a foreign aid project routed calls through an Australian satellite), only a single phone line connected Laos with other countries except for Thailand. The average Lao mails only one letter a year; only 1 in 150 have television; and only 1 in 500 have seen a movie in the past year. A more common diversion is watching battles between rhinoceros beetles, a sport like cockfighting, which is also popularly enjoyed.

Laos is saddled with the distinction of one superlative: it is the most heavily bombed country on earth. During the nine-year secret war against the Communists, during the Vietnam War, the United States dropped 6,300,000 tons of bombs on Indochina, about a third of which fell on Laos. It was the heaviest aerial bombardment in the history of warfare. During the 1960s and 1970s, the United States rained more bombs on Laos than were dropped on Nazi Germany during World War II—three times the tonnage dropped during the Korean War—the equivalent of a plane load of bombs every eight minutes around the clock for nine years. Unexploded ordnance still infests the countryside. Despite the concentrated efforts of international demining organizations, fifteen of Laos's eighteen provinces were still considered significantly "contaminated" and some two hundred "accidents" occur each year.

Abandoned by its secret American supporters after the fall of Saigon in 1975, Laos's government fell to the hands of the Communist rulers who created the Lao People's Democratic Republic. ("The only word in that phrase that is true is 'Lao,'" said Gary, who had patriotically given up his college deferment, willing, though not eager, to fight the Communists if his draft number been called.) Fifty thousand undesirables, such as civil servants, intellectuals, and royalist sympathizers, were rounded up and held captive in filthy, malarial jungle reeducation camps. There, after toiling all day on communal farms, they were forced to memorize the résumés of Communist revolutionaries, the names of battles fought, the numbers of people killed. An excellent student might be freed in five years, but most were held prisoner for ten—if they did not die first of dysentery, cholera, hepatitis, typhoid, dengue fever, malaria, or starvation. Many, upon their release, fled the country. Ten percent of Laos's citizens became refugees, including three-quarters of its intellectuals. It was an exodus that, in the opinion of some historians, set Laos's development back a generation.

But today, Laos's leaders are less draconian in their approach. We had read that they had outlawed dollars, the use of scrap metal, and the use of the letter R. Despised in many Asian countries and usually confused with an L ("We are preased to serve you runch" comes the meal announcement on many an Asian airline), R and L are separate symbols in both Lao and Thai, but both are somewhere in between the Western pronunciation. So the English letter "R" became a victim of Communist oppression.

But we soon learned that such laws are ignored, and the government looks the other way. Dollars are in wide use, houses and fences usually incorporate scrap metal (we found bomb casings used as flowerpots), and Rs adorn menus, hotel signs, and billboards. Laos's economic reforms now allow farmers to sell their crops at free-market prices; teenagers flaunt American fashions; and discos flourish in the capital.

Vientiane, we found, is a city accustomed to accommodation. It is a city of ruin and resurrection. In the eighth century the Mon occupied and then abandoned this city, and next the Khmers. The Lao King Setthathirat moved his capital here from Louang Phabang in 1560. "The City of Sandalwood" it was called—overrun by the Burmese, Chinese, and Siamese until the French found it swallowed in jungle in 1867. Like neighboring Cambodia and Vietnam, it was a colony of France from the end of the nineteenth century till the middle of the twentieth, Laos declaring her independence in 1945.

Many of the old French mansions now seem to be crumbling into dust. Some of them appear to be held together only by vines—as if the spirits of the place have not only accepted, not only forgiven, but actually embraced the city's past. The streaming roots of ficus trees, too, seem to have bonded with the sidewalks—what sidewalks there are. In the main tourist district, dotted with restaurants, bakeries, and Internet cafés, the sidewalks are land-mined with yawning, man-sized sewer holes, giving new meaning to the term "tourist trap." Visitors, addled with the heat, not infrequently fall in, plunging into a soup of Mekong and sewer water that makes any wound go septic.

Gary and I were careful of these holes as we wandered the city, waiting for word from Nee. She had gone on ahead of us to Laos, and was negotiating with the army officers who ran the Tulakhom Zoo for permits to allow us to collect hair from the bears there. Meanwhile, we had been advised to view Vientiane's Victory Arch. Gary van Zuylen had called it "the world's largest vertical runway." It was made of six thousand tons of concrete, originally donated by the U.S. government for a landing strip; instead, the Laotians turned it into a large, square monument that looked like it had dropped out of the sky and lodged incongruously at the center of the roundabout at the end of Lane Xang Avenue. It was intended, we learned, to turn the city's broadest avenue into a tropical Champs Élysées, billed as a cross between the Arc de Triomphe and the Taj Mahal. "The Arch is a splendorous concrete monument and it is praised not only by the Laos people, but also by foreigners who have visited Vientiane," explains a thirty-five-page commemorative booklet, *Victory Arch: Construction · Significance · Prestige* written by its designer, Tham Sayasithsena. The monument was an international critical success. He reported, "Some visitors say: 'The Arch is the most beautiful and no any architectural style of monuments in this region can compare with.'"

We were not among these enthusiasts. To us, Vientiane's charms were more humble. At our hotel, an old French mansion with a courtyard embraced by fragrant, purple-blossomed vines, a nanny goat was tethered to the front gate. Many of the streets are unpaved, and the red mud records the bare footprints of Buddhist monks who wander at dawn with their begging bowls, allowing the people to earn blessings by feeding them. There is a peace, even a serenity, amid the recycling decay on these uncrowded streets. The trees along the Mekong have epiphytes—ferns, orchids, and sometimes even cacti perch harmlessly on the branches— and some, judging from flowerpots beneath them, quilled with spent incense, have spirits. Fig roots hang like hair, chickens strut in the streets, and along the river, people live as they have for millennia in thatched-roof stilt houses. Beside the river, a man shucks corn squatting on flat feet and folded thighs, and a woman cooks in a tin pot over an open fire. Children play checkers with bottle caps and women prepare ginger-scented sauces with mortar and pestle. People carry wares with *habs,* a bamboo pole worn across the shoulder from which two baskets called *kaboongs* dangle on either side. Today you can still view scenes like those sketched by Louis Delaporte, the artist who accompanied De Carne's 1866 expedition. The moments do not seem to travel, as they do in the West, forward in time; instead they hang, heavy and eternal, like the humidity in the air: past, present, and future all at once.

Everyone moves with languor in the dense, moist heat: the young girls selling dried squid and Teletubbies' key chains on the streets, the weary, pale backpackers searching for cybercafés, the women sweeping storefront sidewalks with grass brooms, each movement as soft as eyelashes brushing a cheek. The sidewalks are in ruins, but on the roofs of crumbling buildings, satellite dishes gape at the heavens, like supplicants requesting a boon, and on the hotels and restaurants, tiny Christmas lights wink gaily at one another in the night, as if they have overheard some whispered confidence.

"Poor, empty, secretive, beautiful Laos," English author Lucretia Stewart wrote in her 1992 travelogue, *Tiger Balm.* The country's poverty, emptiness and beauty were readily apparent to us, even that first day. But we were yet to explore its secrets.

* * *

"I wonder what bears think when they look at the Mekong?" Gary wondered. "Now, bears do swim to the ABC Islands, across cold waters with swift current," he continued, referring to the coal-black grizzlies of

Alaska's Admiralty, Baranof, and Chichagof islands, the closest living relatives of the polar bears. "We know this from nuclear DNA data, that indicate regular crossings by males. Do moon bears think maybe there's a female on the other side, and swim across it? Or do they think, man, that's a lot of water?"

Below us, the Mekong stretched like the endless, ancient naga on whose coils the Hindu Creator slept, dreaming the universe into being. We were in the air again, on another Lao Aviation flight, this time headed to Louang Phabang. The city was built by nagas, the legends say. Many centuries ago, two sorcerers, arriving at the junction of the Mekong and Nam Khan rivers, found a paradise here, ablaze with crimson flowers of countless flame trees. The magicians conjured from the water seventeen serpents to construct the city at this lovely spot. It is believed the nagas guard it still.

Louang Phabang has long been a city of miracles. Many generations after the sorcerers summoned its serpents, a baby was born here, possessing at birth a set of thirty-three teeth. Sensing a bad omen, royal advisers convinced the king to exile his son. On a raft, complete with advisers, wet nurses, and servants, the infant was set adrift on the Mekong. A Buddhist monk found the child and took him to the court of the Khmer kings. He was educated as a Khmer prince, married to a Khmer princess—and, provided with an army, fought his way up the Mekong Valley atop a war elephant to found a kingdom of his own in 1353. He named his kingdom Lane Xang, the Kingdom of a Million Elephants, testifying to his royal prestige and military might. Present-day Laos is about the size of Oregon, but Fa Ngum's kingdom extended into northern Thailand and what is now Xishuangbanna Province in China. Fa Ngum made the city of his birth the capital of his great empire, and here established the line of kings that would rule Laos for six centuries.

Buddhism flourished in Louang Phabang. In its beautiful wats, epic poems were composed, sacred texts copied, great murals produced. Even after the kingdom moved its capital to Vientiane, Louang Phabang remained the center of the nation's soul. Until the last king was exiled to a work camp by the Communists, this was the sovereign's principal residence. It is the home of the most sacred icon of the country, the Pha Bang, a golden Buddha whose image is said to have been cast in gold, silver, copper, iron and precious stones overseen by the god Indra himself. Twice Siamese invaders have captured the palladium—and twice they have returned it to Laos, believing it bad luck for the conquerors. The city is named in honor of the image. Louang Phabang, The Great Pha Bang, is now enshrined, as was once the king, in the royal palace.

It is a city of Buddhas. They reside, reclining and standing, granting boons, dispelling fear, dispensing wisdom, in more than thirty wats somehow packed into this tiny city, nearly one on every block, each name itself a sort of incantation—Wat Xieng Tong: Temple of the Golden City. Wat Long Khun: Temple of the Blessed Chant. Wat Cham Pet: Monastery of the Diamond Spire.

Gary and I were eager to explore these wonders, but they were not the focus of our trip. Our permits were not expected to come through for several days, Nee had told us. So in the meantime, we had embarked for the ancient capital of the Kingdom of a Million Elephants on an errand: we were looking for a tiger and three bears.

"There are bound to be forests loaded with moon bears down there!" said Gary, looking over the green swathe surrounding the river below. But the bears we were seeking were in captivity, along with the tiger. Gary van Zuylen had told us he'd heard that someone was keeping them somewhere in Louang Phabang. He'd asked us, if we had time, to look in on them and report on their condition; if they were in distress, perhaps the zoo could rescue them. But where were they?

"Everyone will know where the tiger is," Gary had told us, "and the bears are on the same street." Was there an address? "There aren't any addresses in Laos," he told us. "Just ask around."

* * *

We both felt unwell when we landed. The short flight had been wearying. We'd traveled in what I had dubbed the Menopause Plane. When we'd boarded, it was like a sauna, and the air conditioning had appeared to consist entirely of refrigerated wet cloths the stewardess had handed out to the sweating passengers. Halfway through the flight, though, cold clouds of condensation had begun to pour from the overhead compartments and we froze. This was a preview of the chills and fever to come: both of us were coming down with stomach problems, perhaps from an unwise encounter with ice cubes in the capital.

Nonetheless, we set out immediately to find the animals. We spoke with a driver for the Auberge Catalao. The hotel was beyond our means, but the van had been sent to pick up a tourist named Jennifer who never materialized, so the driver agreed to take us into town. He didn't know about the animals, but suggested we ask at the hotel bar.

"We are looking for a tiger and three bears," we announced to the bartenders. "Do you know where we might find them?"

Blank stares. Our request was incomprehensible. Our sentences were clearly not among those normally uttered by their clientele.

"Tiger? Bear?" we repeated.

"Oh yes!" said the barkeep. "We have tiger—Tiger beer!"

No, no, we explained—we were looking for a real tiger. A live tiger. A live bear.

"Ah—you want the zoo!" offered a barmaid. "For that, you have to go outside Vientiane."

No, no, this tiger is not in the *zoo* . . .

"Tiger in forest?" offered a bellhop. "Maybe, but you will never see them there . . ."

After much discussion, suddenly the barkeep realized what we were saying. "Oh yes. *That* tiger!" It was a cub, he said, the only survivor of three, and it was living at the agriculture department, about a half hour's drive outside of town.

Was it still there?

He didn't know—but he knew who would: a Madame Sin-wee, who is French, works at the agriculture department. Did he have her address? No—but she lives near Wat Khily, whose Buddha image, it was said, broke out in a cold sweat in 1958, signaling the coming war. We should go there.

Louang Phabang is a tiny place, the old city concentrated on a tongue of land only one kilometer long and a quarter kilometer wide. It did not seem a difficult task to find a house near Wat Khily. Gary was confident. We had no fewer than three maps of the city to help us. Gary adores maps and always has piles of them. I, on the other hand, have a profound distrust of maps: when I was a child, a map pulled out of the glove compartment was a sure sign we were lost.

Although Gary could unfailingly locate almost any destination on a map, that did not mean we would ever reach it. There were few street signs, and those that existed bore names that did not seem to resemble anything on our maps. And unfortunately, Gary is the only person on Earth with a natural sense of direction almost as bad as my own.

"I can't understand it!" he said, frowning at the three different maps. "I thought the Mekong was over here, and now, it's over there!"

We wandered, feverish and lost, through the colossal noontime heat. The city was once home to a god-king named Panya Kabilaphom, endowed with a four-faced head, on whom I blamed all our troubles. Legends say he loved to set enigmas for the people. Perhaps he had designed our maps. Panya Kabilaphom used to cut people's heads off when they failed to solve his riddles, until one day a wise man met his challenge and cut Panya Kabilaphom's head off instead. But being a god, his four-faced head, once severed, was hot enough to cause the atmosphere to burn, the rivers to boil, and the land to ignite. For this reason, the people had to keep his head in a cave. It only comes out once a year, nowadays, on which day people parade its image through the town, pouring water on it all the time lest it burst into flame. I wondered if perhaps the four-faced head had gotten out of hand again.

We passed little wooden houses, alive with peeping chicks, and old French villas. We passed children playing catch-the-shoe in the streets, and older boys hitting shuttlecocks with badminton racquets. Occasionally a monk flowed past in orange robes, beneath a black shade umbrella, one of the few possessions allowed other than the begging bowl. And incredibly, we passed an advertisement, in English, for an Herbal Sauna—run, of all things, by the Red Cross. "Jesus Christ!" said Gary, "I don't care what culture you are from, anyone who wants a sauna here is crazy!" We passed wat after wat. Wat Paa Fang: Temple of the Flaming Forest. Wat Aham: Monastery of the Radiant Heart. Wat Paa Huak: Temple of the Bamboo Forest. None of them were spelled like the wats on our maps. Nobody could direct us to Wat Khily. Nobody we met knew Madame Sin-Wee.

Sweat drenched our shirts and socks and underwear and poured into our eyes. Our intestines were knotting with cramps. Finally, we went into a shop selling handmade mulberry paper and found an English-speaking clerk inside. Madame Sin-wee? Oh yes, he knew her; in fact, she lived next door.

We knocked on the door of a white house with light blue trim and shutters inhabited by a four-year-old child and her governess. "Madame is at the oaf-eesh!" the governess told us. But we had the right house—and when we returned that evening, we met "Madame Sin-Wee." Sylvie Dideron, her dark hair pinned up, flour from bread-making on her hands, stood in the doorway and told us that yes, the tiger, a ten-month-old female, was still living at the agricultural station, and that we would be welcome to visit her there next day. But of bears, she knew nothing.

*　*　*

We had wisely asked a bellhop at the Auberge Catalao to write out for us, in curving Lao script, the directions to the agricultural station. This we handed to a tuk-tuk driver and within ten minutes, we were standing before the tiger cub. She was contentedly chewing a rib of beef inside a spacious, metal barred cage. She was in perfect condition: her golden eyes bright, her flame-colored fur lush, and her paw pads smooth and tough. The twelve-by-nine-foot cage contained a live tree, which she used to climb and to sharpen her claws, as well as three different types of floor—dirt, concrete, and wood—which was surely why she had not succumbed to the cracking paw infections that plague many captive animals.

While admiring her cage, we were astonished to learn she had only been in it three months.

"Before, she was with us," said Sylvie.

With us, we pondered. . . . Did that mean the tigress was loose?

"In the oaf-eesh," Sylvie said with her charming French accent.

A tiger cub roamed loose around the office?

"Where did she sleep?" asked Gary.

"She slept with students," Sylvie replied. "The problem is, she is big, and began to catch and kill chickens." This must have been bad PR for the ag station, which was supposed to teach people the art of modern poultry keeping—which surely did not include allowing a tiger to roam freely through the barnyard.

"The neighbors were afraid for their children," Sylvie continued. "So the cage was built."

The tiger cub had been one of three unweaned babies the police had confiscated from poachers, she explained. One of them had died before police even had a chance to bring them here; the other expired despite everyone's best efforts. But no one here really had any experience in raising wild animals, after all.

What about bears? Sylvie asked several of the project staff for us.

"The governor of the province has two bears," Chanphone Keoboualaphet, head of the Section of Livestock and Fishery, told us. "He was given them." The governor, he told us, was a very important man. He discouraged us from visiting his bears. A third bear had once lived at the Phou Si Hotel. "A big one—very big," he told us. But it got sick, and although his veterinarians tried to treat it, the bear died several years ago.

Wild moon bears live in the north of Louangphabang Province, the staff assured us. And tigers—last year a farmer shot a very big tiger who was raiding his chickens. "We say, 'Oh, no, no, the tiger is to protect!'" explained Sylvie. But the farmer never understood. Like many Laotians, he saw a tiger as a nuisance, a bear as a commodity. One younger staff member said that in 1992, he saw for sale a moon bear who was the color of the wood of this door—a golden brown—from an animal dealer. But no, no one had ever brought a bear to the agricultural station. Certainly not!

* * *

Having solved the mystery of the tiger and the three bears, we yielded to our increasingly insistent intestines and took a tuk-tuk back to the guest house. Our hostess was on the phone in the lobby. The call was for us.

It was Sylvie. Someone had just brought in a bear cub. Would we come back and tell them what to do with it?

"We'll be right there," I told her. But first we went upstairs to get the tweezers and vials.

We returned to the ag station to find, behind one of the offices near the chicken hatchery, a tiny cage of chicken wire and wood half again the size of its inhabitant—a fluffy black, blue-eyed male moon bear cub, perhaps three months old. He was so overheated that as a female worker hosed him off, he lapped what must have been a quart of water from the shallow bowl in his cage with his ribbon tongue. Then, exhausted, he dropped his leathery nose into the empty bowl and fell asleep. We checked him gently for wounds. There was a small cut on his nose, possibly from an exposed nail in his cage. I removed a tick the size of a kernel of corn from his ear, and then took four good samples of his fine, woolly hair.

Now what? We had to find a place to keep him. The tiny, frail cage wouldn't do at all. Was there a poultry enclosure we could use? Yes—but it had bamboo slats for flooring. He would be able to chew right through it.

We had to do something soon. We phoned Nee from Sylvie's office and left a message. Outside we heard a terrible wail. Gary assumed it was one of the turkeys who roamed the compound, tail spread with studied pomposity, or a Toulouse goose, its stately waddling interrupted by some avian emergency. But no—the bear cub, having woken from his nap, was wailing piteously, and chewing so frantically at the cage that he had cut his gums and tongue, leaving flecks of bright blood on the wire.

We had to get him out of there. Then I remembered the tiger cage. It had a sliding door in the middle that would allow it to be partitioned into two. We hated to confine the little tigress to a smaller space, but a decent holding pen had to be found for the cub immediately. We slid the barred door closed and erected a sheet of plywood between the two partitions, so the two animals would not see one another, transferred the bear inside, and breathed a sigh of relief. The little bear would be safe, and soon Nee would phone back to tell Sylvie what to feed him. In the wild he would have been still nursing. I suggested Esbilac, a synthetic bitches' milk replacement, and Sylvie laughed. "In Louang Phabang, you cannot even buy dog food!" she said. Dogs are fed scraps. I had no idea how to approximate a recipe for bear milk. But the staff at the Tulakhom Zoo would surely know, and we felt certain that the zoo would soon rescue the little bear.

We left exhausted but delighted. We could not believe our luck: not only had we been able to help a baby bear, but he was scientifically of inestimable value to us. Here we had found a Laotian bear whose capture location could not be more certain—he had been rescued from poachers, police told Sylvie, in Viang Kham District, about ninety kilometers northeast of here, near the border with Vietnam. More important, he had provided us with our first hair sample from this side of the Mekong. The little cub's DNA could help us answer Gary's question of whether the river was indeed a genetic barrier to moon bears.

*   *   *

Back at the guest house, we wanted to celebrate. Instead, we doubled over with cramps.

"Insects, you know, don't get this," Gary noted during a rare moment when neither of us was in the bathroom. We had already taken all the Pepto-Bismol and now were nearing the end of our supply of Immodium. "Insects' excretory wastes are funneled into the digestive system and have no moisture at all!" the professor explained. "They have malphigian tubules that funnel waste into the gut directly, and the lower gut extracts every bit of water . . ."

I was delighted to know that, no matter how we were suffering, insects were not.

"If we are lucky," I said to Gary, "we will come back as bugs after we die."

Our days in Louang Phabang passed feverishly. Each morning, we woke at four to the sonorous gong at the temple across the street. Wat Xieng Mouane, "Temple of the Lively Drum," sounded its gong, drums, and cymbals to keep demons in their lairs, protecting the monks at sensitive times like holy days, full moons, and the times when the men shave their heads.

Though we did not venture far from plumbing those first few days, we revisited the little bear, happy to find him comfortable in his new surroundings. We perused the Dala Market. Nearby, Hmong women, having walked down from the mountains in their black traditional dress, hawked splendid embroidery. The main market offers the usual supplies of jewelry, cloth, and souvenirs, as well as local essentials: plastic bags of yellow sulfur and quartzlike saltpeter mixed with charcoal, for homemade gunpowder. Here, from a Chinese merchant with a cascade of long hair flowing like a waterfall from a conspicuous mole on his cheek, Gary also purchased new scientific supplies: a pair of enormous pliers. He proposed we use these, instead of my tiny eyebrow tweezers, to pluck the dangerous bears of the Tulakhom Zoo.

Already, we had been practicing for this. We knew it might be too dangerous to stick our hands in the bears' cages; we might have to obtain hair in another way. I chased Gary around the hotel room, whacking him repeatedly on the head with a pole to which I had attached a wad of sticky flypaper. Then we would carefully examine it to see if it had obtained a follicle. "I bet the hotel management doesn't suspect what goes on behind the closed doors of their rooms!" he commented.

We awaited word of our permits. Meanwhile, we ate at French restaurants and Swedish bakeries. We wandered through the wats, admiring magnificent murals. We climbed the holy hill of Phou Si and gazed through a grate to see a rock that the locals say records a footprint of the

After trying to put this face through our window,
Stripe, a 250-pound male moon bear, followed
our Jeep through Banglamung. *Gary J. Galbreath*

(right) With their enormous, round, furry ears, moon bears look like no other bear species. *Dianne Taylor-Snow*

(below, right) Prior to our expeditions, only dark moon bears were known to science. *Gary J. Galbreath*

The moon bear's original Latin name, *Selenarctos,* honors the Greek goddess of the moon, Selene, because of the distinctive, pale crescent on the bear's chest. *Dianne Taylor-Snow*

Bear cubs are especially adept climbers.
Dianne Taylor-Snow

(left) Southeast Asia's other bear species, the sun bear, is the more tree loving of the two. The fur is short, the claws long, and the ears tiny. *Dianne Taylor-Snow*

The golden moon bear's astonishing blond coat contrasts with the dark, lionlike mane. *Dianne Taylor-Snow*

(left) Around the globe, for millennia, human cultures have claimed kinship with bears: they are strikingly humanlike, with postures like ours and hands dexterous enough to peel a peach. *Dianne Taylor-Snow*

The golden bear's pale face seemed to shine like a moon from the dark shade.
Dianne Taylor-Snow

(left) After having hiked through land-mined forests and searching two countries,
we found a golden moon bear in a private Thai zoo. *Dianne Taylor-Snow*

A bear's face set in a lion's mane: Bertha was the oldest, blondest, and most magnificent of the golden bears, proof that the golden color was not a juvenile growth stage. *Sy Montgomery*

(right) We discovered that even very young moon bear cubs can be blond. *Dianne Taylor-Snow*

Stripe's unusual markings, dark eye rings and dark forequarters, may resemble an early stage in the evolution of the giant panda's coloration. *Gary J. Galbreath*

Born at a private zoo, this golden cub will spend his life performing for tourists. *Dianne Taylor-Snow*

(below) Captured from the wild as a cub, the thin, sickly golden female stared out at us from her exile on the palm plantation at the foot of the Elephant Mountains near Kampong Som. *Sy Montgomery*

Buddha. Three wats are located on the hill; at one of them I prayed for rain. Outside another temple, we watched the sun set on the shimmering river below while listening to the chants of the monks. The moment they finished, a musical clock in the temple chimed the tune "Für Elise." ("It is from Japan," a novice explained.)

We visited the Phou Si Hotel, to try to find out more about the deceased moon bear. Possibly they had even acquired a new one. To keep the language simple, we used in our inquiries only the present tense:

"Do you have a bear?"

"Yes, yes, bear!" said the smiling maître d', pointing to his right.

"Where?" we asked in astonishment.

"Here!" he said. "Right here!"

Gary and I looked at each other, wide-eyed. Our luck, apparently, knew no bounds.

"Right here? In the *restaurant*?"

"Yes," the maître d' insisted, "in restaurant!" He continued to motion us toward a table. We didn't see any bear. In Cambodia, we'd seen that many restaurants have bears, but they are not usually kept in the dining area.

"A live bear?"

"Yes!" he assured us, "have Lao beer!" And he pointed toward the bar, where a mirrored wall was lined with bottles of the national beverage: "Beer Lao!"

* * *

One day, fortified by antibiotics brought from the States, we fought our way through the stupefying heat to visit the royal palace. Here a Communist-run museum preserves the trappings of the monarchy it extinguished: ceremonial hilts and swords, royal seals and decorations, gifts of visiting diplomats, the king's elephant saddle, or howdah. To our astonishment we also saw paintings of the kings: Oun Kham (1872–89); Kham Souk (1890–1904); Sisavang (1905–59) . . . and no more. "They don't have the rest because they murdered him and his family," Gary noted angrily.

No one really knows how the king and his family died. The Communist government did not officially acknowledge that they were dead at all until in December 1989. In Louang Phabang, as journalist Christopher Kremmer observed in his investigation of the fate of Laos's royal family, *Stalking the Elephant Kings,* "history is spoken in whispers." This much is known: an army truck removed King Savang Vatthana, Queen Khamboui, and Crown Prince Vong Savang from the palace and deposited them at Louang Phabang airport in spring 1977 to be sent to a prison work camp. Various sources claim that the crown prince died of dysentery, and the king of malaria and starvation, in May 1978, and the queen wasted away three years later. Others say the king died six months after the queen. The monarchs are said to be buried in unmarked graves at the base of a big *kok leung* tree along the Houey Path River.

We saw the famous Pha Bang, in an unlit room inside a curtained shrine, behind an array of elephant tusks, plastic flowers, incense, and a crystal chandelier. The Buddha's arms are held out with flattened palms, like a policeman halting traffic. With this gesture, legends tell us, the Buddha once subdued a rampaging elephant.

But far more moving, and far more troubling, were the walls of the Palace Throne Hall.

The murals here are spangled with colored mirrors set in a wall of crimson, created in the 1950s to commemorate the twenty-five hundredth anniversary of the historic Buddha's passing into Nirvana. One wall depicts a battle scene. It could be from the *Ramayana,* the Hindu epic, or it could be any of the ancient battles from Laotian history, from Fa Ngum's victories to the invasions of Vietnamese, Siamese, and Burmese. Sword-bearing soldiers are busy lopping heads off. The heads fly from the necks cleanly, like a shuttlecock from a badminton racquet or a golf ball from a tee. In one corner of the room is a case filled with ivory-handled swords, which may have been used for this task. Here, Gary dispensed another gem from the treasure trove of his biological knowledge:

"You know, it's neurologically possible that some consciousness persists for several moments after beheading," he said. "Theoretically at least, these people might have been able to see their own headless bodies as their heads flew through the air and rolled on the ground."

Would you have the time to actually understand the sight? What would one's thoughts be at such a moment? I wondered.

"Probably," Gary replied, "there is sufficient time to think something like 'ouch.'"

In the palace of a murdered king, we stood in a room decorated by scenes of monstrous cruelty, dedicated to a saint. But perhaps the Buddha would have been pleased. The central tenet of Buddhist teaching is not obedience, nor salvation through grace; it is compassion. Com-passion: the words mean "with suffering." Anyone who has loved knows passion as a twin of pain. The Buddhists call it *dukkha;* in the folk language at the time of Buddha, it referred to a cart wheel that cannot turn properly because something is wrong at its very hub. Suffering, this state of profound disharmony, is at the heart of earthly existence, Buddha taught. Compassion does not quench suffering, but marries it.

And so, perhaps, it was no accident that these scenes of suffering are painted in mirrors. In the images of ancient, ruthless cruelty, we see our own faces. Other scenes in the mirrored glass depict ordinary activities: people planting rice fields; plowing with water buffalo; riding on elephants. During the Vietnam War, the nation to which Gary and I owe our allegiance dropped 6,300,000 tons of bombs on farmers like these. In 1965 and 1966, our Air Force rained 200,000 gallons of poison on Laos's forests and rice fields. We bombed elephants as transport vehicles. We might prefer to view the scenes on these walls "in a mirror darkly," as the Apostle Paul wrote of the unenlightened of his day: the soldiers and the farmers, the victims and the kings, these people are not *us*. But as the Apostle exhorted, as the Buddha taught, in the spangled walls of the Throne Hall—as in the faces of doomed war prisoners, the eyes of captured animals—we cannot escape our own reflection.

* * *

The rain, when it came, was a great, cool balm, like a mother's soft hand on the forehead of a feverish child. It carried the heat away like the lustral water in which the Pha Bang is ritually bathed each April, at the start of the Lao New Year; it extinguished the fire of Panya Kabilaphom's severed four-faced head. On this day, the Mekong shone rosy as a polished copper kettle, and we traveled upriver on a long-tailed boat to its confluence with the Nam Ou, to the Buddha Caves.

In the mist, it is easy to imagine the nagas the sorcerers conjured here. Their images guard many of the temples, their scaly bodies lolling down the banisters of the temple staircases. In their gaping mouths, the monks place small offerings, balls of sticky rice and bits of fruit. By morning, the offerings are always gone.

The river trip afforded us a chance to view potential bear habitat. To either side of us, the forest looked regal and refined, like silver filagree—less monstrous than the Amazon or the Congo. The bamboos splay like water sprayed from a palace fountain; on the vines, huge leaves are strung like Chinese lanterns. Big rocks clutch the riverbanks like the toes of a giant.

There are two hills ahead, coiled one against the other like sleeping lovers. Our young guide, who was once crowned "Miss Louang Phabang" in a beauty contest, tells us this is, in fact, how these hills came to be. They are the stone reminders of Louang Phabang's Romeo and Juliet. Forbidden lovers, they ran away to the forest, took poison, and died, clasped in each other's arms, forever joined.

We traveled an hour before we reached a huge pale cliff face, the site of the Buddha Caves. "During the war, many Buddhas burned," says our pretty twenty-three-year-old companion. The Tham Ting and Tham Phoum caves were the sanctuary to which the damaged icons were taken—a refuge for injured Buddhas.

The Lao people, too, took refuge in caves during times of strife. During the rain of bombs and defoliants of the Vietnam War, caves offered the safest shelters. The Communist Pathet Lao's shadow government operated in a network of caves in Houaphan Province, complete with a hotel cave, a hospital cave, and even a theater cave.

Because these Buddhas were damaged, no longer could they be venerated in a temple. So they were brought here, to a large upper cave and a smaller, lower grotto. There are some four thousand Buddhas in all. Some stone, some bronze, some ceramic; some lacquered; some covered with gold leaf. Some are nearly a story tall; others, only inches. Some have burn marks, or missing limbs. From their position standing or sitting, they all seem to look out of the cave, facing the Mekong, serene, smiling, eternal. In this limestone hole literally eaten by time, they are timeless. They stay here, bestowing blessings, dispelling fear. Several of the images depict the Buddha seated in the lotus position, reaching forward and touching the earth with his right hand. This posture testifies to the Buddha's enlightenment, symbolizing his victory over the demons of desire, a mudra known as Calling for the Earth to Witness.

On the second day of the New Year, the Lao of Louang Phabang come here to ritually bathe the Buddhas, as they do the Pha Bang. But most of the time, the Buddhas wait in their dark cavern refuge, absorbed in the bliss of inner illumination.

They contemplate eternity in the company of spirits far older. Long before King Fa Ngum brought Buddhism to Laos, our guide told us, this cave was already sacred: it was the abode of nature spirits, she said. Those spirits are still here. From the ceiling, I feel something fall softly on my head. I shine my flashlight above me. And here, on the ceiling of this natural Sistine Chapel, we can see the winged guardians on this holy place: little nature spirits who, in this particular incarnation, have taken the form of bats.

* * *

Finally, our permits came through, and with them, the day we had been awaiting—and dreading. When we arrived back in Vientiane, Nee told us more about the bears we would pluck. Because for much of their lives, they had been starving, through the widely spaced bars of their cages, they frantically seize in their claws any object they might possibly consider food—otherwise another bear might get it, or the food might pass them by. In this way, one of the bears had so savaged the arm of a female zoo worker that it had to be amputated.

My coffee cup trembled as I set it in its saucer that morning. But we couldn't pass up the opportunity. These were some of the most geographically crucial bears of the study, Gary reminded me. Almost all of their capture sites were known. One had been captured in Namtha, in northern Laos near the borders with China, Thailand, and Burma. Another had come from Xaignabouli—near where Bertha and Dave had been captured, on the same side of the Mekong; this bear, a female, was important not only to test the veracity of Dave and Bertha's haplotype but also to see if they were genetically distinct from the Namtha bears caught across the river. And several came from various sites in the Annamite Mountains: four were from Bolikhamxai Province, at the very top of this remote mountain chain—and these might quite possibly turn out to be a very distinct haplotype, if not a new subspecies—or even a new species.

The zoo was nearly deserted when we got there. As we waited for Nee, Gill, and a new volunteer, Claire, we saw a pretty Laotian woman, with a wide, sweet face, walk by with a folder in one hand. She had only one hand. One arm was missing.

The zoo was an attractive spot, situated on twenty-five acres and built in 1991 on land owned by the Lao Army. Nee, Claire, and Gill appeared and led us past a large, leafy enclosure for binturongs, a pool with turtles, and grassy outdoor cages for muntjacks. We passed a field where workers were busy mixing concrete and digging—an area slated soon, thanks to Gary van Zuylen's organization, to be a large outdoor bear exclosure like those at Banglamung.

Nee introduced us to the army officer in charge of the zoo and to several of the zookeepers, none of whom spoke English. Next we met the bears. First, in a cage detached from the others, was the huge, tame Elsa, a former pet of a German expat who had obtained her in Ban Lao Meuy, in Namtha. I plucked her hair with no problem. Next we met Miggy, another sweet adult female, with an astounding face: her snout, instead of being long and doglike, was squat and bunched. "A perfect pig bear!" Gary said. We were told this was the result of a deformity that left her always panting. Miggy, one of the two survivors of the "Culture Park," also yielded gracefully to my tweezers, even seeming to enjoy the attention.

But the other bears were progressively more difficult. Two small females from Oudomxai Province were very wary. I was able to retrieve only a few hairs from the back of one's leg while Gary fed them both bananas through the cage bars. A large female cub in another cage was too skittish to approach, and was known to attack people. She was from Louangphabang Province, and as we already had hairs from the little cub we had just visited, we didn't chance it. Besides, the most critical bears—and the most dangerous—were still ahead.

These were the bears from Bolikhamxai and Xaignabouli provinces—among them, the bear who had savaged the zoo worker's arm. Two of the bears had been sent from Lak Xao, the town where George Schaller and his team had discovered the Sao la and the giant muntjack. The bears lived in a series of cement-floored, adjoining steel cages we called "the blockhouse." The cages were arranged in such a way that we could duck beneath a steel beam and stand surrounded on three sides by cage bars—through which six bears were threading their huge paws, trying to grab us. Their desperation was terrifying. No matter how well they were fed for the rest of their lives, they would never forget nearly starving. Would they forever feel anger, too, toward our kind?

Our position gave us the feeling of being in a cage ourselves. Our movements were severely restricted. If you backed up more than a step or two in any of three directions, you were within someone's swatting range; and as each cage contained two bears, there was never a point at which, even directly in front of you, there was only one bear to worry about.

Each attempt at gathering hairs carried a different risk. The tweezers required very close contact. The giant pliers allowed more distance between the hand and the bear, but the implement was so big and clumsy it could jam on the cage bars if you didn't withdraw it properly—leaving your hand stuck inside. We tried the pole-and-flypaper method. Our target, one of the subadult Xaignabouli females, caught it in her paws.

Now we were horrified the bear would try to eat the flypaper and choke. Eventually we fished it out. All the while, Western, Thai, and Lao companions were shouting advice in various languages—usually something like "watch out!" in response to which you could not leap away, or you would land in the outstretched paws of another bear.

Meanwhile, we were baking. The sun ate into our skin like acid; the humidity pressed on us like flesh. Sweat poured off our faces and stung our eyes and made our fingers slippery. But somehow, eventually, we secured hairs from at least one bear from each of the localities—all except the important pair from Lak Xao, which I couldn't seem to nail. Seeing our dismay, two of the zookeepers, Nuan Tohong and Bun Thum, threaded their bare hands through the bars, and with lightning-quick grasps, came up with a dozen hairs each. Gary stuffed them delightedly into vials.

Drenched with sweat, dizzy with relief, I was the first to stagger out of the blockhouse. I smacked my head on the steel beam and saw stars. It was oddly appropriate: long before Western astrologers named the constellations Ursa Major and Minor, people all over the world have looked at stars and seen bears.

We flew back to Thailand with vials full of hair and hearts full of hope and sorrow. Scientifically, our expedition was, so far, a huge success. The desperate, rescued bears at Tulakhom, the orphaned cub at Louang Phabang, all were great boons to us. We hoped what we learned from their DNA would one day help restore captive bears to their rightful homes. But I couldn't shake the sorrow of knowing that our data was only made possible by their tragedies.

Beneath our plane stretched forest, rice paddy, river, temple. The forests seemed forgiving, deep, like a secret kept, a vow honored. The paddies below shimmered like the mirrors on the mosaic at Louang Phabang's royal palace: green, copper, and gold, winking up at us with reflected light.

CHAPTER TEN

The Empty Forest

"Ah! Good news," Gary said to me, looking up from the *Bangkok Post* at breakfast the morning after we returned to Thailand.

"Really?" None of our reading material had provided much cheer of late. As Gary was reading the paper, I was going over a report we had picked up at the International Union for the Conservation of Nature's office in Vientiane. "The sad fact is that all recent wildlife surveys indicate that wildlife throughout Lao PDR is declining," read the introduction. I was eager for some happy news.

"Well," the professor said cheerfully, "it's a particularly torrential monsoon this year."

"Yes . . . ?"

"And it has hatched an unusually large crop of mosquitoes."

"Yes . . . ?"

"So now there is an epidemic of malaria . . ."

"Are we at the good part yet?" I asked.

We were not.

Gary and I were now in Chiang Mai, the thirteenth-century capital of the former northern Thai kingdom of Lanna, 150 kilometers from the border with northeast Burma, or Myanmar. The newspaper story, which Gary read me aloud, adding his own commentary as he saw fit, concerned the warring tribes of the Wa and the Shan. Some two dozen groups of ethnic rebels had been fighting the Burmese government along the border; the Wa and the Shan were among those tribes who were merely fighting each other.

The Wa, or the Wild Wa as they were once called, "are well, but not favorably known, for their embarrassing custom of cutting other people's heads," we had learned from an account written in the 1950s by a member of the Royal Siamese Provincial Gendarmerie, "which they exhibit in the skull avenues of their strongly fortified hill villages." These days, however, the Wa were better known for manufacturing much of Asia's illegal amphetamines and heroin. To expand their operations, the tribe was eyeing territory now held by the Shan, whose creation myth claims they are the descendants of a great white tiger, who still sometimes walks the length of Shanland, followed by fifty ghost leopards. The Shan are not inhospitable people; one of the stories collected from them tells us that small tremors are caused by subterranean dwarves who, feeling lonely, knock on their ceiling; to this, the Shan respond by rushing from their homes, kneeling on the ground and crying out, to reassure them, "We are here!" But even the solicitous Shan did not appreciate the Wa's incursion into their territory and customer base, and were zealously preparing for war—one that "threatens to send thousands of refugees across the border into Thailand," the paper said.

"I'm still waiting for the good news," I said.

"I'm getting to that," said the methodical professor, and he read on. "Some five hundred Wa militiamen have died of malaria in the last few months in the disputed district, and the heavy rain is hampering both groups' drug operations, the muddy roads forcing them to move amphetamines and heroin through the jungle on motorcycles."

The happy news was, because of flood and disease, the two tribes had agreed to postpone their turf battle. Which meant, for us, that our progress was not likely to be impeded by warring, drug-selling headhunters. Once we met up with Gary van Zuylen that afternoon, we would be able to travel, as planned, the 200 kilometers southwest from Chiang Mai to Mae Sariang, 150 kilometers north to Mae Hong Song, and on to the Salaween Wildlife Sanctuary, along the Burmese border.

*   *   *

On the twisting, mountainous drive to Mae Sariang in Gary van Zuylen's four-wheel drive Isuzu, the Australian told us about the Salaween sanctuary, and his hopes for releasing captive bears there. We wondered, was a sanctuary on the edge of a war zone really the best place for this historic reintroduction?

"Salaween was badly hit by poachers," he answered. "You've got rebels, half a dozen ethnic minorities, Burmese troops up there. And they all come into the park." Thailand has more than a hundred national parks, ranging from three thousand square kilometers to less than fifty; all but four of them have human settlements within their boundaries. Most of the people are refugees.

Half a million people, mostly known collectively as hill tribes, live in Thailand, but apart from the Thai. They originated farther to the north and northwest, from the mountains of south China, from northwest China, from Burma and Tibet. Like the moon bears whose lineages we were now tracing, they have been migrating south for centuries—displaced by invaders, by warfare, by political whim, by famine, and by drought.

In Thailand's national parks and sanctuaries, they continue their traditional way of life as best they can: hunting, cutting wood, planting opium. "They're a nightmare for the parks people," Gary van Zuylen told us. "They really tear up the place. And once it's ruined, they move on to deforest another area. But you can't move thousands of people."

About six years before, some ten thousand Burmese refugees illegally settled in camps inside the Salaween National Park. But the section he had in mind for the release was not in the park, but in the Salaween Wildlife Sanctuary. Wildlife sanctuaries, of which there are forty in Thailand, are set aside for conservation alone, not recreation, and they are under different and somewhat stricter administrative control. Visitors are not encouraged. The Salaween Wildlife Sanctuary is relatively secure. "Soldiers from Burma occasionally cross," the Australian said. "But they just hang around. There's the odd shell . . ." That, of course, wouldn't

worry *him* . . . the only problem was they would be unable to use air-
planes to track the released bears with radio-telemetry, "because the
Burmese would take pot shots at us."

But that would be a minor inconvenience. Gary van Zuylen had never
seen the place: he would do so for the first time on this expedition. But
even sight unseen, the Salaween sanctuary offered two shining advan-
tages over most of the sites he has considered. One was that it had no hill
tribes. The other was its director, his friend Preecha Rattanaporn.

"Preecha is an absolutely all-right guy," he told us—which meant he
was a man of rare integrity. In the Forest Department, where an official
could become rich from simply looking the other way at the right moment, Preecha was scrupulously honest. Further, he had vision, and was
willing to try new things. With Preecha, Gary van Zuylen did not face the
problem of entropy that he had grown to understand was endemic to
Third World government agencies: "The official who does nothing," he
told us, "does nothing wrong."

Any release of formerly captive bears carried a number of risks—risks
few officials were willing to take. To minimize them, Gary van Zuylen
planned to first acclimate the bears in a large, outdoor fenced area within
the sanctuary. Before release to the wild, he planned to radio-collar the
bears, to track them and make sure they didn't wander into villages outside the sanctuary. Initially, the ex-captives would be provisioned with
food, which would be gradually phased out as the bears learned to find
food in the wild for themselves.

But would this ever happen?

The scientist was optimistic. Even now, we were driving through what
appeared to be magnificent forest: the beautiful Route 108 snakes upward into the mists of mountains covered with giant trees. This is not
rain forest jungle, but a type known as "mixed deciduous monsoon
forest," dominated by teak, with its straight, strong, termite-resistant
trunks and monstrous broad leaves, each as big around as the face of an
ox. In the dry season, many of these trees' leaves would turn brown and
drop. But now is the season of promise and plenty. The rains have

brought the teak into bloom, with its huge clusters of light yellow puff-balls, and many other trees are in fruit: the logans and durians and custard apples, with their velvety cream flesh and watermelon-like seeds. "This looks like perfectly gorgeous bear habitat!" the scientist said to our host. "There should be thousands or tens of thousands of moon bears in these forests alone!"

Gary van Zuylen looked shocked. "There are no bears here," he said.

Now it was the professor's turn to look shocked. He turned to me in the backseat. "Can you imagine a forest this big in North America with no bears in it? Can you imagine that poaching has been *that* thorough?"

But Gary van Zuylen was adamant. "There were plenty of bears once—but they sure as hell aren't anymore. They've all been hunted out by the hill tribes, their gallbladders sold in the market, or they've gone off in the back of someone's pickup to be sold to a restaurant ten years ago."

It seemed too awful to consider. Wasn't there somewhere—any park in Thailand—where there was a chance we might see a bear—a wild bear living free?

"See a BE-AH?" Gary van Zuylen parroted in astonishment—as if we had just asked if we might bump into the Pope at a gas station. "Nobody *ever* sees a be-ah! The parks department who are looking for them for years don't see a bear. The only ones who ever see a bear are poachers."

Thailand's moon bears are refugees among refugees. There might be 150 bears in Forest Department breeding centers like Banglamung; perhaps some 40 in zoos; and maybe another 100 remaining in private hands. But in the wild? "We spent a year looking for bears in this one sanctuary," he told us, where Forest Department workers had rigged up cameras to snap a picture of any animal who crossed in front of them. Not a single bear turned up. "We talked with rangers, who used to shoot them," he told us. "'Oh yeah, there are bears,' they'd say—and then you find out they're talking about when they saw one nine years ago.

"No, I don't think there are many bears left. If you're going to look for a bear out there, you're going to have a goddamned hard time."

* * *

We established our base at a dingy little hotel in the modest town of Mae Sariang. The ambitiously named Samsri Resort featured Chinese-style showers, i.e., with no door or shower curtain. Turning one of its faucets merely dribbled cold water out of a hole in the wall, but the other sprayed fountains of hot water everywhere. It sprinkled the sink and the Western-style toilet, soaked the single, ratty pink towel, melted the cardboard-like toilet paper (when there was any), and nourished a breathtaking floor-to-ceiling jungle of black mold. But the hotel staff was kind, serving us luscious fruits with our breakfast, and the place was convenient to Mr. Preecha's forest headquarters, less than half an hour's drive away.

Unfortunately, Mr. Preecha was not in. He was expected back the day after tomorrow, we were told. So the next day, our host planned to take us to Om Koi Forest Conservation Center, where some dozen confiscated or donated moon bears were living out their lives in captivity, the luckiest of whom were in a big outdoor enclosure built by TSCWA.

The Garys went on without me. Though my scientific companion's stomach problems had abated, mine had thickened into nausea, augmented by a raging sore throat. The men drove for hours in the Isuzu through gorgeous, bearless forest and returned elated. With the enormous pliers purchased in Louang Phabang, the scientist, aided by facility staff, successfully plucked hairs from no fewer than nine moon bears. For most of them, at least the confiscation sites, if not the capture sites, were known. Station records indicated that two came from Mae Sariang, from a border policeman who had kept them as pets. One, partly blond, may have been transferred from another Forest Department facility, outside the town of Hot. Three more bears were from Phrae Province, south of Nan—near the border with Laos, and near where Colonel Wirat said Bertha had come from, a report Gary was coming increasingly to doubt. If it were true, then Haplotype II extended over an enormous range. But Gary van Zuylen considered it very unlikely that anyone would have brought a bear confiscated at the Laotian border to Lop Buri, so far away. Gary Galbreath couldn't find Ban Pang Kae on any of his maps, and we wondered whether Colonel Wirat could have been mistaken, or if somehow what he had meant to tell us had been lost in translation. The DNA in these hairs would help solve that mystery.

We spent the next day in the familiar Asian holding pattern, waiting. At our midday and evening meals at a Chinese restaurant down the street, Gary van Zuylen alternately amused and horrified us with tales of bureaucratic incompetence: "So they raised the money for a satellite dish for the school, but guess what they don't have? Electricity!" He told us of some of the red tape he faced working as a foreigner for a Thai charity: "At one point, I had to sign a paper saying I wasn't authorized to sign documents!" No wonder he was still awaiting approval from the upper echelons of the Forest Department to proceed with his reintroduction plans; "Thailand's development has developed pear-shaped," he said, "just developed enough to screw things up. We might end up doing a reintroduction in Laos and not in Thailand, because Laos won't be such a circus. How bizarre would *that* be?"

The professor and I spent most of the day continuing to comb through documents we had obtained in Laos. *Wildlife in Lao PDR: 1999 Status Report* was a litany of horrors: army officers shot endangered gibbons for food; in Vientiane, people hunted birds on Buddhist temple grounds; poachers took their booty past the front door of at least one prominent conservation organization, unmolested. It seemed no species in Laos was exempt from human hunger for food or for money. Under Asiatic Black Bear, we read that though historically, the species was common, in their years of surveys, IUCN and Wildlife Conservation Society scientists had seen only skins and skulls: "This is the only large carnivore with no recent wild sight records in Lao PDR." In other words: "See a BE-AH? You're going to have a goddamned hard time."

But the depressing report also contained a short paragraph that made our hearts pound: "In the Central Annamites, villagers often report two sorts of 'Asiatic Black Bear,' which are said to differ in size and color of the chest pelage. This may explain the findings of Duckworth . . . where informants reported two sorts of bears, but stated differences between them were not the obvious morphological ones between Asiatic Black Bear and Sun Bear."

"We are hearing the same sorts of things over and over," the scientist said to me, electrified. "The Hmong in Chicago say there are three kinds of bears, two of which are probably moon bears. And they are hunters; they should know. IUCN says their informants tell them there are two kinds of moon bears, one of which is bigger than the other." Further, he had heard something similar from a colleague in Vietnam with whom he had an irregular e-mail correspondence: the Vietnamese forester had written that hunters "are always recording a 3rd species of bear." A bear living on the border with Cambodia, he wrote, was considered distinctive not only for its appearance, but also for the qualities of its bile.

"Either there is something causing all these different people to mistake these things for two different kinds of moon bears," he said, "or else there really are two species. And the haplotype information will be able to tell."

* * *

The following day, we collected more samples. This time, we drove north to Mae Hong Song. Before the road from Chiang Mai was completed in 1965, the town was known as "The Siberia of Thailand" and considered a dumping ground for disgraced bureaucrats. Now tour operators market it as "Thailand's Shangri-La" and it receives more than 200,000 tourists a year.

They come to trek in the beautiful, mountainous forest and gracious, green valleys. And they come to view the colorful "natives," people dressed in embroidered traditional costumes and elaborate headdresses, heaped with silver bells or decorated with coins or adorned with distinctive necklaces, earrings, and wrist bangles. But they are not natives; Mae Hong Song's population is only 2 percent Thai, in the sense of Siamese. Fifty percent are Shan—originally inhabitants of Burma or of the ancient kingdom of Lanna in what is now northern Thailand—and the rest are hill tribes.

Among the most popular tribes on the tourist agenda are the "Long-Necked People" or "Giraffe Women." They are members of the Padung tribe of Burma, a subset of the Karen people. What distinguishes the Padung is their women have for centuries worn tall coils of brass, sometimes weighing twelve pounds, around the neck—a custom that makes the neck appear nearly a foot long. Placed on the neck in childhood and lengthened as the girl grows, the ornament does not, in fact, stretch the neck, but pushes down the collarbones and rib cage, causing the shoulders to slope. The result is "eerily graceful," a *New York Times* travel writer wrote, "the head floating above the shoulders like the crown of a dandelion, the chin projected forward as if in perpetual curiosity." We saw their pictures posted prominently in many of the tour offices in town.

Many of the Burmese Padung have abandoned the neck coils, which once served as a way to secure family wealth from theft. But today, among the refugees, the women themselves are the valued commodity. Tourists pay about six dollars apiece to enter their villages. Some say these villages are little more than human zoos; but meanwhile, some twenty thousand Karenni refugees are living in poverty, crammed into a series of camps along the border, or squatting illegally in national parks and sanctuaries.

And while the human refugees spill into the wildlife parks, the native bears live in the zoo.

All eight moon bears at the Pang Tong Open Zoo, we were told, were local "contributions." They'd been born wild in the forests nearby. From their cages, the bears could see the thick, handsome plantings of bamboo and flowering ginger on the zoo's well-tended grounds. They could smell the fruits ripening in the forests. Perhaps they could smell them from many miles away. Lynn Rogers tells how one American black bear he was watching responded to a wind change: "He just turned his nose and loped directly toward the best hazelnut crop I'd ever seen." Guided by scent, the bear traveled all night and much of the next day, beelining to a lush hazelnut stand more than *forty miles* away. To the bears, perhaps such scents are like the fragrant blooms of the heavenly Parichart trees—

transporting them to recall former lives. If so, like human refugees, the zoo bears may have dreamed of returning to their homelands.

Since all the bears were from the same area, it seemed unnecessary to bother all eight of them. We concentrated on getting hair from those who seemed friendliest: three large female cubs, perhaps siblings, with markedly different crescents on their chests. As I snaked my tweezers through the wire aimed at one clambering cub, I noticed something big moving in their cage. It was one of the keepers, who just walked up to each of them, one by one, and pulled hair out with his hands.

The scientist was pleased with the harvest. In the twenty-eight vials he carried constantly with him in his camera bag, he had now amassed samples from bears from much of northern Thailand and Laos. Our map was filling out. In town, our host took us for an elaborate Thai meal to celebrate.

We careened back to our hotel in the dark. Dodging dogs, snakes, and other vehicles, we looped down the mountain roads through a forest both beautiful and bereft—emptied of bears, and full, instead, of people who didn't want to be there, but who had no place else to go.

* * *

The Salaween River: born, like the Mekong, on "the roof of the world" in the frigid mountains of Tibet, its source is said to be protected by a naga sent by the gods of the sea. Earthquakes, say the Shan, are born of the wagging of the tail of a great fish who lives beneath its waters. It boils with rapids, swirls with sediment, and pours for 2,784 kilometers through a deep trough encased in steep mountain walls, running south to the Indian Ocean.

The Salaween is before us now. Across it, atop a wooden building with a metal roof, white letters on a red background spell out in English: UNION OF MYANMAR. We stand beneath a leaf shelter at one of the gateways to the Salaween National Park, watching the river swallow the rain.

After multiple delays, it's taken us several hours to get here. Over zigzagging, tortuous roads, we had traveled in two separate vehicles: Mr. Preecha, a stout, cheerful, confident man of fifty-five, captained a Forest

Department four-wheel-drive truck, bristling with seven soldiers armed with M-16s. Gary van Zuylen's Jeep followed, driven by the Salaween substation chief, his belt holding a large combat knife, a revolver, and two extra clips for his rifle. The Australian held his M-16 between his legs in the front seat, while the scientist and I squashed into the backseat.

We'd forded two rivers along the way, nearly miring in one. Now we were waiting for our boat. Mr. Preecha dispatched a solider to find it.

The Garys marvel at the forest across the river in Burma. "This is not secondary forest!" Gary van Zuylen says in surprise. He had expected to find the Burmese side intensively logged, as logging has destroyed two thirds of the country's original forests. "I thought it would be like a sand-bank!" he exclaims. "It's basically virgin!"

The other Gary, though, is transfixed by the roiling river. He wonders aloud: "Do you think that a bear could swim across that?"

Our long-tailed boat arrives—forty feet long, low, open, wooden—a canoe, essentially. The long propeller sticks out the back (its "long tail") attached to a 1.6-liter diesel car engine. For more than an hour we travel the river, surrounded by a green wall of trees and vines and rain. We arrive at the sanctuary field station sodden, but exhilarated.

We climb a muddy hill toward the station. The first thing we notice are the logs.

Some two thousand of them, each thrice the circumference of a telephone pole, lie in neat piles beside the boat landing. Mr. Preecha found them two years ago, shortly after he had been given charge of the sanctuary. Illegal loggers had left them scattered all along the river to pick up later. He never found the poachers, he said; "I just met the logs." He had to hire elephants to drag the logs nearly to the front steps of the forest substation building. If the poachers returned to reclaim their booty, his men would catch them. But they never came, and this spoke volumes: Mr. Preecha's soldiers were a powerful deterrent. Each log, he said, was worth twenty thousand bhat. A million dollars' worth of teak is lying here, and in two years, no one has returned to touch it.

We're amazed at the integrity of the forest we have seen. On both sides of the river, for our entire journey, we've been surrounded by a cascade of foliage, vines pouring out of giant trees—sensuous, luxuriant, like a woman's long hair trailing down a backless dress. "It's very wild," the scientist says. "There are no tracks on either side and so few houses."

Gary van Zuylen is eager to take us into the forest. He is hungry for our opinion: could bears who had spent most of their lives in captivity remember how to survive in the wild? Could they do so here?

Disappointingly, our explorations are confined to a muddy track, surrounded by soldiers. Time allows only two hours for a walk. We do not glimpse a single mammal the entire time, not even a squirrel. We see very few birds. The scientist and I could not reasonably assess the forest for bear habitat. But we remembered something we had seen at Banglamung, and it gave us hope.

Two weeks before, we had witnessed an event for which Gary van Zuylen and his staff had spent weeks in preparation. A new eight thousand-square-meter outdoor enclosure had been built for sun bears, rimmed with electric wire. Juliet, a subadult, was to be its first resident, and the guinea pig to see if the fence would hold bears.

Gary might not admit to it, but Juliet is his favorite bear. With a brilliant orange setting sun on her velvet black chest, she is a beautiful, sweet animal who'd been hand-raised as a cub by owners who later gave her to police. She had sometimes frolicked outside under human supervision. But much of her life had been spent in a large cement-floored cage. It was handsomely appointed, with green painted bars, climbing logs, and a shallow pool—but a cage, nonetheless. On this day, we would see that change.

Because sun bears can climb almost anything, the only fence that can keep them in is electric wire. But animals do not always react to electric wire the way we expect. If the initial shock of the electricity does not particularly impress them, they may decide to go through the fence anyway, and never learn to fear it. Or the shock may simply enrage the animal, and instead of backing away, it will plow through. How will Juliet behave?

"This is a major milestone," Gary van Zuylen said to us as the sleek little bear emerged confidently from her cage into the enclosure. After a few dozen paces, Juliet sat with her back to a mimosa tree. Then she approached the electric fence. She stood, touching it with both paws. We heard the crack of electricity. She cried out—an angry moan, just like a person—and raced behind the tree. "That's it! That's perfect! That's exactly what I want!" shouted Gary van Zuylen, genuinely overjoyed.

But what happened next was the real breakthrough—one so subtle, almost no one noticed.

Juliet stood behind the tree, her two front paws steadying her as she peeked out from behind its protection—staring in wonderment at the invisible danger, trying to smell it, to hear it. She had received, on her sensitive orange hands, the maximum amount of shock—thirteen thousand volts. Because it was delivered in a pulse it can't damage her physically. But it hurt, and she wanted to get farther away. She found another mimosa trunk and climbed it, lunging and gripping. She arrived at the crotch of the tree, about fifteen feet up. And here she began to break branches with her hands, dropping some, but placing most of them beside and beneath her in the crotch of the tree.

I gasped. "Do you realize what she is doing?" I asked Gary van Zuylen. He assumed she was simply destroying the tree, like the logs and tires she had shredded with her long claws for amusement in her cage. But no. This is a well-known, complex, and completely natural behavior in arboreal bear species, including the American black bear. George Schaller described it in moon bears in his studies of the species in India and in China.

Juliet was building what we in New England call a "bear basket"—a springy nest to cushion her weight as she rests and feeds. With her forepaws, she pulled a small branch toward her, and then pushed it beneath her feet. A larger branch required a bite to break it. Holding each branch securely, she sniffed the ends of the twigs, sometimes nibbling at the leaves, then stuffed it beneath her, methodically building her platform.

She had almost certainly never witnessed another bear doing this; she was captured as a very young cub. (Mothers don't usually build bear bas-kets when their cubs are young; the fruits and nuts are not yet ripe, and most of the food is on the ground, not in the trees.) And Juliet herself had never attempted to do this before.

But now, offered a small measure of freedom, she has located the river of instinct that has been flowing inside her and allowed it to carry her away from her fear. Less than half an hour after her release, she had re-connected with her ursine heritage, joining her with her ancestors in bear-knowing that stretched back beyond the Pleistocene, back beyond the Pliocene, to the ancient knowledge that runs deeper than learning, deeper than reasoning, deeper than thought.

This is what gave us hope as we trudged down the muddy track in the empty forest. There were surely few if any bears left here, Mr. Preecha as-sured us. Thailand's laws had been passed too late to save them; on the rare occasion his men caught someone with a bear cub these days, it was coming to Thailand from Burma. The Salaween Wildlife Sanctuary could be as bearless as the new lands those pioneering moon bears might have found in the early Pleistocene, as they had migrated south from China.

But emptiness bodes well for any new crop of colonists, as the scientist pointed out; the biggest danger to any bear who enters new territory is that another bear already owns it. For the ex-captive moon bears, the sanctuary could offer a clean slate, a new Eden. *If* Gary van Zuylen was able to secure permission from the Thai government to proceed with a release; *if* Mr. Preecha could continue to keep poachers at bay; *if* the moon bears' natural instincts had not been extinguished by their years in captivity . . .

Surrounded by forest, enveloped in rain, and flanked by hope and de-spair, our boat puttered back down the Salaween, along the troubled border.

CHAPTER ELEVEN

Soul Wandering

Gary van Zuylen spent much of the drive back to Chiang Mai telling us there *was* no Elephant Training Center. "It's a joke," he said. "It's put on only for tourists. There are no elephants being trained to do anything anymore." But we had read about it in a guidebook and resolved to go anyway.

The scientist and I were both debilitated by illness and soul-weary from sorrows. I was beset by nightmares. Empty forests, captive bears, human and animal refugees had warped their way into monstrous, greedy dreams that would not let me go. My screams were so loud they would wake sleepers in adjoining rooms as they echoed down the halls. "It's just a dream—a dream," the biologist would say to comfort me, "a human, right-brain phenomenon!" But even as I would try to pull my consciousness back to my body, I felt the dream still trying to claim me, like a shark rising from the ocean, pulling me away from shore. And this was why I so wanted to see elephants: Gary and I both adore them, and I hoped the blessing of their presence, time-honored throughout Asia for their wisdom and strength, could set my restless soul at ease.

After Gary van Zuylen drove on to Banglamung, we hired a car to take us to the Thai Elephant Conservation Center just outside Chiang Mai, at Hang Chat. We were greeted by a delightful parade of some thirty pachyderms. Young and old, the elephants walked beside their mahouts toward the training ring and greeted delighted visitors like politicians shaking hands with a crowd. They reached out their trunks to us, and we reached toward them, relishing their moist, pliant, delicate touch as they explored our faces and hands.

The training show *was* touristy. We sat behind a wall of shrieking children, trying in vain to learn something from the brief, English translation broadcast after each burst of Thai commentary. The elephants picked up logs in their trunks; knelt; bowed with trunks curved into an S against their foreheads; trumpeted on command. Afterward, we wandered about the grounds, and down a dirt driveway, stumbled into deeper sorrow. We found the Elephant Hospital.

I had read about one of the patients here. Motola, a thirty-eight-year-old female elephant, was being treated for injuries sustained when she stepped on a land mine while illegally logging in Burma. My mother had clipped and sent me a one-inch squib from the *Washington Post.* But in Thailand—indeed, throughout large parts of Asia—Motola's plight had been front-page news for months.

No creature in Thailand elicits such sympathy as a wounded elephant. Until 1948, when Siam changed its name to Thailand, the elephant was depicted on its flag. Simply walking beneath an elephant is believed to erase bad luck. Later, at one of the elephant camps where TSCWA provides free veterinary care, I would meet two motorcyclists who came after a traffic accident for just this reason. One, with a bandaged forehead and swollen eye, the other with a gashed cheek and scraped knee, they passed three times beneath the elephant's belly, carrying offerings of coins, leaves, candles, and incense. The young men were visibly relieved afterward.

In the absence of horses, elephants carried monarchs into battle, cleared land for cultivation, and were seen as the saviors of the kingdom—especially the so-called "white elephant," which is not an albino at all, but marked with spots of light color, such as white toenails, white palate, white hairs on the tail. Specially trained monks determine whether a "white elephant" qualifies as a sacred bearer of good fortune. This entails more than just looking for light markings; even the elephant's snore is scrutinized. (A weepy snore is a bad omen, but if it sounds like wind being blown through a conch shell, this is a boon for the kingdom.)

So after Motola stepped on the land mine on August 15, 1999, she became the object of a national outpouring of sympathy.

With her left forefoot in shreds, the elephant and her mahout had walked for three days until reaching Thai territory. There, she was brought by truck to the Elephant Hospital, at the time the only one in Thailand.

Her foot was beyond repair. After ten days of injections and poultices, prayers and press, the hospital vet amputated the foot in an operation from which she roused from anesthetic three times, even though she was given enough sedative for seventy humans.

In the weeks following her injury, well-wishers thronged the hospital. "It was crazy here," an Irish volunteer, Ann Marie Eaton-Evans, told us. "We had to have the place barricaded. You almost couldn't get in for all the press and milling people."

People came to pray for Motola and to leave donations for the hospital. Her condition was broadcast on the national news every night. Hundreds of visitors brought bananas, sugarcane, grasses for her to eat; they offered incense and flowers to the hospital's spirit house. Her mahout stayed with her for three months—without pay of course—before finally leaving her side. For weeks, a crane and hoist system eased pressure on her remaining feet.

Now she occupies the westernmost of the three elephant sheds in the compound, with a soft sand substrate to sleep on, as well as a concrete floor. Because of the direction she was facing, we could not see right away that her left front foot was missing. But then, we saw it—the stump encased in a cast covered with plastic so it won't get wet from her daily bath. Her right front foot was clearly sore, swollen from the strain of her four-ton weight. Normally, elephants place more weight on the front legs than the back. She picked up some grass, swished it in her trunk to shoo away the flies, then pressed her trunk against the padding on the metal rail to which she was chained by the neck. She was essentially doing a headstand to take pressure off the front foot. Then she eased back down to face her agony again.

While we were standing with her, a bus disgorged seventeen Thai tourists who came to visit. "Motola! Motola!" they cried, going directly to her. They pointed and asked questions in hushed voices of their tour guide. One woman turned her face toward me after hearing the answer, in Thai, to one of her questions. Her face was pure anguish, one with the animal's suffering.

The woe of an elephant is an enormous thing, like the weather. In fact, Hindu legend tells us elephants were born of clouds, and no wonder: they rumble, transmitting infrasonic messages that travel miles away, that resound in your chest like thunder. They walk so softly on their tiptoe bones inside their soft round feet, that it is sometimes impossible to find their tracks in the grass, as if they float, cloudlike. But Motola will walk no more in shallow elephant tracks. She is to be fitted with a prosthesis, it is hoped, but she will never again be whole. And she is young—younger than Gary and me, only thirty-eight—though she was born to live past seventy. An elephant's age is always mentioned in Thai newspaper stories, just as the *New York Times* does with a person. And like the *Times*, which always refers to people on second reference as Miss, Ms., Mrs., Mr., or Dr., adult elephants are endowed with honorific titles, bestowed to tell us something of their lives. Pang is the honorific for lady elephant, who in the Asian species does not bear visible tusks. Pai connotes a tusker; Sidor, a tuskless male.

At an outdoor display near the entrance to the hospital, we read some of the news stories about the patients. There is Pang Bomee, fifty-five, a former amphetamine addict, who was forced to take the drugs to give her greater energy for illegal logging. Pai Bet, forty, has a broken rear leg. He fell down a hillside and hasn't had the leg pinned yet because he is too weak for the operation. Pang Tentong, sixty, is nearly blind, entirely so in her white left eye, and she is enjoying being hosed down by a volunteer.

We read of another elephant, Thong In, thirty-eight, whose left front foot was shredded by a land mine blast when he strayed outside a logging camp near the Mae Sot District, according to a May 11 *Bangkok Post* article. He, too, was treated at the hospital, but we could not find him. He was not among the seven patients there. Ann Marie explained, "He collapsed. A crane came to lift him, but he couldn't support his own weight. He lay so long he became paralyzed." He died on June 5.

"It's only a question of time," she said to me, "before we get another land mine case."

That night, the nightmares returned. It had nothing to do with elephants or war or captured bears. The content didn't matter; it was its *force* that was real. I felt as if, in my sleep, my soul were trying to get away from this place, but in its wanderings, found sorrows everywhere, inescapable.

* * *

Next, we embarked on what might have seemed like another tourist's errand: a visit to the Tribal Museum. We went to learn more about the hill tribes—potential sources who we hoped could help us corroborate or dismiss reports of an unknown species of bear.

A video at the museum called them "people from another time." Many travel guides feature the hill tribes in a field guide format, which, like Roger Tory Petersen's bird identification system, show you the salient "field markings" that will allow you to identify the people. For instance, red boas and dark turbans distinguish the Mien or Yao; the Aka are known for their helmet-like headdresses, with long strings of beads and coins hanging down like hair. We watched the film in one of the hot, airless office cubicles on the museum's second story. It featured six tribes celebrating traditional festivals and rituals: the exuberant New Year's dances of the Lisu, the giant swings used in Aka festivals. It showed a horrifying Hmong exorcism, in which a puppy and a cat are torched in order to rid a house of illness.

Such cruel practices, though, are not what has made the hill tribes so unwelcome in Thailand, the museum is careful to point out. It's their penchant for growing opium, so deeply ingrained in the cultures that, among the Hmong, the poppy product has for centuries been used in place of money. Outside pressure from foreign countries over opium production prompted Thailand's first hill tribe development program in 1960, later to become known as a Thai-ization program.

To create the opium fields, the hill tribes practice slash and burn agriculture—which in the words of King Bhumibol Adulyadej himself, in a 1974 address quoted in the museum, called "methods which if left unchecked could bring the country to ruin." An entire floor of the museum is devoted to national, Buddhist, and royal projects aimed at dissuading the hill tribes from these practices, and encouraging them to grow alternative crops—which, unfortunately, do not bring as much money. A royal crop substitution program underwrites the farming of fruit trees like lychee, guava, and passion fruit, as well as bracket fungus, from which a soft drink is made. The products of the program are marketed under the Doi Kham label, which means Golden Mountain.

We already knew, of course, that hill tribes deforest parks and sanctuaries; but our interest stemmed from the fact that they also hunt, some of them prodigiously—especially the fierce, dog-grilling Hmong. And we learned of another tribe revered for its hunting prowess: the Lahu Na, or Black Lahu. Some say these Yunnanese mountain people, who manufacture their own muzzle-loading rifles, are master practitioners of black magic, and are feared by other tribes. So this is where we ask a guide to take us next: to the northwestern mountains between the Huay Nam Dang National Park and the Lum Nam Pai Wildlife Sanctuary, in which the Black Lahu hunt bears in the large forests where the Chan Yoma mountain chain intersects with the Burmese border.

* * *

Our round-faced, balding guide of thirty, Samkait Reinpathomsak, has been guiding tourists for more than a decade, but he has never had a request like this. "We want to talk with Hmong and Black Lahu hunters about different kinds of bears," Gary told him, and he was immediately intrigued. Luckily for us, Samkait's English was excellent, and he was good friends with a Black Lahu family with whom we could stay; on the long, mountainous drive to their village, we could stop at two Hmong settlements and talk with the people there.

The first Hmong village was far from "traditional." Ban Huay Luk, with a population of eleven hundred, was a muddy huddle of graceless, metal-roofed cement buildings and ugly electric wires. The wires were part of the Thai-ization program: where electricity comes, television follows, theoretically enabling people to learn to speak Thai. Chickens scratched and a few skinny dogs fought for scraps among the trash scattered in the sticky red mud. Dirty children were running everywhere, watched over by toothless old women. The place looked ugly and untended. But there were signs of prosperity. A large number of brand-new pickup trucks roused Samkait's ire.

"I work hard for ten years, and have only a motorcycle!" Samkait said.

"Where do they get the money for this?" Gary asked. "What do they do for a living?" Came the answer: "Amphetamines."

Samkait had made our request to a young woman at the village gate, and she led us to a cement-floored, garage-like building. Past a chugging washing machine, she took us to a middle-aged man repairing a child's toy gun with a screwdriver as three little boys feinted at one another with plastic swords. The man's name was Pao, his age, fifty, and yes, he told us, he could tell us many things about bears.

"When I was twenty or twenty-five, I would kill them a lot," he told us through Samkait. He had killed perhaps twenty of them in his life. That was when the forest was full of bears—and tigers. The tigers, though, he did not hunt. Bears were dangerous enough, but tigers were another matter: "The bear is running," he said, "but the tiger is jumping!"

But the bears run and the tigers jump no more. He hasn't seen or heard of a bear near the village for fifteen years. But, he said, he remembered them well.

He knew how to track bears in the forest. He knew from the dung if a bear was fat or skinny—if fat, the dung was firm and shaped like a ball.

Sometimes, he would come upon a bear in a tree, resting and feeding in a springy "bear basket" like the one Juliet had constructed. "If it is in a tree, you must wake it up, make it angry, bring it close," he told us. "To hunt the bear, you must be strong inside," he said, "because the gun is not strong." Muzzle-loading rifles don't shoot far—and if you miss or fail to kill the animal, you have a problem. His uncle was mauled to death by a bear he had wounded who attacked him. But the Lahu people, he said, were the bravest when it came to bears: he told us that to protect themselves against misfortune, they will go right up to a bear and hit it on the nose.

We asked if he knew different kinds of bears, or if they were all the same kind.

"There are three kinds of bears," he said firmly, and then he elucidated:

The biggest bear is *Mii khwai*. It raids the cornfields, prefers open, higher-altitude forest, and the hair on the neck can appear parted. Surely, we thought, he was describing a moon bear. The parted hair, we thought, was surely its characteristic mane.

Next in size is *Mii muu*. It prefers denser, lower forest. It is about a foot shorter than *Mii khwai*. The crescent on the chest is a thin line. On its neck, the hair is like a pig's. Was this Shuttong Vang's pig bear? we wondered. It sounded to us like this could be the sun bear, as the size and habitat description matched. Or was it something else?

A third kind, the smallest, he called *Mii nghen*. He said it was the size of a dog, lives in a tree, and it smells bad. It has a longer tail than *Mii muu*. Clearly, Gary decided, this was a binturong. But I was not so sure. Did it use the tail to climb? I asked. He said no—which seemed to me to rule out the binturong. This, I thought, could also be a sun bear, the most arboreal of Asia's bears, who looks so like a dog. If so, what was *Mii muu*?

Next Gary brought out his Rogues' Gallery of Bears. Pao examined them carefully. To our annoyance and confusion, he identified both the sun bear and the moon bear, as well as one of the brown-backed moon bears, all as *Mii khwai.* The other bears weren't in the book, he said. And immediately, he rejected the picture of the grizzly. "That is a bear I have seen only on TV," he said. "Those bears eat fish. Why," he asked the biologist, "do not our bears eat fish?"

*   *   *

Samkait next insisted on taking us to the Chiang Dao Wildlife Sanctuary. He was sure the biologists there could help us, though we doubted it, and he had taken the trouble to call them in advance. So we removed our shoes and climbed the stairs to the sanctuary's administrative office. The room was paneled in flow charts, indicating the levels of responsibility: for education, protection, public relations, etc.

Samkait introduced us: Gary was a biologist, he explained, and I a writer. We were seeking to learn what kinds of bears inhabit the sanctuary. A balding man in red socks reached for a bound publication. He had to look up the answer. It listed sun and moon bears. Sun bears were rarer here, we read, and not found farther north, as they preferred lowlands to mountains. Did the man in red socks have anything to add to this? Samkait translated: inside the sanctuary, he told us, there are ten villages—Karen, Lahu, Lisa, Hmong—and since the villages came, "it is very difficult to see a bear."

Then the forestry worker asked Gary a question in English. "Can you tell me," he asked, "about the bear's residence?"

*   *   *

We traveled on, to another Hmong village, Chum Yen, much smaller than Ban Huay, with only about 250 people. Most of them were out harvesting logan fruit. But we did find a very short, spritely older man, wearing a large coin earring in his left ear like a gypsy, who was happy to talk with us. He had never hunted a bear, nor seen a live one wild, but his brother had killed many. "When you see a bear, you must cover your face, or you will be attacked," he warned us. But from his brother, he knew there are three kinds of bears: *Mii khwai,* the largest, with a white patch on the chest; *Mii muu,* a midsized bear with a white chest patch and short tail; and *Mii maa,* with a patch on the chest he called "brown" and also, most important, a short tail.

He looked in our book and, to our surprise, like Pao identified sun and moon bears alike as *Mii khwai.*

We left, puzzled, and drove for hours on roads that coiled through the mountains like pythons, up into the mist. When we arrived at Bo Kreit, the Black Lahu village, it was dark, the mountain mists covering the moon like an eyelid.

*   *   *

Our hosts are Jaa Bet, thirty-three, and his pretty wife, Na La, thirty-nine, our guide's friends. We remove our shoes in the dark and climb the ladder to their bamboo and wooden house, built on stilts so the animals do not come in. Jaa Bet is handsome, taller than Gary's five nine frame, with thick wavy hair and a great white smile. The couple wears traditional Black Lahu dress: black trousers with a dropped crotch, a black jacket enlivened with insets of colored cloth.

Jaa Bet was born in Burma, where he used to work as porter for an opium caravan. "He could run through the forest like a tiger," Samkait tells us by the hearth of the spacious kitchen, where metal cooking pots are stored in a corner and we sit cross-legged on the bamboo mats Na La has woven by hand. "These people know the forest even without a trail," Samkait says. "They close their eyes and know where to go—you and I would be lost in ten meters."

At age fifteen, Jaa Bet began hunting, with a group from his village. Whenever anyone saw an animal footprint near the fields, they would gather their friends to track and hunt it—three, four, sometimes as many as fifteen people in the party. Almost any kind of animal was fair game, and would be shared with everyone in the village. The foreleg would go to the village headman, the neck for the blacksmith who made the knives. The hunter's father-in-law would get the haunch. Everything but the eyes is eaten—the tongue, the ears, the nose. Only two kinds of animal are not eaten: bear and goat. It was bad to bring this meat into the village, he told us, although they hunted and used parts of both animals medicinally. The bears were hunted for the gallbladder, and the fat was used to heal burns; goats were valuable for their urine, mixed with whiskey, to ease joint ailments.

While corn roasted on the fire and tea brewed in the kettle, as crickets throbbed and frogs clicked like castinets, Jaa Bet told us about bears.

Here in the mountains, he told us, were two kinds: *Yeah paa,* the larger, and *Yeah meuay,* the more aggressive. He has killed two *Yeah paa* and one *Yeah meuay* in Burma and two more *Yeah paa* and one *Yeah meuay* in Thailand. We show him the picture book of bears. Like the Hmong we visited earlier, he does not recognize the difference between the sun bear and moon bear.

We are perplexed—and excited. Clearly he recognizes two kinds of bears in the mountains—although we are fairly certain that sun bears are not found here, and besides, they prefer lowlands to mountains. Nobody, so far, has recognized the pictures of the sun bears as a separate species. We are generally impressed with the hunters' knowledge: they all tell us the bears make nests in the trees, that the babies are born in dens, and they all seem to know what they eat. What is the smaller bear, if not a sun bear? Gary asks if Jaa Bet has a skull or a skin of either bear. No, he answers, via Samkait—why would he keep such a thing? The skin—well, maybe people from the outside might buy that, but he never kept one. Tomorrow, he said, he would take us to Lu Kalam, another Black Lahu village, where the people have killed many bears, and maybe they can answer our question.

* * *

In the morning, Jaa Bet took us to see a bear sign—claw marks on a tree. I expected we might walk with him deep into the forest to see it, but no— here it is, just a ten-minute drive from the village, right next to the curling macadam road. Some forty meters up, along the arrow-straight trunk of a light-barked tree he called *Go-gu-gene,* we see the distinctive, deep gashes carved by the claws of a climbing bear. What was a bear doing so close to the road, we ask? Another twenty meters up, and we could see the answer: the yellow skeleton of a giant honeycomb still hanging from the underside of the tree's lowest branches.

"Every big tree with a bee's nest in it has claw marks," Jaa Bet told us through Samkait. The hive was vacant now—the bees all leave before the rainy season, he explained. They come back again when the logan flowers bloom at the end of January, and by April the combs are heavy with honey. Much of the traditional medicine is mixed with April honey, Samkait told us, "with the sweetness of so many flowers." There are several species of bee in the forest, but the big ones, who make these giant combs, are called *pung yie.*

We imagined the bear who had climbed that tree—the sweet scent of the honey calling her, calling to her bear-knowing back through so many lifetimes. We had read a report from one researcher, I. Johnson, who gleaned through interviews with Thai villagers that sow bears guzzling honey were sometimes so rapt with delight that people could capture the cubs without the mother's notice. Usually a bear tries to knock a honeycomb down with the swipe of a paw, so it can escape the attacking bees. For hours, a bear might lick the honeycomb once it was on the ground. We imagined the sweet, hot-breathed ursine pleasure as the bear savored the honey in her mouth, the ribbon tongue licking up a feast of juicy, fat-rich bee larvae. It gave us such delight to see that claw mark—the first bear sign we had seen in two trips to three countries. It felt like a completed pilgrimage, like Buddhists make to see the Buddha's footprint at Phou-Si at Louang Phabang.

Again, Gary voiced amazement that there had been a bear so close to the road. "Oh, but the road wasn't there then," said Jaa Bet. When the bear had climbed that tree, there was only a muddy track here, for the one truck a day that might have ventured this far north from Mae Hong Song.

So how long ago was that? I asked.

Jaa Bet wasn't sure, because he wasn't even living here back then. The claw marks were at least twenty years old.

* * *

We drove on, the macadam giving way to a horrendous gully of red mud that was the road to the village of Lu Kalam. Like Bo Kreit, it is actually inside the Huay Nam Dang National Park. Bo Kreit has just over two hundred people—though Jaa Bet remembers when there were just six families, when he first moved here, before his three children were born. But Lu Kalam is much larger. Some four hundred people live there, we were told.

We mounted the ladder-stairs to the first house to which Jaa Bet pointed us. "Voodoo—this is the voodoo," said Samkait. We thought he was referring to the latticework bamboo stars outside the bedroom of the house. Jaa Bet's house had one, but this one had dozens. They are called *leh-o*—spirit guards to repel ghosts and other evil spirits—especially the worst kind, the bad death spirit, being the soul of a woman who died in pregnancy or childbirth.

Everyone knows how to make leh-o, said Jaa Wat, the sixty-seven-year-old owner of the house. And then we realized that Samkait was not calling the spirit guards "voodoo"—he meant Jaa Wat himself, who was the village shaman. Each leh-o has seven holes, or eyes, because ghosts have seven eyes. With six eyes watching around and one in the center, the leh-o can't fail to spot an evil spirit, nor can a spirit think it can sneak past unnoticed. People bring him the ornaments when they visit, as a show of their respect.

Jaa Wat spread out for us a woven mat of yellow and green with a chicken design on it. The women here are master weavers. We sat in the hearth-room as the fire smoked and the kettle boiled. And here, he told us, again, there were three kinds of bears:

Yeah paa, a large black bear with a white chest crescent. He had seen only one, shot twenty years ago.

Yeah meuay, a smaller bear, which raids corn. It's called *Mii khon* in Shan, the northern Thai dialect that Samkait used when speaking with Jaa Bet.

Yeah meh tooey is the smallest bear, with a long, grasping tail—obviously the binturong.

Out comes the picture book. Again, the sun bear photos don't register. Is this the *Yeah meuay*? we ask, pointing to first one, then the other sun bear picture. No, he says—the *Yeah meuay* has a more doglike head than the bears in the pictures.

A long suite of questions ensued. How large are the ears? How long the fur? Can you show us the shape of the chest mark? The color of the chest? None of these questions yielded answers that made sense to us. One bear was larger, one was smaller, that was all. How do you know that one bear isn't just a young one, and a large one older? Oh, they are different—you can tell right away, we were told. We were puzzled. One thing seemed sure—no one knew of the sun bear. What now?

Having exhausted Jaa Wat's bear knowledge, Samkait asked if we wanted anything further from the "voodoo man." I asked if it were possible for him to give us a blessing. Perhaps he could release us from the cycle of frustration, dispossession and death, captivity and cruelty we seemed to encounter everywhere we went. But of this, I did not tell him. I merely asked if there were some ceremony he could perform to help our bear study succeed.

Jaa Wat's leathery face brightened, and his lips spread into a smile showing his eroded, betel-blackened teeth. Why yes, he told us, he would be delighted. And he began to detail what he would like to do: first, he told us through Samkait, he would kill a chicken for us, and then if that didn't work, he would sacrifice another, and perhaps a third, and finally, a pig would be killed . . .

"A barnyard holocaust!" I whispered to Gary and Samkait, trying not to betray my horror to our generous host. The solicitous Samkait knew, from having asked us about our dietary needs before provisioning our expedition, that I was vegetarian, and that I didn't want to be responsible for any animal's death even to eat it; he gracefully managed to ask Jaa Wat whether there is a ceremony he could perform that would not entail killing any animals.

Yes, replied Jaa Wat, though he looked disappointed. He could not read the details of our future without examining the holes in the bones of sacrificed chickens, he told us; but he could at least perform a soul-binding ceremony.

He asked us to write our names and ages on a piece of paper, which we handed him. We waited in the hearth room while Jaa Wat fetched a bowl of uncooked rice, and took it into a backroom and began to chant over it, facing a cupboard-like piece of furniture we realized was an altar. His chant rose and fell in intensity, like smoke from a fire in the wind. He offered the rice to the spirits of the place—to the mountain spirits, the tree spirits, the guardian spirits of the village—and especially, he told us, the water spirits. "If the water is clean, you are clean," he told us, "but if the water is angry, you will be sick."

He returned to the hearth room, and lit two candles, which he set in the bowl of rice. He dispatched a young man to catch two young white chickens, and asked him to hold one in each hand. Then he took out a ball of string, and holding the thread taut, wiped Gary's palm with it thrice before circling it around his wrist five times, closing the circle firmly with knots. He did the same for the other wrist. And he did the same for mine.

He was tying our souls to our bodies.

"Soul wandering" is a problem that often plagues the migrants and refugees of Southeast Asia. The ritual of tying strings to bind the soul more firmly to the body is common to all hill tribes. The Lahu and Hmong believe the soul is vulnerable to wandering from the moment of birth. The soul is playful, easily frightened, and apt to wander off. It can be enticed away by sweet smells or bright colors and get lost. Because loud noises can scare away a baby's soul, Hmong mothers give birth in utter silence. Then the mothers embroider soul-restraining designs on their baby's clothes, like spiderwebs and pigpens.

But soul loss can strike at any age, at any time. It is a dangerous condition. Wandering souls are prey to malevolent spirits, including vampires, were-tigers (the Asian version of the werewolf), and "bad death" spirits. But the soul may also be stolen by normally benign spirits who are made angry for some transgression on the part of the human. A person curses after tripping on a jungle trail and offends the trail spirit. He kicks a rock and angers the rock spirit. He disturbs a termite hill, and the termite hill spirit retaliates—by capturing the person's soul.

The different hill tribes have devised a number of ways to recapture a wandering or stolen soul. Among the Aka, the spirit priest, or *pii ma,* is specially trained in the art of soul-calling. Incantations uttered by the *pii ma* will call back the wandering soul; then a different kind of shaman, the *nyi pa,* is called in to negotiate with the offended spirit for the soul's release. Ceremonies are often required to make amends with the spirit who captured the soul, such as offerings of food, music, the sacrifice of a dog, pig, or chicken, and special prayers.

To retrieve the wandering soul, it may be necessary to build a soul-calling bridge, at the junction of three tracks, just outside the village, or over a stream. The person whose soul has wandered waits on one side. Among the Lahu, musical gourd pipes are played during the day-long ceremony. The low drone tone is thought to ascend to heaven all the way to G'ui sha, the supreme Lahu being. Among the Yao, a pig is slaughtered and cut into five pieces as an offering to the sky spirit to secure the soul's release.

Gary and I were not that far gone yet; our souls were not yet lost. But Jaa Wat correctly recognized the danger that they might go wandering: Gary's regularly visited the Pleistocene these days, and mine fled into nightmares, trying to escape waking sorrows. "You travel around, around everywhere," Jaa Wat said as he drew the string around and around our wrists, "but in the end, you will come back—your spirit will always come back." He held our hands so gently, his touch dry and soft as autumn grass. A calm settled over me at that moment, with my wrist in those strong, gentle, careful hands; and I felt my soul return in that moment—restored and whole.

As Jaa Wat wrapped my wrists, he stared at them intently, and began to speak to Samkait. "What is he saying?" I asked.

"He is saying maybe there is one person in a thousand with a future like this," Samkait replied. He was reading my fortune in the veins of my wrist. "He says you are very happy. Even if something bad happens, you will always be all right. This is very lucky. He has not seen anything like this before."

I was pleased but not surprised. I have encountered fortune-tellers around the world, in India, the Amazon, and Africa, and although I seldom ask them to read my future, because I am so often a stranger in their land they often do so as a courtesy. They all say the same thing: you are a lucky person. They do not always predict a long life, or great wealth, and no one has ever predicted children, even though these are the standard blessings for which most native people pray. My luck is of a different kind. I have always been grateful for it: although I don't always recognize it at the time, I have been blessed again and again with the luck of being in the right place at the right time. Despite the nightmares and sickness and sadness, I realized at that moment, I was meant to witness the suffering and hope revealed to us on this journey, no matter what the data brought, and that it was my great privilege to be here.

Jaa Wat examined my other wrist and found it equally marvelous. He kept pointing to them and saying to Samkait, "Look at this!"

He also looked at Gary's wrists, at my request, thinking the scientist would otherwise feel left out. "You will have troubles to overcome," he told Gary gravely. And indeed, Gary, who seemed always cheerful, had already overcome more than his share of troubles. His initial Ph.D. project, which was to have taken him to Africa, to study colobus monkeys, had been stymied after two years of meticulous preparation; the federal grant he had won was withdrawn at the last moment, when the White House had cut the budget supporting postgraduate studies. He'd had to design a new study of a new animal at a new study site—and today he is still recognized as the world's top expert on the nine-banded armadillo. He'd traveled widely despite his back injuries; was renowned among friends and students as a good listener despite hearing loss. In the various neighborhoods he had inhabited in Chicago, he had dealt with muggers, burglars, and gangs. Despite his heavy teaching and administrative duties, he had managed to keep his research career alive. And now, at age fifty, the resilient scientist was living his dream: following an enigmatic species back into time, charting its past and its future.

There would be troubles ahead, assured the shaman. "But in the end," he told the skeptical biologist, "you will be happy."

CHAPTER TWELVE

Seeing

Plodding through the mud past chickens, pigs, dogs, and children, we visited house after house at Lu Kalam. We would remove our shoes, climb the ladder-like steps, and sit in a circle with Jaa Bet and Samkait on the woven mats our hosts unfurled. As children stared at us wide-eyed and silent, as our hosts spat, between the slats of the floorboards, gobs of saliva reddened by chewing betel nut, we would sit by the smoking fire drinking proffered tea, and learn of different bears.

An eighty-six-year-old insisted there were four kinds of bears: the big *Mii khwai,* the smaller *Yeah paa,* the little *Yeah meuay,* and finally the dog-sized *Yeah meh tuey.*

Another Lahu told us that just among the *Yeah paa* alone, there were three different kinds: the regular *Yeah paa,* a large *Yeah paa lu,* and the smaller *Yeah paa beh.* That seemed to augment the number of bears the Lahu knew to six—which we knew was unlikely, as there are only eight known bear species on the Earth.

Even apart from the binturong, our informants told us, there were at least three kinds of bears; one was a really big bear they knew from Burma, but which wasn't found in Thailand. Then there was the moon bear, found in both Thailand and Burma. And finally there was a small bear that lived here, and wasn't recognized from our sun bear photos. Could it be there was an unknown, giant bear in Burma and an unknown, pygmy bear in Thailand?

But then, a twenty-nine-year-old hunter told us very firmly there were only two kinds of bears: one big, one small.

As the numbers of bears waxed and waned with each interview, the names for bears proliferated: not only were there *Mii khwai* and the three *Yeah paas*, the *Yeah meuay* and the *Yeah meh tuey;* there was also a *Yeah boo,* a *Yeah kay kai,* and a *Mii khon.*

"You would think you could not even walk to the latrine without falling over a bear!" I said in annoyance.

What was worse, we could not seem to get clear or consistent descriptions of the different bears. All of them were black. None were brown or golden. Two young hunters, though, told us the *Yeah meuay*'s chest mark was not white like the others. Was it orange, like the sun bear's? A calico kitten was dozing in the hearth room, and they pointed to one of the colors of her fur: they bypassed the orange fur, and pointed to a patch that was beige.

Typically confusing was twenty-nine-year-old Jaa Tehrun's response: there were only two bears, he said, but the only difference between them was size. The size and shape of the ears, the length of the fur, the shape of the face, the length of the legs, the color and shape of the chest mark—we quizzed him on every body part and he said, no, the two bears do not differ in these characteristics. And yet, he insisted, like the shaman, when he sees a bear, he knows immediately which kind it is. He shot one of the large ones three years ago, and had seen one of the small kind just last year—a sow he watched for many minutes just twenty yards away with her two cubs. One kind of bear was not, he said, just a younger, smaller individual of the same species as the other. When we showed him our bear pictures, he recognized the moon bear, declared the smaller bear wasn't pictured, and said he had never seen anything like the sun bear. "No, that bear is not here," he told us, looking at two different photos of sun bears, "except maybe on television."

We would return to Bo Kreit in the afternoon, by turns intrigued, excited, skeptical, confused, and frustrated. "When we ask about what bears people see," said Gary, "and once we exclude the binturong, they say there are at least two. What are the two bears here? *What the hell are they??*"

As we drove up the hill to the village, the people were coming home, too. As the men and women returned from tending their fields, I took a short walk to clear my mind and get out of Gary's way. He needed to think. I needed a break from words. Instead, I let the sounds of the village afternoon wash over me: the coos of caged turtle doves, the calls of cocks, the clucks of hens, the peeps of chicks, the clicks of the little gecko lizards who drizzled down the walls of every house like drops of rain. I listened to the slap of water pouring from a spigot from the village spring, where we washed in the morning, the sounds of women doing laundry, and of footfalls in wet mud. A boy was carrying a honeycomb as big around as an end table, like the one we had seen at the bear tree; another child toted a battery-powered plastic truck. Except for the plastic toy, the scene could have been from a hundred years ago, in China or Burma: smoke drifted from the wood and thatch kitchens like the clouds that flowed across the mountains—mirroring one another as the human and spirit worlds do. Men and women walked by, carrying handmade baskets tethered to their foreheads, wearing the traditional smart black suits, formal as tuxedos— except for the T-shirts beneath them, advertising soft drinks and rock groups. One T-shirt says GUESS? And this is what Gary is doing as I return from the rain-washed afternoon.

He is sitting on Jaa Bet's porch with Samkait, puzzling over the bear book.

"Now this sun bear, *Ursus malayanus,* seems to be confusing people," he said to our guide. "People don't seem to know the sun bear. They take it as a *Mii khwai,* a *Yeah paa beh,* or a *Yeah paa.* The *Mii khwai*'s huge ears, versus the sun bear's almost invisible ears, seems to me an obvious differ- ence. Do you think there is something about this picture that is causing people not to recognize the sun bear?"

Samkait replied that the top picture of the sun bear, which showed the animal in profile in a tree, may make the front legs look longer than they really are.

"But the *ears*! How can you look at a moon bear's giant ears and the sun bear's invisible ones and not see that difference?" I interjected.

"There may be something about cultural identifiers here," Gary said. "Or maybe to most people a bear is a bear . . ."

He looked off into the mountains.

"No skulls. No skins. No captive bears like in Banglamung, or in Cambodia, or the Tulakhom Zoo in Laos—where are bears when you need them?" Gary lamented. "Out in the stupid forest."

* * *

On our last evening in Bo Kreit, a number of hunters, as well as the village shaman, visited Jaa Bet's hearth after supper, lured in part by a bottle of whiskey Gary had purchased for the occasion. (He kept the receipt, considering whether he could write off its cost on his taxes under "consulting fee.") In the flickering shadows, as everyone cheerfully swilled down alcohol, they all tried to help us sort out the mystery bears.

Both Samkait and Jaa Bet helped to translate. Samkait spoke Thai and the northern Thai dialect of the Shans. Jaa Bet also spoke Shan as well as Black Lahu. One of our guests was Red Lahu, a related tribe with its own dialect.

Some of our informants used the Thai name for moon bear—*Mii khwai*—for their largest bear. Others used the Black Lahu moniker: *Yeah paa*. These big bears were black, with white chest marks, everyone agreed. They looked like the moon bears in our book of photos, they said.

No fewer than five different names described small bears—four of which may or may not have all been the same species. *Yeah paa beh* means "smaller bear" in Black Lahu; *Yeah kay kai* is Red Lahu. *Mii khon* means "man bear" in Shan. They might have all been words for the sun bear—except almost no one had ever picked out the sun bear pictures to describe it. Another of the Lahu's "small bears" was the *Yeah meh tuey*, whose long tail identified it as the binturong.

Then there were names applied to bears according not to size, but behavior: *Yeah boo* is Black Lahu for "bears come together"—these bears were often seen in groups, they said. And the mid-sized bear is also called "the annoying bear," presumably for its propensity to raid crops. (Although it could have also annoyed hunters if it objected to being shot. The Sao la is known among Hmong as "the polite animal" because it is easily killed.)

In the small, smoky room, we were dealing with five languages, six cultures, and two, three, or four species of bear—all of them colored by different ways of seeing, different memories of creatures and cultures both present and ancestral.

The Lahu originated in southwest China's Yunnan Province—where Gary had seen his first golden moon bear—and migrated south through eastern Burma. Most of the older people we spoke with, in fact, had been Burmese-born. And almost everyone had lived in several other villages before coming to settle in Bo Kreit. They carried with them tales, memories, and names that stretched back for generations, crossed national borders, and were tinged with the languages and customs of neighboring tribes.

In central Yunnan, the scientists say there is only one kind of big bear: the moon bear. But as Gary pointed out, this was not necessarily the only bear the Yunnanese Lahu would have known. At the edge of the Tibetan Plateau, including part of Sichuan, there are Tibetan blue bears—*Ursus arctos pruinosus*—grizzlies that are tan or blond when young, with a huge white yoke extending to the shoulders, darkening to black when adult, except for the head, which remains blond. They are greatly feared for their ferocity. The Lahu of Yunnan may well have known of these bears, or even seen skins, from their commerce with neighboring peoples. They may have heard of pandas, from the border of Sichuan and other provinces further north, living in the fragmented bamboo forests of western central China. It was even possible that, if the subspecies actually did exist, *Ursus arctos shanorum*—the name bestowed on the grizzly specimen secured from an animal dealer in 1906, and thought to have originated in Burma—would have been known, too, to the Lahu or their recent ancestors.

"I would love to think we're dealing with an extra kind of moon bear, or finding evidence for *Ursus arctos shanorum*," said Gary. "A really big bear that isn't here and doesn't live here, is brown with a hump on its shoulder—that would fit *shanorum*. But no. It's a big bear from Burma, but it's black with a white mark on its chest. So what do you do with that?"

Too, the Lahu would have known about sun bears, hog badgers, binturongs, and even red pandas. As the people migrated south over the generations, they may have kept the ancestral memories of all these creatures, and carried their names with them into new countries, applying the old names to new species. Here, what *is* and what *was* are not as sharply divided as in Western culture: Samkait explained that even in Thai, the past tense is denoted by adding a word like "already"; in story telling, one begins with words like "a long time ago" and the story proceeds in the present tense.

It was not unlikely that newcomers would expect to see, and in fact report, species in their adopted country that existed only in the homeland they had left behind. Such was almost surely the case in a chronicle Gary had read describing the fauna of Hainan, the island off Vietnam's west coast in the South China Sea. Though there is no evidence that any but moon bears ever existed there, the author, Kiung chow fu, reported that informants told him of four kinds of bears. They reflected the ancient Chinese classification of bears that Hainanese people had inherited from their ancestors: the horse bear, the dog bear, the pig bear, and the man bear—though the man bear, the gazetteer admitted, "is rarely seen."

* * *

In Homer's *The Odyssey*, a captive Odysseus, longing for his beloved wife and homeland, gazes mournfully upon the "wine-dark sea"—an Aegean scene we can view today. But to our modern eyes, the sea looks nothing like wine.

We would describe the sea as blue. Yet in Homer's epics, the sea is never blue. In 1810, Goethe first pointed out this curious absence in ancient Greek poetry. Why, in these lengthy, evocative, sensuous poems, is there nothing blue? In his lovely book on sight, light, and mind, *Catching the Light*, author Arthur Zajonc suggests that the ancient Greeks saw the world so differently from us that they lacked the experience of blue.

Color theorists translate the Greek word for blue as *kyanos*, a word identified with the blue stone, lapis lazuli; but Zajonc, a professor of physics, argues persuasively that *kyanos* means dark. Hector, slain by Achilles, is described as having *kyanos* hair. The goddess Iris, ashamed, took up a *kyanos* veil, because "there is no darker garment." Similarly, the Greeks may have also lacked the word for green; *chloros*, the word from which we name the green pigment in plants, chlorophyll, is applied in Greek poetry to describe grass and leaves, but also honey, tears, dew, and blood—substances that are clearly not green at all. A better translation for *chloros*, Zajonc suggests, is "moist." The "lifeworld" of the ancient Greeks, he argues, was so profoundly different from our own, that they and we, looking at the same physical world with biologically identical brains and eyes, did not see the same thing.

Even today, human perception is profoundly colored by culture. In a paper in *Psychological Review*, University of Michigan psychologist Richard E. Nisbett and colleagues Kaiping Peng, Incheol Choi, and Ara Norenzayan present the vastly different results of East Asians and Americans on a battery of perceptual tests. In one, Japanese and American students were shown animated scenes of fish and underwater objects and asked to report what they saw. A typical American's first response: "There was what looked like a trout swimming . . ." But Asians instead first described the background, or total environment: "There was a lake or pond." On Rorschach inkblot tests, European Americans are far more likely to focus on a single aspect of the card, while Chinese Americans tend to see the whole field—responding not to a single salient aspect, but its Gestalt as a whole. And on tests of causal attribution and prediction, Americans explain human behaviors—acts of kindness or cruelty—in terms of individual traits: the actor was reckless or sympathetic. Faced with the same accounts, Hindu Indians and Chinese Buddhists explain them in terms of situational, contextual, or even societal factors that may have been at work.

"The East Asians and the Americans responded in qualitatively different ways to the same stimulus situation in study after study," the authors write. The implications of their study for psychology are profound: "These qualitative differences," they conclude, "indicate that literally different cognitive processes are often invoked by East Asians and Westerners dealing with the same problem."

Nisbett and colleagues contend these differences reflect an ancient philosophical divide between the Greek and Chinese systems of thought. Both were cultures of remarkable sophistication: the Greeks forged the new sciences of physics, formal logic, axiomatic geometry, surgery, and rational philosophy. The Chinese invented porcelain, the magnetic compass, irrigation systems, ink, stirrups and (beating Edward Jenner by a millennium) a vaccine against smallpox. The achievements of the two civilizations were equally impressive, but very different—arising from vastly different worldviews, the authors argue. The Greeks emphasized personal autonomy. The Chinese valued group harmony. The West employed formal logic. The East relied on intuitive, direct perception, grasping the whole at once. The Greek language allows each word a meaning by itself, usually understandable independent of its context within a sentence; but many Chinese words cannot be translated at all when divorced from their context. To the Greeks, the world was composed of discrete, individual objects with specific properties. To the Chinese, the world was made of continuities and relationships, a collection of interpenetrating stuffs. Chinese medicine is holistic, as health is seen as dependent on the balance and flow of natural forces throughout the body; oriental medicine was quick to embrace the concept of immunization, but considered surgery heretical.

No wonder our informants did not "see" the same bears we did. Looking at a photo of a moon bear, Gary and I saw it in pieces: the tall ears, the thick mane, the long black fur. A sun bear, to us, could be identified by a series of field markings: the tiny ears, the short velvety coat, the long claws for climbing trees. We had seen far more bears in photographs and in films than we had alive. To see a live bear was, for us, a rare event—perhaps as rare as for the Lahu to see a picture of one. And no wonder they had such trouble describing to us how their bears differed: to break an animal into constituent parts was to disassemble it into nonsense. The Lahu saw their world, and the animals in it, whole, not in pieces, and animate, not in two-dimensional images. Each species was known by a Gestalt they could immediately recognize—but perhaps not easily conveyed to us.

*　*　*

During the manly nighttime discussion about hunting bears, Jaa Bet then added the evening's missing ingredient: a gun. Into the tiny, crowded, smoky room full of men swilling whiskey, he brought, to my profound dismay, a five-foot-long, twenty-pound black powder musket. Gary's face lit up. I could see how he longed to shoulder it—like a woman longs to hold a baby—but, as he told me later, in such a small room he felt to do so would be "indelicate." Instead, he held it admiringly in his lap and sang its praises. "It's a fairly safe gun," he assured me. "Imagine fifteen guys all running after a bear with their fifteen muskets—why don't they all end up shot? If anybody's in the way, you're liable to bump them with the barrel. And it's very steady," he said. "A lot of target weapons, often the barrel is deliberately heavy to steady it. This is a little more like a modern flintlock, but it's pretty much what the American Revolution was fought with."

Tongues loosened by whiskey and by a growing friendship bolstered by shared admiration for firearms, the scientist and the Lahu hunters talked on into the night. By morning, Gary felt certain he finally understood what everyone had been trying to tell us: the only bears the Lahu recognized in their current hunting ground were the sun bear and the moon bear. The third kind of bear—the very large one—was only reported in Burma by two of our previous informants. No one in this gathering seemed to regard it as different from the ordinary moon bear. "The

Lahu have at best a traditional knowledge of a large bear to the north," he said, "but I don't see any evidence for an extra bear here in Thailand." The big bear might be a new species, but it seemed equally likely it was a very big moon bear, a fading memory, or a myth.

But the Hmong were another matter.

On the long drive back to Chiang Mai, we returned to Chum Yen. There we met again with our earlier informant, the man with the coin earring. Unfortunately, his brother, who, he had told us, had killed many bears, was again out harvesting lychee. But our informant had conferred with his neighbors about bears and assured us that the consensus was as he had told us: there are three kinds of bears, all three living in Thailand. All had short tails (ruling out the binturong) and all could climb trees (ruling out the hog badger). He was quite sure of this.

Next we stopped at Ban Pa Nok Kok. It was a large Hmong village, of five hundred people, and well established, having been founded thirty years ago. Unfortunately, here, too, most of the men were out picking fruit. One middle-aged man had stayed behind, possibly because he had an earache; his ears were plugged with cotton. "The chief of our village killed a bear ten years ago," he told us. "I have eaten the meat, but I don't know what it looked like. I have only seen bears at the zoo." But he, too, insisted upon three kinds, and gave us the three names we had first heard from the Hmong in Skokie: the horse, pig, and dog bear. We spoke with a very old man wearing a green beret. "Three kinds," he told us, all bears of different sizes, all in Thailand. Each, he said, had a head like that of its namesake.

"I think, on the whole," said Gary, "the evidence over the past few days weakens the idea for three bears. But if there is a third species of bear, it has more to do with Hmong knowledge than anything else. And there are some things that bother me too much to just let it go."

One of them was Babe, the small bear with the brown eye rings at Banglamung. She was, to his eye, "a weird-looking bear": she had an un-usually flat head and a pointed muzzle—doglike, you could say. She was smaller than the other moon bears, though she was an adult.

And the other was simply this: the list of countries where people claimed more species of bears than were supposed to be was getting just too long. Besides Thailand and Laos, there were similar reports of "extra" bears from Sichuan and Nepal. In *Something Hidden Behind the Ranges,* a book that began as a quasi-scientific expedition to try to find the Wild-Man, or Yeti, author Daniel Taylor-Ide discussed at length Nepalese reports of two types of very furry, dark-coated bears found in the Himalayas: a smaller "tree bear," *Rukh Bhalu,* and a larger "ground bear," *Bhui Bhalu.* In the end, convinced by the famous grizzly biologist John Craighead, he dismissed these claims—but perhaps too hastily, Gary now suspected.

"People in Southeast Asia have been saying for years there were more kinds of muntjacks than there were known to science—and they were absolutely right," he said. "The same with the Vietnamese warty hog. They always said there were two kinds of wild pig." The stories about unknown species that have been proved wrong by science tend to be those in the spirit realm: things like the Yeti, which was supposed to be able to become invisible, or the Cobra Grande in South America, the giant snake supposed to make whirlpools, the *Mkele mbembe* of the Congo, a dinosaur-like monster.

"This goes beyond science for me," Gary resolved as we headed back to Chiang Mai, toward air-conditioning and hot water. "I've been reading whodunits all my life, and I want to solve the mystery!"

We turned up the driveway to our riverside guesthouse in Chiang Mai. Two women were walking side by side down an alley. I pointed to one of them. "That one," I said to my companions, "has bigger ears."

Samkait dissolved into laughter. But Gary, ever the scientist, looked first to see if it were true.

PART THREE

Lost Worlds

"Y<small>OU GO</small> royal palace?" the cabdriver we'd hailed in front of our Bangkok hotel asked. "You go Floating Market?"

"No," we replied—we were bound for neither of these well-known attractions. Instead, we handed him a scrap of paper on which was written, in Thai, the circuitous directions to our destination, some forty-five minutes out of town: a private museum dedicated mostly to a collection of antlers.

The driver had never heard of it. "Why you go there?"

We had heard of the antler museum from Gerry Schroering, who was a friend of Forbes Lewis, a man we had met weeks before at our hotel in Vientiane. In the short time we had known him, Forbes, a professor of computer science at the University of Kentucky, had given us nothing but excellent advice. "Don't eat the fried grasshoppers in Bangkok," he'd warned as we'd breakfasted in the vine-shrouded courtyard of Le Parasol Blanc. "They are killed with DDT." With his lady friend, Mai, Forbes had traveled extensively in Southeast Asia, but the only time he had ever gotten sick was after a gala send-off thrown by his Thai friends, which involved eating insects and drinking a lot of beer. "They were all eating fried grasshoppers, and it seemed like a great idea at the time," he said. He was sick for three days.

Forbes had also recommended the convenient, inexpensive hotel at which we were now staying in Bangkok, days before our scheduled return to the States. And learning of our interest in bears, he had put us in touch with Gerry.

Gerry, an outsized six foot five Louisville native of fifty, earns his living exploring for oil, but his passion is the natural history of Southeast Asia as explorers found it. At his Bangkok apartment, which he shares with his Thai wife, Tina, he keeps an extensive library, encompassing several languages, of old European travelers' and hunters' accounts, detailing the wonders of the jungles and mountains of Southeast Asia. To our delight and astonishment, some of them reported more than two species of bear. Some of the hunters, Gerry told us, claimed to have seen, shot, or even eaten animals that most scientists insist could not have been there: grizzlies and sloth bears; the snow leopard; and the tapir—a large, long-snouted, pig-shaped creature with a trunklike upper lip, who whinnies like a horse, and whose accepted range is well south of the region. One 1933 source described seeing an animal that Gerry was convinced was the Sao la, well to the north of its known distribution. Gerry had once visited a market in Cambodia and seen for sale the annulated horns of a Khting vor. When he examined them carefully, he noted a polygonal shape at the tip, as if they had been held in a vise or worked with a file. "Yeah," the vendor admitted. "They're fake. They come from Vietnam." The merchant then went on to describe how they had been manufactured from ox horns, softened in hot oil, and then twisted into their spiraling shape.

Still, though, Gerry fervently hoped that the Khting vor roamed the forest. And so, he hoped, might many of the other creatures the early explorers described—even some believed extinct. He spent much of his spare time talking with locals in remote corners of the region and searching small markets for evidence that they might survive—and if so, where they might be found. Hence his interest in the antler museum. Long after midnight, when we left his apartment loaded with library references, he insisted that we visit the place.

* * *

The antler museum is little known, and even with our Thai directions, our driver stops several times to get his bearings. Finally, along an ordinary-looking Thai street, with its fruit stalls and clothing shops, its 7-Eleven and spirit houses, we see a red and yellow sign, in English: The Biggest Museum of Wildlife Antlers Deers in Asia. But the sign on the street isn't attached to a building. Where is the actual museum?

A metal grillwork gate that seems to lead toward the museum is closed. A young woman in a ponytail spots us. *"Farang!"* our driver calls to her—and that explains everything. The woman points down an alley.

We wander into an apartment building. A hallway is lined with doors, the owners' shoes exiled outside. A flight of stairs looks promising. We mount them, find an identical floor, and then climb another flight, and another. At the fifth floor, a single, heavy wooden door with a long wooden latch looks as if it might open into a castle. But what we find behind the door is even stranger. As it is opened, by a young girl of perhaps twenty, we see a foyer crammed, floor to ceiling, with antlers.

We wander into the first few rooms. Antlers are mounted and nailed to the walls, piled on the floor. The Thai names of the animals are carefully labeled in both Thai and English: *Wou khwpree*—the kouprey. *Kray Pa Ma-Hong Su*, the wild buffalo. *Wou ga tong*, the gaur. *Kvang pa*—the sambar. *Gang*—barking deer. *Laong Kow Lamung*—Eld's deer. *Nuesaman*—Schomburgk's deer, a species extinct for 60 years.

The kouprey, too, is extinct in Thailand, and rare, if any still survive at all, in Cambodia. Scientists and conservationists, including our friend Hunter Weiler, have looked in vain for them in Cambodia. But there are 150 pairs of their antlers here. In all, the museum houses seven thousand pairs of horns and antlers—mainly from the strange and beautiful Asiatic members of the antelope and deer tribes, like the little barking deer or muntjacks, with their primitive, razor-sharp fangs. The teeth are in this collection too: "A successful Hmong hunter might wear a crown of 100 barking deer canines," we read on a label beside one of these ornaments.

There are other natural history treasures here as well: the skulls of sun and moon bears; the skulls of one- and two-horned rhinoceroses; the tusks of elephants and of extinct mammoths; the mounted heads of African springbok; and moose antlers from North America.

They represent the lifelong collecting passion of Prassert Sriyinyong, a fifty-eight-year-old jeweler who has been accumulating his trove since he was a child. "This is my museum," he announces in well-pronounced English, appearing from behind a door down the hall. The museum is in his apartment. In fact, he owns the whole apartment building, but he keeps the top two floors to house his wife, his family, and his seven thousand pairs of horns and antlers.

Learning Gary is a biologist, he is delighted to offer us a personal tour. "Everywhere, antlers, deers!" he says expansively. "I go to kitchen," he says, directing our attention to its open door, "I have!" Antlers are mounted above the toaster oven, horns piled by the refrigerator, and more antlers crowd a blender on the counter. "I go to toilet," he says, opening the door to the water closet, "I have!" Although it is a large bathroom, the only open space is a slender path from door to toilet—every other available space is piled with antlers. Above the commode perches a magnificent pair from the extinct Schomburgk's deer. "I go to bedroom," he continues, "I have!" Pulling open another hallway door reveals his wife and daughter, bewildered by our intrusion, beside the king-sized bed, surrounded by a forest of antlers, as if they were among a herd of deer.

Mr. Prassert proudly introduces us to his specimens as if they were paintings of his recent ancestors. "Kouprey," he says, pointing to a giant set of crescent horns on one wall. The tips of the horns are tasseled, but not with hair; it looks as if they have splintered. "Get from fighting," he explained. "Attack the rock, attack the tree. Kouprey extinct Thailand eighty year." Seeing our crestfallen faces, he added, "Sorry."

Not that he was personally responsible, he wants us to know. "I no like hunt the wild animal," he stresses. Everything in his collection, he insists, is antique—at least eighty years old. He next offers to show us something very special. Using a key, he opens a cabinet and directs his young daughter to remove what looks like a wad of bedding. She kneels at one end of the long central hallway, and begins to unwrap, and then unroll, the object. "Reticulated python," our host announces, as his daughter continues to unroll the skin's seemingly endless length. When she stops, Gary paces off its size; our host's measurement of 13.5 meters—about 45 feet—seems accurate. Later, Gary would look up the world's record for the species: there was a report, considered dubious, of a reticulated python thirty-three feet long from Sulawesi, but the largest known specimen ever exhibited was about twenty-five feet long. Our host tells us the skin itself is perhaps a hundred years old, and the animal who had worn it had probably been alive for a century when it was killed.

From the skin of the python, I look to the skin of our host. Although he is nearly sixty, there are no wrinkles on his face, no gray in his hair, no calluses on his hands. His are the hands of a jeweler: pliant, precise, soft flesh yielding to the facets of the glittering gems, hard, sharp-edged, everlasting.

He trades in objects prized for their durability. "A diamond is forever." But what he enshrines here in his museum he considers far more precious: the testament to breathing, blooded, vanished lives.

The eccentric jeweler shares a passion with Gerry, as he pores over explorers' accounts; with Hunter Weiler, as he searches Cambodian forests for kouprey and Khting vor; and with Gary and me, as we seek Pleistocene refuges and unknown bears. Our trophies are different: historical references, or antlers, or teeth, or DNA. But what we are searching for is the same: the hope of retaining lost worlds.

CHAPTER THIRTEEN

Hearing

"What do you really think are the chances for a third species of bear?"

Gary and I had asked each other this same question for months—on the flight back to the States from our second expedition, after each foray into the historical literature, after each new communication from Gary van Zuylen, Sun Hean, Lisette, Gerry, and Forbes. Our estimates had, at various times, sunk to one in ten, and soared to one in five. Now it was December, and as we began the nineteen-hour trip to Bangkok, on the way to our third expedition, Gary asked me again.

"I want this so much, I don't want to scare it away," I told him.

"Me, too."

We sat silent.

"I think," he finally said, "the chances are one in three."

What did I think? I didn't know how to leave my own desire out of the equation. But I tried, impassively, to review the data we had accumulated so far:

Nothing in Lisette's latest laboratory work suggested a new species of bear. We'd been mortified to learn that the nucleotide sequencing of most of our second batch of hair samples had failed. We had discovered in Chiang Mai a source of silica gel, and, as a colleague had previously suggested, this time we'd added the desiccant directly to the tubes containing the hairs. As it turned out, that was a mistake; Lisette later explained that adding the silica directly to the hairs actually removes their DNA. This, to our profound distress, had rendered useless all the hairs we had plucked in Laos—including those bears' in the Tulakhom Zoo captured in the Annamite Mountains, the area we had expected might yield the most dramatic genetic variation. But Gary van Zuylen came again to our rescue. After we discovered the disaster, his team finished building the outdoor exclosure at Tulakhom Zoo. When the bears were sedated before moving into it, a vet pulled hairs for us to send on to Lisette's lab. These samples were yet to be sequenced.

However, French explorers' and hunters' accounts, to which Gerry had directed us, suggested an unknown species of bear may well have been present—at least during their travels in the early twentieth century. The big-game hunter Henri de Monestrol reported in his 1925 book *Les Chasses et la Faune d'Indochine* three kinds of bears: a short, stout "Malay bear" with short hair and a yellow chest crescent; a mid-sized bear with a pale crescent, upright ears, long fur and mane; and the largest, an entirely black mountain bear. Three decades later, in a different book, he reported he had examined "remains" of this giant animal—though it may have been only a single specimen—and claimed it was twice the size of the moon bear. Fernand Millet, a forest warden and hunting adviser based in what is now south Vietnam, wrote in 1930 he had seen two kinds of bear, clearly the sun and moon bear. But he also knew of another—a large, "fauve"-hued bear the local people called the "horse bear," who lived in the mountains. Millet was a shrewd listener and skilled observer. That he dismissed as fanciful reports of mythical animals—such as a rhino with a phosphorescent horn—rendered his reporting particularly credible. And he had also included in his 1930 volume an excellent description of the giant muntjack, six decades before the species was officially recognized by science.

In a 1939 book, Guy Cheminaud, an overseer for a logging company floating teak down the Mekong, enumerated four bear species in Laos: a large, maned "pig bear" with a long, flat muzzle, shovel-shaped jaw, and small, rigid ears; a smaller "dog bear," which lived in the mountains, with gleaming black fur and a dirty gray chest mark; a "honey bear"; and a big bear like a grizzly with dark brown fur. And J. Bordeneuve, a forester,

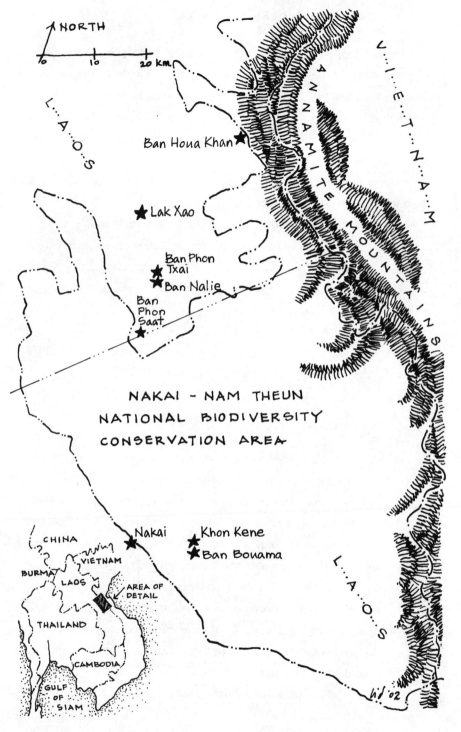

Annamite Mountains

writing in 1925, claimed there were no fewer than five kinds of bears in Indochina: two types of "honey bears," found in the lowlands (at least one of which was surely the sun bear); and three found in the mountains: a grizzly-like, dark mountain bear; a "collared bear," whose illustration resembled a moon bear; and a completely dark bear with no chest mark, illustrated with a drawing that looked like a sloth bear.

It seemed to both Gary and me that if there remained a new species of bear to be discovered, it lived in remote mountains. George Schaller, who had discovered several of the new species in Southeast Asia, had (at a dinner to which I'd brought a squash pie that he commented "would make an excellent tracking medium"), actually suggested years before what we should do. "If you want to find new species," he had told me, "go to the Annamite Mountains of Laos."

Indeed, this was where Gary and I were now, hopefully, headed. There, a new species of bear seemed at least a reasonable possibility—whether we could find it or not. And thanks to a contact that Gerry had generously provided, we had an excellent starting point for planning an expedition.

As we'd tried to make sense of the summer's Hmong and Black Lahu interviews, Gerry had e-mailed us in November with more valuable advice. "There is a linguistic anthropologist in Vientiane who has used animal names from the villagers all across Indochina for his studies," he wrote us. "He probably has a better understanding of what the villagers are saying than any of the past surveyors. His name is Jim Chamberlain. He is absolutely brilliant. I would think that he could help clarify many of the conflicting reports and the problems thereof."

Through the e-mail address Gerry had thoughtfully provided, we'd gotten in touch with Jim. Not only was he a renowned linguist, expert in the very languages that were giving us trouble; among his many studies, we discovered in our correspondence, was the first and only modern survey of the tribes of the Nakai-Nam Theun conservation area of the Annamite Mountains of Laos.

Once a royal hunting preserve, the 3,700-square-kilometer Nakai-

Nam Theun National Biodiversity Conservation Area is the largest protected area in Laos and boasts the highest biological diversity of any site surveyed in the country. Among its wet and dry rain forests, old growth pine, fragrant cypress forests and riversides, some three hundred wild Asian elephants still roam, along with tigers, clouded leopards, rhinos, and both sun and moon bears. Here, and just across the border in Vietnam, the Sao la, the giant muntjack, the other new barking deer, the zebra-striped rabbit, and the Vietnamese warty hog had been discovered. More than four hundred species of birds have been cataloged, the greatest variety in the country. And, unknown to all but a small handful of researchers, small communities of people, speaking seventeen different languages but all belonging to a branch of Mon-Khmer known as Vietic, have also been living here for thousands of years. Unlike the Hmong and Black Lahu, the Vietic people still inhabited the homeland that birthed their language and their understanding of the world. "Many of the groups are hunter-gatherers or were until recently; their familiarity with the animals and their habits is quite amazing," the linguist had replied to our e-mail queries. "At any rate," he wrote us, "if there is a third species of bear, they would know."

The question I pondered now, on the way to Bangkok, was whether we would be able to organize, on short notice, an expedition into the Annamites. Securing permission to travel in this border area might be impossible. Although happily, we were traveling in the dry season, when the rutted tracks used as roads in the Annamites might be passable, we would need to locate a driver who would know where to go. And, most crucial of all, we would have to find a translator able to communicate both with us, in English, and with Annamite tribes—someone willing to venture into a dangerous and politically-turbulent area. The chances, I estimated, were one in two.

* * *

We met Jim our first morning back in Bangkok. Through a happy coincidence, he was in town on business, and we were staying at the same hotel.

The man we met at the hotel coffee shop did not look the part of the jungle explorer: a balding, heavy fellow of fifty-seven, wearing a pink button-down shirt, he was a plainspoken, mild-mannered Midwesterner, who when truly surprised, might be moved to exclaim "Well, I'll be darned!" He seemed like the sort of guy you might sit next to on a train commute, hidden behind a newspaper, both of you too shy to start up a conversation. But we were so eager to meet him—and Jim, perhaps, so hungry to speak English with people who understood and appreciated his somewhat esoteric work—that we instantly plunged into the heart of what brought us together: the people, the landscape, and the animals of the wildest areas of Southeast Asia.

Our tools and fields of study, of course, were vastly different. Gary's focus was on science and animals. Jim's was on language and people. But our work was not only complementary, it was astonishingly parallel. Exactly as we were using DNA to try to trace the travels of ancient moon bears back in time, Jim was using language to find the ancestral homelands of Southeast Asian peoples. He had learned to hear the unspoken history of words. Charting the changes accumulated in the words of related languages, just like mapping the changes of nucleotides on DNA molecules, he had been able to trace origins of the Tai languages back to the lower Yangtze valley of China. Similarly, he had determined the Proto-Vietic homeland to be the Laotian provinces of Bolikhamxai, Khammouan, and a province just on the other side of the Annamites in Vietnam. And using a linguistic method not dissimilar to our "molecular clock," Jim had determined that the "linguistic time-depth" separating the Vietic-speaking of the Annamites from the speakers of modern Vietnamese was at least two thousand years. For two millennia, these little-known Vietic peoples had lived relatively undisturbed in the homeland in which they had carved out their unique and previously unknown cultural and ecological niche.

Through their language, Jim was exploring the "life world" of unknown peoples. He was bringing to light a highly sophisticated understanding of the biology and ecology of a rich and imperiled world largely unexplored by science.

"Nothing else exists like this in Southeast Asia," he told us. "These people are a living, breathing part of the ecosystem whose languages and cultures are far more endangered than the most threatened of all the endangered animal species. There is so much to learn from them!" The Vietic peoples, he believed, could well hold the key to preserving their homeland—for themselves, for the forest, for the animals, for the nation of Laos, and for the world. But since his last trip there in 1997, no one had followed up on his research. He did not even know if the most endangered of the peoples still survived. Of one tribe he discovered, the Mlengbrou, only eleven people were left.

"There is so much more work to do!" he said. "But no one is interested. No one is listening. And soon, I'm afraid, they're going to be gone—and with them, everything they know."

Over coffee and eggs and porridge and steaming noodle soup—and then more soup and sandwiches and bowls of chilled lychee fruit—we did not move from our seats until deep into the afternoon, so transfixed were we by his story.

* * *

Jim Chamberlain grew up in Lansing, Michigan, a country boy prowling the woods and swamps for frogs and butterflies and animal sign. Once, he recalled, a particularly forward beaver grabbed hold of his canoe paddle when he was exploring a swamp. "It was a marvelous place for wildlife," he told us. "It was one of the few places you could find the tiger salamanders," he said—gorgeous, giant black amphibians with gold spangles, who grow thirteen inches long. His uncle kept a pair in the basement that lived for more than twenty years.

Jim's father, the son of a bookstore owner, was always reading him exotic stories: he vividly recalls Rudyard Kipling's *The Jungle Book*. He developed a hunger for travel. A bad teacher had turned him away from a career in biology, so he pursued languages and literature instead. He had a natural ear for languages. Words played in his head like music. Both his parents were musicians; his father, a CPA, played cello, and his mother, viola. In college, Jim studied both French and Hausa, a northern Nigerian coastal trade language.

He got to Laos, he explained, "by default": after completing undergraduate studies in comparative literature in 1965, he joined International Volunteer Services, a precursor of the Peace Corps, to avoid the draft. He planned to go to Algiers, having mastered French, but ended up living right next to the war he had sought to avoid: in the small, quiet village of Vang Vieng, Laos.

The village where he was sent to teach English was halfway between Vientiane and Louang Phabang. There were no electricity or running water. "Vang Vieng was total culture shock," Jim told us. He recalled his first encounter with the Southeast Asian passion for chewing betel: "Ladies are spitting out blood onto the sidewalk—everybody's got some disease! My God, what a terrible place!"

Then he began, intuitively, to speak and understand Lao. As the charms of the little village grew on him, he fell in love with Laos—and with a local girl. When the American director of U.S. AID objected, he married her anyway, and the couple moved to the capital, where he worked teaching English at an international school.

He has since divorced that wife and buried another (a Cambodian woman who died of complications of diabetes). Four years ago, he married a third Southeast Asian lady: a Black Tai–speaking Laotian whose mother was a former opium dealer "back when it was respectable." He has earned a master's degree, then a Ph.D. in linguistics. And, although he has twice contracted dengue fever (a disease also known as "breakbone" fever, whose agonies I knew well from having suffered them in Borneo), as well as malaria, he wished to live nowhere else. In Laos, he has found an extraordinarily fertile area in which to carry out his special brand of ethnolinguistics.

"Laos has 240 ethnic groups," he told us. "Linguistically, Brazil has two basic ethnolinguistic families, Laos has four, and Vietnam has five. In

Laos, ethnic minorities are actually seventy percent of the population!" That's a figure you never read; for, he explained, non-Lao ethnic Thai groups are all included in the official count of lowland Lao people.

The land is as varied as its peoples. "Every valley has its own eco-system," Jim explained to us. The International Rice Research Institute has identified 13,600 genetic varieties of rice in Laos—number two in the world behind India, with one hundred times the land area. The rich-ness of Laos's peoples is tied directly to the richness of the land and its creatures. This fact was lavishly illustrated by Jim's Ph.D. thesis, which he had completed in 1977, "An Introduction to Proto-Tai Zoology," com-paring the zoological references of thirty-five related languages and di-alects in the Tai language group, spoken in Laos, Thailand, Burma, Vietnam, and six Chinese provinces. The study was, he explained to us, an examination of "early Tai's ways of looking at, behaving around, naming, and thinking about animals."

Strikingly, he found, more often than not, folk taxa correspond to sci-entific categories. The early Tai speakers were extraordinarily gifted stu-dents of natural history. So detailed was their knowledge of the natural world that they often named plants or fungus after animal body parts (*Auricularia polytrica:* "tortoise intestine mushroom"; *Jussiaea caryo-phyllea,* "eel gall vegetable") or even animal excrement (*Gymnopetalum monoicum,* "crow shit"; *Urena cordifolia,* "bamboo rat shit").

But the naming of plants and animals reveals more than biological knowledge. In his thesis, Jim quotes from psychoanalyst Jacques Lacan: "The function of language is not to inform, but to evoke." The Chinese, he notes, once believed that each human had two souls, one dark and one light. The dark one, a changeling, looked like a frog. Like the Chinese soul, each word has an unspoken twin: there is the thing the word repre-sents—the "real" natural world—and the changeling, the human rela-tionship to that thing—the imagined natural world—which gives it meaning within a culture.

The Tai languages reveal an ancient reverence for animal powers that are evoked again and again not only in words but in worship, diet, even architecture. The Black Tai speakers of the upland valleys of north-western Vietnam, for instance, build houses whose roofs are rounded over the veranda, mimicking the shell of a tortoise, for it is this creature that controls the rains that give life to the rice paddies (a belief shared by the southern Chinese).

The study of a language, says Jim, allows its student to hear a people's "interpretation (or misinterpretation) of messages from environment to human." The spoken word reveals, upon reflection, that to which its speakers first chose to listen, then ponder, then live by.

Understanding this ancient relationship between nature and culture "is terribly important for the future of Laos," Jim told us, "but it's not getting a lot of attention."

So it was with Jim's groundbreaking work in Nakai.

* * *

As part of surveys preparatory to the construction of a huge new dam, CARE International and IUCN had sponsored Jim's work in the central Annamites. In pursuit of hydroelectric power to sell mainly to Thailand, the World Bank–financed Nam Theun II project (there was no Nam Theun I) was scheduled to begin construction within five years of his first survey. Upon completion, scheduled for 2006, the fifty-meter-high dam would create a 450-square-kilometer reservoir, flooding one quarter of the Nakai Plateau. Not only did the entire cachement area of the dam lie within the "protected area" of the Nakai-Nam Theun National Biodiversity Conservation Area, with its seventeen globally threatened animal species; the project would also flood more than a dozen villages, forcing the eviction of more than four thousand people. The organizations sent Jim there to find out something about the people whose homes the project would obliterate.

Equipped with a helicopter, a translator who spoke Brou, the lingua franca of the region, and a Phong speaker who had also learned some of the local languages, Jim embarked on his first expedition in January 1996. In the first village where they set down, Jim documented no fewer than three completely unknown ethnic groups. On trips between December 1996 and July 1997, during his contract with IUCN, he discovered two more. The new groups were all rain forest hunter-gatherers, among the last of their kind in Southeast Asia. One group, the Themarou, was still wearing bark cloth, pounding loincloths and blankets from fibers of the same tree from which they extracted their arrow poisons. Their tools were few. The people cooked in hollow bamboo tubes, sewed with vines for thread, washed with a rain forest fruit that served as soap. Except for the two months of the rainy season, when they lived in more substantial structures by a river, the people sheltered in temporary leaf-structures in the forest that they would occupy for a few days at a time and then move on.

Another new group, the Atel, used sharpened sticks to hunt out hog badgers, with the help of dogs, from their holes. Other Vietic people, like the Cheut, used primitive crossbows. But mostly the forest people hunted by following the rare, foxlike Asian wild dogs, the dholes. Early humans, including *Homo habilis,* were thought to have secured meat in this way, Gary observed—not actually hunting, but scavenging, relying gratefully on the skills of another, fellow animal.

Jim did not have time in his frenzied surveys to observe such a hunt, but he was able to collect several descriptions. The people would follow the pungent scent of the wild dog, or else they would follow the crow. These family-living birds, like people, love meat, and like them, often take advantage of dholes' kills. When the people would hear the crows making a commotion, or see a crow flying with meat in its beak, they would follow it, and often find the dholes' kill. If the carcass was still fresh—two or fewer days old, before maggots would hatch in it—they would take the meat. The dholes would run away, but not far. This, the people understood; and so, before taking away the kill, they would remove a front leg of the slain barking deer or sambar to leave it, with their thanks, for their hosts, the dholes. They would take the rest home to roast over an open fire.

Only a few Vietic groups still said they hunted with dholes when Jim visited, but he found the ancient relationship was still honored even where it was no longer practiced. No one hunts or kills dholes or crows, because the people remember: the more than one dozen Vietic-speaking tribes living in the Annamites were all hunter-gatherers until about 1700. At that time, Katuic-speaking Brou and Tai-speaking Sek peoples appeared, fleeing war and persecution and bringing swidden and paddy agriculture. But for at least two thousand years, all seventeen of the Vietic tribes—from the village-dwelling Maleng to the nomadic Mlengbrou, have lived in relative isolation, interacting with non-Vietic groups only to trade wild honey for tea and tobacco.

Or so they did until 1976. After the Communists took power, they began to capture Laos's forest peoples and force them to live in villages as part of a national program of village consolidation. Though brutal and abrupt, the program's goals were not dissimilar from those of the recent "Thai-ization" programs, or the U.S.A.'s "Americanization" classes offered to immigrants in the early decades of the twentieth century. Laos's leaders hoped to assimilate all their people into a national unity, an effort they saw not as the annihilation of native cultures, but as a noble endeavor to share the benefits of civilization.

But in the Annamites, this was an agenda few of its supposed beneficiaries would survive. "I estimate perhaps eighty percent of the population just died," Jim said. Many succumbed to new diseases; some fled to return to the forests. When Jim met them, the Atel numbered only five families totaling sixteen people. The Themarou's population had been reduced to a bit over thirty; of the Mlengbrou, only eleven were left.

"Compare that to the Sao la," Jim said to us, "the emblem of endangeredness on the nonhuman side. There are supposed to be one thousand of them left." In his report, Jim pled for protection of the rights of the ravaged hunter-gatherers and urged further study of their cultures. They "represent a cultural type that is virtually extinct in Southeast Asia, and is found nowhere else on the planet," he wrote in his eloquent and detailed report, *Nature and Culture in the Nakai-Nam Theun Conservation Area.* Theirs is "a way of life that demonstrates, in a way that no other can, the intimate relationship between nature and culture."

But none of his recommendations were implemented. No follow-up surveys of the people have been planned. And none of his findings were published or publicized.

How could that be? Gary and I were astonished. "If you had found the new species of warty hog," I noted, "it would be considered huge news. And this was the equivalent of discovering new species, morally!"

Jim sighed. "I wish I'd had you here to say these things," he said. "The problem is basically, it got very polarized. The social against the biological. And my whole point was we shouldn't separate things out like that." The organizations that sponsored Jim's surveys saw nature and culture as antithetical. "The biologists wanted all the people moved out of the reserve. The government wanted to bring civilization to the people." In the carnival of controversy posed by the Nam Theun II dam, in the scramble to balance "sustainable development" with the preservation of globally-endangered wildlife, the needs and knowledge of the native people of the Annamites have simply been ignored.

* * *

Of course, in learning all of this, what Gary and I wanted to know most was: what did the people say about bears? How many kinds of bears did they know?

And this, said Jim, was not easily answered.

His work on the plateau was painfully hasty. He was trying to get a basic vocabulary, including the names of wild and domestic mammals, birds, insects, and plants, as well as collect myths, map territories, sketch lifestyles, and establish histories for seventeen different ethnic groups, each of whose language was as different from the next as French is from Portuguese. "I would be getting into the helicopter and still asking people, "and what about the tigers? And what about the deer?" he said, laughing softly. "We barely scratched the surface."

Only the Liha and Ahlao people seemed to make a generic level distinction between the sun and the moon bear, the two bears for which he tried to collect names in his Vietic vocabularies. But distinctions like this could be misleading, he warned us. "These people's relationship with the land is so intimate and so detailed," he told us, "that it is almost beyond the Western imagination."

Jim had asked one group, speaking to them in Lao, to list for him the types of hornets they knew. "And they were completely perplexed. I thought this was crazy," he said—he knew that the people were quite familiar with all the different kinds of bees, wasps, and hornets; as bears did, the people ate many of the larvae and relished their honey. He finally figured out what was wrong: "In Lao, I had used the word hornet. But they have so many different kinds of hornets, they each have separate names—there is no one generic name that means hornet!" Then he began to collect the names: "These are the ones that build their nests in the ground, then there's the big one that lives in stumps; there are the ones that live in the trees, then the small ones that live in the ground, and each has a different name!" Similarly, the Mlengbrou had no generic name for fish. "They name each separately, as a separate creature. They are living *so close*." So it could be with bears. "People may see different bears as such distinct animals there is no generic word for bear." It could well be, he said, that they knew of a third species of bear, but that they had not spoken to him of it, as he did not ask the right questions.

"And then there's the other problem," he told us. "There's always complications!" And he began to tell us how he had, at the eleventh hour of his research, discovered how much the Vietic peoples communicated in silence and in code.

"At the very end of our research up there, we discovered there are naming prohibitions," he told us. "Prohibitions against speaking the name of the animal out loud. The name of the animal is secret. The reason is, when you walk into the jungle, if you name the animal, the animal will know you are coming and run away. And there are euphemistic names as well as secret names. There may be up to twenty different names for one animal! So there may be at least three names—the real name, the secret name, and the euphemistic name." Usually the secret names consisted of a single word with no other meaning: the euphemistic or concealing names were often descriptors. Among the Ahlao, for instance, the elephant is called "floppy ears" or "big foot"; the bamboo rat, "red teeth," the scaly pangolin, an ant-eating mammal who looks like a giant pine cone, "toothless." In fact, among at least two of the groups Jim interviewed—the Mlengbrou and the Kri—the bear is a sacred animal; it is forbidden to eat its flesh. The very people who might know most about the bear might not be willing to speak the animal's name.

That was, if we were even able to get to the people in the first place. We met with Jim daily in Bangkok and then flew, following the linguist, to Vientiane. Gary and I took up residence again at Le Parasol Blanc (whose nanny goat, we noted, now had two kids). Jim came to meet with us over coffee in its vine-covered courtyard to finalize the logistics of our expedition.

We would need to rent a Land Rover and driver—more easily said than done. There are only a handful of vehicles in the country reliable enough to travel what passes for roads in the Annamites, he told us, and few drivers who would know the area. Both were expensive. But if we were able to secure them, we'd be able to reach, by car, a number of villages hosting different ethnic groups Jim thought could help us. "The Liha—they're pretty savvy," he told us. Also we could reach groups of people from several other tribes, and, if we wished, speak with more Hmong. Unlike the people Jim had needed a helicopter to reach, these groups live in established villages. We would not need to wander around in the forest looking for temporary leaf structures built by people who had just left.

What about permissions? The area was rife with conflict. Despite unexploded ordnance left over from the war, Vietnamese poachers routinely invade the area, usually armed with automatic weapons. "A well-organized network in Vietnam takes wildlife, mostly alive, to China and much of this comes from Lao PDR," we had read in the 1999 IUCN/WCS status report on Laos's wildlife. Animals were not the only targets; wood, rattan, and fish, too, were so sought-after that turf wars sometimes broke out over the booty. While Jim was on his first expedition, two rival groups of Vietnamese wood poachers were seeking *Mai*

Heuang, insect-infested wood used for incense by Arabs, and very valuable. In an effort to keep all the wood for themselves, the rival groups had first tried to poison one another, then held a shootout. Finally the last of them were killed by Lao workers with a rattan concession.

Also, the Lao government was concerned about Hmong insurgents. They were blamed for the latest bombings in Laos, which had included the capital's morning market, the central bus station, the Nam Phou Plaza (where we had eaten sandwiches and drunk fruit shakes at the Scandinavian Bakery), and the parking lot of the Lane Xang Hotel (where we had watched performances of traditional Lao music and dance). Though the Hmong who had recently moved into the Nakai-Nam Theun area were not insurgents, they brought social conflict and ecological disaster: "They leave no trees standing," wrote the authors of a 1998 revision of the management plan for Nakai-Nam Theun Cachement and Corridor Areas. " . . . usually the barren hills that remain leave little hope for natural reforestation during human planning timeframes." The newcomers treated their neighbors' landmarks with no more tenderness than they treated the trees. In one incident, newly arriving Hmong had taken over a neighboring Maleng cemetery and dug it up to plant rice in it, prompting another shootout.

However, despite these troubles, Jim told us we would need no permits to travel to Lak Xao. This had long been on our hopeful itinerary: at its marketplace, George Schaller had found the meat of the Sao la for sale, and Rob Timmins had purchased the skins of a zebra-striped rabbit that turned out to be new to science. There was also a menagerie, owned by a Lao general, where scientists had found two new species of muntjack, one large and one small. We could even stay in hotels in Lak Xao, Jim told us, with electricity and running water, built to accommodate the many dozens of foreign consultants hired by the consortium planning the Nam Theun II dam. Because there were so many foreigners about, we were unlikely to attract unwelcome attention from authorities. From Lak Xao, we could probably travel to a number of communities within the province of Bolikhamxai without special permission, Jim guessed.

There was another large town we could use as a base to explore villages in the adjoining province of Khammouan, Nakai. To our amazement, we would be able to stay in hotels and eat in restaurants the whole time.

The only real discomfort we could count on, said Jim, were fleas and lice in the villages, which the people get from sleeping alongside their chickens and dogs. It was unlikely, he told us, that we would arrive during one of the dramatic rat plagues that occur every six to eight years—but that would certainly be something to see: "The rats carve highways into the forest," he said. The local people told him that the plagues are caused when a certain species of bamboo drops its flowers into the water, causing the fish to turn into rats. This unlikely story actually reflects the keenness with which the people observe the natural world, Jim told us: this type of bamboo, it turns out, only blooms every six to eight years. Its nourishing flowers make the rats extraordinarily fertile.

CHAPTER FOURTEEN

Appetite

"Boiling Special Veal Following Soup," I read from the menu at the Thip-pavangxay Restaurant at Lak Xao. What could it be?

Gary and I were often mystified by the English translations of menus in Southeast Asia. It seemed anything might show up on your plate or in your bowl. Finding an insect in your food, you couldn't be sure if it was supposed to be in there or not—grasshoppers, certain grubs, even preda-ceous diving beetles are all relished. In Bangkok, Ian Glover, a specialist in Southeast Asian archaeology, had told me restaurant patrons some-times dispense with the menu entirely. In Vietnam, he'd seen diners at one restaurant pointing to animals pictured on IUCN endangered species posters, and telling the waiter, "I'll have one of those, and one of that, and one of these. . . ."

Soups proved particularly treacherous. In Cambodia, one night when Sun Hean was not with us, I had ordered what I'd assumed to be a safe, vegetarian item: "Fragrant Flower Soup." But instead of blossoms, the en-tree that ensued featured a thin bouillon in which floated at least five dif-ferent digestive and excretory organs. Gary, ever the biologist, had helpfully fished each out onto a plate for better viewing, cross-sectioning some with his knife to confirm the identification.

The soup offerings at the outdoor restaurant where we found our-selves our first morning in the Annamites seemed equally mysterious. Taxonomically speaking, "Boiling Special Veal Following Soup" appeared to be a subspecies of "Boiling Soups" to which also belonged "Sour

Boiling Eel Soup" and the enigmatic "Tasteless Boiling Soup." I was almost afraid to ask, for fear it might—shuddering horror!—result in ordering the item, but finally, I could not resist:

"Panh," I asked our translator, pointing to the menu, "what is in this Boiling Special Veal Following Soup?"

Panh Phomsombath, fifty-eight, paused for a moment in his ceaseless, elegant smoking to find the right words in the right language. He spoke at least four—Lao, Brou, French, and English—of which the latter was, unfortunately, not his forte.

"It is some-zing coming after *le veau*, you know," he answered.

Jim had mentioned we might have some trouble communicating. "Panh is really good," he'd told us, but cautioned, "His English is okay. His French is better than his English. He'll understand most of what you're saying."

Gary and I had hoped to persuade Jim to come with us. Though he said he would have loved to, upon returning to Vientiane, Jim found an important contract had come through that he had to see to immediately. But he had arranged for us the next best option: Panh had been one of Jim's translators in the Annamites. Not only did he know the languages, he knew the people, too, as well as our own objectives.

This is not always the case with translators. Fernand Millet, in his 1930 book for hunters, *Les Grands Animaux Sauvages de l'Annam: Leurs Moeurs, Leur Chasse, Leur Tir,* advised his readers to learn two hundred words of the Coho language before embarking on the hunt; if one does not have time to do this, "one can have recourse to the service of a native servant or an interpreter of the Annamite race, as many of the Moi understand that language," he wrote. "But then one is exposed to all sorts of problems and one finds oneself at the mercy of the native; for, if the Annamite is not a hunter, the Moi is not much any longer and, unless one then can get accustomed to clearly understanding and to directing the hunt oneself, one must rely only on accident and luck."

But Panh understood perfectly the sort of hunt we were planning. Panh and Jim had worked together for three decades. The two of them had set up an arm of Laotian national studies, the Division of Minority and Ethnic Research, funded by the Asia Foundation, in 1973. (Two years later, though, the Communist revolution put an end to it. Panh then worked for the resettlement program—counting himself lucky, he told us, not to have been sent to a reeducation camp.) Both linguists were now working freelance, mostly as cultural brokers to foreign nongovernmental agencies—or, as the calling card Panh handed us put it, beside the face of a Federal Express–like eagle, "Consultant, Socio-Economic Development."

When we had met him the day before, at our hotel in Vientiane, we saw immediately that Panh was a man of great learning and refinement. We could see this even in the way he held his cigarette—pinkie slightly crimped and held aloft. It was a gesture I imagined he had acquired in France, where he'd earned his baccalaureate in its language in 1965. Besides his general elegance, we noticed two other things about him: one was that he was a sharp dresser. When we met he was wearing a denim vest that said KANSAS on the back, a short-sleeved shirt, new shoes, and two rings. One ring held four diamonds, one for each of his children—three of whom were in college in Australia, studying electrical engineering and computers, he noted proudly.

The other thing we noticed about Panh was he had a terrible cold. This did not help our decoding of his accent, or his hearing of our numerous questions and requests.

"*Le veau,* you know," Panh continued congestedly, "the baby is coming. And what is following ze baby, that is in ze soup."

I thought for a moment and then understood: the soup's main ingredient was, as advertised, what follows the "veal" out of the birth canal: bovine afterbirth. Panh asked solicitously, "You would like to try it?"

"No, thank you," I said with all the grace I could muster. Instead of this item issued from a cow's vagina, I ordered instead for breakfast what had recently exited a chicken's cloaca: "I'll have eggs."

* * *

The previous day, we'd had ample opportunity to witness the eclectic Southeast Asian appetite, when we had strolled through the Lak Xao market in the golden afternoon light. Upon our arrival in the dusty, timber-boom town, we had first tried to visit General Cheng's menagerie, but were told that the animals there had been moved to another facility, which was closed until morning. The Lak Xao market, too, was winding down for the day, but still there were plenty of women beneath umbrellas in the dust, squatting before their dwindling stock: a handful of red chiles; a bowl of giant water bugs; a pile of snails; a small pyramid of tree fungus. A middle-aged woman in a conical hat was negotiating a sale with a much younger woman. She was selling roasted rats. The shopper, wearing a neat black and white *sin*, the traditional round, slim skirt common to Thailand and Laos, carefully inspected each of the carcasses, squeezing and probing them as if they were melons, to be sure to select the finest, the fattest, and the tenderest of the five rats on display to cook and feed to her family.

Another vendor, a woman in a green shirt, was selling smoked bats. They probably had lived in caves in the limestone karst whose jagged limestone cliffs we had passed earlier on our drive. Cave dwelling makes bats extremely vulnerable to overharvesting, because so many can be taken in a single evening, as they emerge en masse to feed. The IUCN wildlife report had mentioned its contributors saw large vats containing several hundred bats being cooked for sale at markets north of Vientiane, thousands being smoked at one village, and over three thousand of them sold to a single passing truck. "It seems likely," the report said, "that most species of cave-dwelling bats in Lao PDR have suffered very serious population declines over the past few decades."

Along with the bats, a smoked civet was for sale, its graceful, fluffy tail singed naked. Alive, civets are among the most appealing animals imaginable: lithe climbers, with soft fur adorned with bands or spots, they race up and down trees at night, their huge, light-gathering eyes set in inquisitive, catlike faces. This was probably a palm civet, among the commonest of the fewer than one dozen civet species in Southeast Asia—an animal the Chinese had called "wind-raccoon dog" because they move with such grace it was thought they waited for the wind to blow them to the next tree. We also saw tortoises for sale, and snakes, and other mammals whose bodies had been so hacked and charred that not even Gary could identify them.

"There seem to be few if any taxa of wild vertebrates not used by some (and in many cases, many) ethnic groups, be it for food, medicine, or in trade," the IUCN wildlife status report had told us. In fact, throughout Laos, most animal protein consumed—according to one survey, some 82 percent—comes from captured wildlife.

"The killing of wildlife in Laos was unlike anything I had seen elsewhere," reported Alan Rabinowitz, the biologist who led the WCS team on the first wildlife survey of the Annamites in 1993. "The skies were virtually empty of birds, and many of the rivers seemed to harbor only the smallest of fish." Hunters use every method imaginable: snare lines, nets, and traps; dogs, catapults, and crossbows; homemade black powder muskets and automatic and semiautomatic weapons; poisons and explosives hidden in baits. Children shoot squirrels out of trees with slingshots, and professionals hunt around the clock, exposing nocturnal species with powerful spotlights. Trees are felled to remove pangolins, lorises, monitor lizards. Trees with promising crevices are even felled speculatively. And while the widespread hunting of animals is a very ancient practice here, never before in history has there been such financial incentive to do so.

The sale of these wild animals, the report said, was the second biggest income earner for rural families after fishing. The trade grew exponentially in the late 1990s. "Trade is driven by entrepreneurs in response to market forces," we read. One researcher reported that on several occasions, he was told by Lao villagers that they would not hunt so much if the Vietnamese did not want to buy wildlife. As a result of both foreign and domestic hunting pressure, the report continued, "visitors from other countries in the region generally comment on the scarcity of wild birds, bats and other land vertebrates around Lao towns and villages." With neighborhood wildlife largely exhausted, the hunters turn to parks and sanctuaries for their larder. "No experienced wildlife observer can fail to notice the low densities of wildlife in Lao PDR's protected areas," the management plan for Nakai pointed out. "The intensity and efficiency of the hunting is quite remarkable."

On this one afternoon at the Lak Xao market, we caught but a tiny glimpse of the immense trade in wildlife. Because of its proximity to Vietnam, the Lak Xao market had once been notorious for its open sale of endangered species. International pressure had brought a crackdown. Unfortunately, as a result, "much activity became clandestine," our report noted. "It is now much more difficult to monitor the volume and species range of trade."

Knowing this tore at our hearts as we surveyed the market. We would look up from the corpses of slain animals to angelic faces. The vendors offered us beautiful, welcoming smiles, even though they surely realized there was little chance of selling us their bats or rats or smoked civets. One shopper pointed me out to her baby. I was probably one of the few Western women the mothers had ever seen. The infant stared at me wide-eyed, in the startled way all babies take in everything in the strange, hungry new world.

* * *

The clouded leopard sprang as if he were flying and caught the chicken in mid-air. He landed upside down, clinging by his claws to the wire mesh ceiling of his cage, pinning the dead bird that had been tossed to him between his teeth and the wire. Soon a thick orange fluid dripped down his black lips, staining his spotted chest. The hen had an egg inside her.

The leopard's name was George, the young woman who escorted us through the little zoo told us. She led us down the dirt paths that wound through jungle-like vegetation to introduce us to the inmates. Though the zoo was now open, the man who ran the place was not in that morning; we would meet him later that afternoon. Meanwhile, his assistant showed us the animals, although we were forbidden from taking pictures, or plucking any hair.

Next we came to a large cage of binturongs, including three young. They were so tame we could put our hands through the mesh and stroke them, and inhale their lovely, fruity musk. But the rest of the animals weren't so lucky. The zoo also had four masked palm civets in a cage so filthy that their feces had grown a coat of purple mold. Cages housing three leopard cats and a golden cat were also tiny.

The facility had once been supported by an American-based wildlife charity, Carnivore Preservation Trust. We had read about it in one of the reports. It said this zoo, which was supposed to be a breeding center for endangered carnivores, held sixty-seven individuals of nineteen species. Where, we wondered, had they gone?

Lastly we were led to the cages for the bears. Jim had visited four years ago, and told us there had been quite a few bears. The cages were tiny. Two sun bears were caged together, and a third, very thin, paced psychotically in his twelve by twelve-foot enclosure. "I don't have a good feeling about what happened to all those bears," Gary told me.

There was only one moon bear—a medium-sized adult male, who looked at us with benign interest as we approached his cage. Clearly he wanted to come over to the side of the cage and sniff us. But in horror, we soon realized why he did not: his hindquarters were paralyzed. He had been in this condition for a month, the zoo assistant said. Nobody knew what was wrong. He had not been seen by a vet.

Later, when we returned to meet with the manager, a pleasant young man named Kito Sihorat, we learned that in 1998 there had been nine bears. That year, the Carnivore Preservation Trust had withdrawn its support. "We don't have enough funds," he told us through Panh. "They ate the honey, the meal—now we don't have enough." Five bears had died of starvation. "At the moment," he said, "still alive are four." Gary and I gave him our last hundred-dollar bill and asked him to buy food for the animals.

* * *

Lak Xao, like many modern towns, was founded on appetite. Each side of the border hungers for the products of the other: Vietnamese want the wildlife and timber products of Laos. Laotians want the manufactured products from Vietnam. Laotians buy Con Soc (Squirrel Brand) batteries, and Vietnamese buy live and dead squirrels from Laos. Lak Xao had been carved out of the hills in the 1980s by Phoudoi, the military-controlled logging company—the only one in the country exempt from a logging ban enacted in 1991—to facilitate border trade with Vietnam. Phoudoi, it was clear, owns the town. We noted immediately the Phoudoi Hotel, the Phoudoi Restaurant, Phoudoi Transportation, Phoudoi Guest House. We learned that since the Carnivore Preservation Trust left, the timber concession had also taken over the zoo, where the animals were starving.

The town is full of machines. Chainsaws buzz, trucks roar, dust flies. Earthmoving equipment is everywhere, and sunbaked plastic bags spill like tumbleweeds across the treeless landscape, catching only on barbed-wire fencing surrounding pretentious cement homes. Lak Xao is an ugly place in a breathtakingly beautiful setting, a tumultuous commercial wound in a sanctuary that had served for eons as a refuge from turmoil.

Once we'd left Vientiane, we'd watched the landscape float by as if in a dream. Cement houses give way to stilts and thatch and bamboo; to fields recently cleared by fire; to wallowing water buffalo, their skins luscious with mud; to ponds abloom with pink lotus. This time of year is known as "the scented season," Panh told us, because so many flowers are in bloom. But gone, along with the stupefying heat, are the emerald fields of young rice of summer. It is the dry season now, and many of the trees' leaves have turned brown and fallen. When we got out of the car to stretch, the leaves crunched like potato chips beneath our feet.

At the wheel of our immaculate Toyota Prada (the Laotian brand name for the Land Cruiser) was Boun Jahn. Like Panh, he is originally from Louang Phabang. He is a much younger man, strong and burly, whose sparse hair stands out on the sides of his head like the spines on a hedgehog, or a durian. He speaks no English, and we no Lao, so we simply smiled and nodded at one another, hoping he knew how grateful we were for his skills. On he drove us along the winding roads, past startling, jagged limestone cliffs, like those on Chinese scroll paintings. Below us coursed the brown Nam Theun River, peppered with dugout canoes. Around us loomed a forest dark and deep: huge trees roped with lianas; bamboos, their stems and leaves in sprays as wide as fireworks; and the fluffy white seed heads of the grass the Lao use to stuff mattresses. Along one hairpin curve, Boun swerved to avoid a giant truck that had jackknifed and spilled its cargo, a yellow bulldozer, onto the side of the mountain below. Two men squatted in the shade of the fallen monster, playing cards.

"This is the kind of country that Cheminaud claims the dog bear lives in," said Gary. The scientist had painstakingly translated much of the French overseer's 239-page memoir *Mes Chasses au Laos* from the French: "This active, elongate, supple bear lives on the high plateaus of the annamite Cordillera, getting rarer to the south until it vanishes," the hunter wrote. "In the north . . . these bears can be hunted when they descend to the bases of plateaus during the dry-and-cold season between November and March. They are usually then seen in pairs, less often in small groups . . . Standing on two legs, this species is about the height of a small man. Its postures can resemble those of a dog. The black thick fur gleams . . ." Unlike the sun bear, the dog bear boasted large upright ears and a narrow face. In fact, Cheminaud said he had examined similar stuffed specimens in a Tashkent, Uzbekistan, museum, which had been labeled as moon bears, *Ursus thibetanus.* But the dog bear, he claimed, had shorter hair, and was also much smaller, scarcely attaining half the 140 kilos listed at the museum, with a mean length of a meter without the tail and a height of about .40 meters.

Is this the same dog bear the Hmong described to us? Is it a new species of bear? If so, why has it still remained undiscovered by science?

Maybe, ventured Gary, a few hundred thousand years ago, a third species of bear went extinct in the climatic fluctuations of the Pleistocene—everywhere but here.

"Most people think of the Pleistocene as the Ice Age," he explained. "But really, it was a time of great climatic change, not just cold." In Europe, true, the Pleistocene included periods so cold that great sheets of ice spread over much of the continent. But these glacial periods were interspersed with warm, wet times—called interglacials—during which tropical forests grew and spread for millennia, and along with them, animals we think of as tropical, too.

During one recent interglacial, a period known as the Eemian, a hundred thousand years ago, the world so warmed that hippos lounged in the Danube and Thames. Gigantic straight-tusked elephants, standing fifteen feet high at the withers, overran northern Europe; enormous cave lions spread from Africa into northern Asia, North America, and South America as far south as Peru. The moon bear then thrived as far into Europe as Germany, along with grizzlies and cave bears, and the beetle-browed Neanderthals may have hunted them with their fire-hardened yew spears.

But another glaciation soon followed. Much of the world's water was locked up in ice. The temperature change altered worldwide rainfall patterns. In Asia, the Tibetan Plateau and the Himalayas (which began to rise when the Indian subcontinent hit Eurasia in the Miocene, and are still rising today) created the updrafts that sculpt the monsoons; but during glaciations, these forces were disrupted and the life-giving southern monsoons failed. Cold, dry winds whipped up black blizzards across China. The Danube dried to a trickle, the hippos retreated, the cave lions vanished. In the tropics, thorn scrub grew where rain forests once flourished.

In the past million years, the world has undergone such sweeping turmoil some dozen times. The huge temperature changes were, in a way, the least disruptive of these transformations. Anything that survived the temperature and habitat changes also had to deal with the resultant disappearance of important food and prey items, and the invasion of new predators and competitors. It was not heat or cold that vanquished Neanderthal man during the minor glacial retreat between 40,000 and

30,500 years ago, but the arrival of Cro-Magnon man, the first Homo sapiens. With their invention of the atlatl, or spear-thrower, these invaders from the south outcompeted their predecessors. Homo sapiens alone, among the species of humans, survived through the next cold glaciation in Europe, the heyday of the European mammoths and reindeer.

Only a very resilient, adaptable fauna could survive such tremendous flux. Unless it could find a refuge to which to retreat and wait out the centuries-long storm.

Such a refuge, Asian wildlife experts believe, was the Annamite Mountains.

"This part of the world has persisted longer than most of the Amazon," Gary told me. "During much of the Pleistocene, much of the Amazon's present rain forest was grassland. But in the Annamites, the montane forests would have been large and resilient, and the bears would have found habitat."

Perhaps a new species of bear had arisen during one of the early glacial periods, when Southeast Asia's rain forests were fewer and farther apart, separated by vast oceans of scrub and grassland. "Barriers between the different populations, setting them apart, is what creates more speciation," Gary explained. "A little bit of climate change can promote diversity—too much, of course, and you lose what you have."

So the third kind of bear might have disappeared through most of its former range during one of the climatic upheavals. But it could have persisted here. Such is the theory explaining why the Sao la, the Vietnamese warty hog, the two new muntjacks, and the zebra-striped rabbit persisted here and only here.

On the other hand—and Gary always considered each new theory along with its opposite—perhaps the moon bears didn't make it to Southeast Asia until quite recently. Perhaps they had come in separate groups from different parts of Asia. After all, he pointed out, moon bears today have an enormous distribution. Unlike most other species of bear, the moon bear overlaps its range with many of its fellow ursines: sun bears, grizzlies, even pandas—even though those species each prefer different altitudes and habitats within the same general range. Moon bears could have entered Southeast Asia from almost any direction except the south.

"So much of this is intuitive," he said to me. For Gary, hypotheses seemed to wink on and off like fireflies. One idea would appear, and then, immediately, its opposite, yin and yang, darkness and light. "I agree with Robert Ardrey," Gary said: "A good scientist has the duty to be wrong. If you think about hypotheses, some of them are going to be wrong. If you're too scared to be wrong, you're never going to do anything important. And if you don't have hypotheses," he said, "it's impossible to interpret data—or at least that's what Sherlock Holmes says."

* * *

On the way to Lak Xao, we had stopped for lunch at the village of Ban Pakkading, at a tin-roofed outdoor restaurant serving fried vegetables and meat and rice, and sat beneath a great tree where women were selling dried fish, bananas, dried buffalo meat, and coconuts. Along the dirt path leading to the restaurant's latrine, I discovered a black-and-white sow who had given birth to her three piglets so recently that one of them was still covered in afterbirth. Two older, black piglets ran loose through the little dirt compound in back of the restaurant, among strutting turkeys, a stately white goose, and a curly-tailed, black-faced white dog. I raced back to interrupt Gary's lunch and show him the piglets. He watched them respectfully and with great concentration. When we got back in the car, the scientist said, "Seeing the pigs really helped."

Yes, I agreed: what could be more helpful, more jolly and uplifting, than the sight of a pig—the unlikely bulk mincing along on tiptoe hooves, a fat lady in high heels; the sensuous, flexible nose disk, capable of uprooting small trees with one gesture. And it is always delightful to watch a pig eat. What other event offers such a chance to see someone so thoroughly, so greedily engrossed in appetite? Pigs remind us of ourselves. Indeed, they are so like us their bodies are used to study human physiology, and their skin and the valves of their hearts are used for human transplants. The proto-Tai speakers of the lower Yangtze shared an appreciation of pigs; Jim's thesis mentioned a pig god, Chang Ta-Ti, worshiped in A.D. 265–317, as the creator of wet rice agriculture. Which, Jim pointed out, the pig was: by rooting in the low-lying swamplands, pigs in effect plowed the land for the farmers.

So for many minutes, it did not occur to me to ask Gary: what *specifically* had improved in his life due to seeing the pigs?

"Seeing that blunt snout," he told me, "now I can really see the pig analogy in sun bears."

But as we were to discover the next day, after I had finished my eggs at the Thippavangxay Restaurant, and George, the snow leopard, had finished his at the zoo, our original information about the pig bear turned out to be wrong—and learning this, our quarry transformed once again.

* * *

The first village we visited was a Hmong settlement of thirty-six families. It was a raw-looking, dusty little village, many of the stilt-houses new; the people had moved here only eleven years ago. "Always they move because of ze paddy field," explained Panh. "Maybe next step they move over here, or over here," he said, pointing to the forested hills where perhaps the last of the mystery bears still survived. Gary and I shuddered at the thought.

Jim had told us that the Hmong, while excellent hunters, were not great taxonomists. "The Hmong are newcomers," he reminded us. "They are very nice people, they are good hunters, but they're completely out of place here. I would view anything they tell you, taxonomically, as suspect. They hunt first and name later." But still we wanted to confirm what we had heard in Skokie and in northern Thailand.

Unlike the Lahu, the five young men who greeted us when we came to their village immediately recognized our pictures of the sun bear. But they called it *Dais dev*—dog bear. Immediately, too, they knew our picture of the moon bear—and this they called *Dais npuas*—pig bear. It was exactly the opposite of what we thought Shuttong Vang had said. If what they told us was true, the "new species" of bear was not the dog bear at all.

They hunted both kinds of bear, the men in short black pants told us. "Very good eating!" Panh translated. Everything, in fact, was good eating—everything except snakes, which they killed but did not eat, and baby mice. (The most terrible of evil spirits, they believe, the *dab quov av* or *dab ntxug,* live underground, and not infrequently assume the form of helpless baby mice if you happen to surprise them by turning up the stone underneath which they live. These are never killed, for if you do so, someone in your family will surely die.)

Our informants did not know of golden bears, and had never seen anything like the golden bears in our pictures. But they knew of another kind of bear, they said, though no one among them had ever seen it. They called it *Dais neng*—the horse bear—for it was a giant. It lived further north, in Xiangkhouang Province.

To thank them for their time, we gave the men each a pack of Camel cigarettes. They examined the drawing on the pack carefully and with much interest. "What sort of creature is this?" asked a balding man with gold teeth. "Where do you hunt it?" I pictured them setting snares in the jungle for Joe Camel.

* * *

"Giant bears," Gary said aloud to the empty room, as I came to retrieve him for dinner. Most of the time, when he's thinking like this, Gary is utterly silent. Once I had found him staring out the window of a hotel room. The window was curtained closed. Now, once again, I had come upon the professor lost in thought. What was he thinking?

"For months I have been thinking about pygmy bears," he told me. "Now, it looks like the third species, if there is one, is a giant."

During our first few days in Bolikhamxai Province, two Hmong villages plus a Hmong we met along the roadside had provided the same information. There were three kinds of bears. One was clearly the sun bear. Another was clearly our moon bear. And there was a third, much larger, as long as a horse and so heavy it took six to eight strong hunters to carry the corpse away.

Is it a new species? Or just a larger, montane form of the moon bear? Or perhaps just big, old males? This we don't know. The Hmong do not keep skins or skulls. It is possible that we already have the specimen we need: four samples taken from moon bears originally from Bolikhamxai Province are now at Lisette's lab, awaiting analysis, which might prove so different from the others as to constitute a third species, or a subspecies.

Even the giant bear's meat is different, we were told by one informant, Yawnu, thirty-nine, from the village of Ban Phon Saat, whose father had killed one some years ago. The gall is superior, too, he told us: not only does it supply enough bile to fill a beer can but it is more curative, he insisted, than the gall from the sun or moon bear. It lived on Phou Viang Mountain. There was once a road there, but it washed out. Jim Chamberlain later told us this might be a mountain about a day's walk from the Hmong and Liha villages we had visited the day before.

Does this bear still exist there today? Oh yes, our informant assured us. Just two years ago, when the Hmong were clearing new land for their cornfields, they found its footprints. They are unmistakably huge. He looked around for something for a size comparison. He settled on Gary's size-ten Converse All-Stars. "They are as big as that!" Panh translated, as we all—all but Gary—marveled at the unfathomable enormity of the feet of both the giant bears and the silver-haired Western scientist.

Other than the Hmong, none of the other villagers in the province knew of the giant horse bear. Interestingly, when we asked about bears, the other villagers had told us to ask the Hmong—they were the best hunters, everyone seemed to agree. But what the others had to tell us spoke eloquently, and elegiacally, of the fate of species known and unknown, and the fate of the people themselves.

* * *

The *pii-com-coy* is invisible, but you can hear him: "Chap! Chap! Chap! Cong! Cong! Cong!" the creature calls in the night. Even if you have already made camp, even if your nighttime fire is already blazing, if you hear it, you should move on. If you stay, the *pii-com-coy* will eat you, the young Liha warned us. And he knew the *pii-com-coy* was real; he had heard its eerie calls himself, just this year, as he had camped near its lair, in a cave near water in the mountains.

You must be careful not to disturb the spirits of the forest, the men of Ban Houa Khan told us. Besides the *pii-com-coy,* who is invisible, there is another greatly feared monster, the *pii-nya-why.* It looks rather like an ordinary gibbon, but you can be sure it's a spirit, all right: this creature cannot be killed—not even with an AK-47! And if you anger him, he will create storms and wind, rain, and darkness. He lives in the mountains, and the people are careful not to invade his forest home. Even now, the men told us, if you go to that big mountain, the *pii-nya-why* will see you. "The wind and rain comes," Panh translated, blowing smoke like a magician, "and it will be like night."

To the Liha, the forest is more than one great grocery store, a source of income or a repository of resources to serve their appetites. The forest is a place of mystery and inspiration, alive with its own appetites and desires. Long ago, before the people lived in the village, the Liha had lived as hunter-gatherers, Panh explained to us. He knew because he had been to this village before. In fact, Ban Houa Khan had been one of the very first villages he and Jim had visited on their expedition to the Annamites four years earlier. Panh received a warm welcome when we alighted from our car in the neat, pretty settlement, with its stilt homes walled with woven bamboo, set among trees whose leaves can be brewed for tea, little gardens and dirt paths and peeping chicks. We took off our shoes, climbed the ladder, and were welcomed into the great room of one of the larger stilt houses, where a woven cradle hung from a rafter, corn dried above the hearth, and black iron kettles were stacked neatly by the fire.

We asked what bears the people knew. They described the sun and moon bears. They like to eat both of them, they told us, especially relishing the paws. They used the gall for medicine. We asked if they had any stories about bears to tell us and they said no. Was there a bear spirit? I wondered.

"Our spirit animal is the dhole," one of our informants, Pho Phay, sixty, told us through Panh. This Panh already knew, for it was here that he and Jim had collected the one surviving myth possibly common to all the Vietic peoples—one that Jim determined was the key to understanding Vietic culture. The myth, as Jim tells it in his report, goes like this:

"Most people died, but there was one old man who had lived three hundred years and still had not died. So they (the ones who had died) went up to Mphloey (the chief heavenly spirit) and complained that they were always dying whereas there was one old man who had lived three hundred years and was still alive.

"So Mphloey sent three children down from heaven to inquire after the old man. They went and found him fishing.

"'Hey, old man,' they asked, 'have you ever seen stones floating upward?'

"'Ohhh, you youngsters,' he answered, 'I am more than one hundred years old and still haven't seen this.'

"'Are you the one who is three hundred years old?'

"'Yes, that's me.'

"'Then, come with us.'

"But first, the old man had to see after his companions, a dog and a chicken: 'I must take my dog and chicken home first.'

"The heavenly children would not wait. But they asked him what they should do to look after the animals.

"'No one must destroy my dog and chicken,' he replied. 'Whoever shoots them will get impetigo; if you shoot and miss, may your flesh rot. Do not shoot them; do not hit them. Let them go.'

"The people took the old man away. He did not return home. But to this day, the dhole and the crow cannot be killed or eaten."

* * *

Because the myth may be common to all the Vietic groups, Jim had told us, it speaks to us across the ages of an ancient and sacred relationship between animals and hunter-gatherers. It is a tale that tethers the people to each other, to the animals of the forest, and to the nourishing abundance of the Earth. The tale tells us of animal powers: in it, the dhole is no less than the intermediary between life and death, transforming living creatures into food for the people. The crow is his sacred emissary. To forget this, as the old man warns, is to incur grave consequences.

And those consequences, we were to learn, are already upon us.

For centuries, the myth has served the people, reminding them who they are; and it has helped the dholes, too. These foxlike wild dogs, with their bushy, black-tipped tails and reddish coats, have been persecuted to near extinction almost throughout their enormous range, from West Asia to China, India, Indochina to Java. Most hunters consider them rivals, for they are highly efficient killers. Two or three dholes can kill a 110-pound deer within two minutes, attacking from behind and disemboweling the prey. Dholes usually hunt in family packs, usually five to twelve animals but sometimes up to forty, keeping together by communicating constantly by whines, growls, screams, shrieks, and whistles. They are excellent swimmers who often chase their prey to water. They will take down deer, pigs, antelopes, even animals as big as the buffalo-like gaur. And some say they will even kill tigers, leopards, and bears. In the dholes, the Vietic people have found creatures well worthy of emulation: they are brave and strong, honor family ties, and have learned to cooperate among themselves to survive.

Gary and I would have loved the chance to spot a dhole. Could any of the villagers here take us to see some?

"Before, there were a lot in this area," Me Phay, fifty, told us through Panh. "There were fifty of them living near some years ago," he said. Many different animals—tigers, bears, deer—used to inhabit the forests here, he said. "Now, we don't know where they live. We live in a society where buffalo are killed, and dholes would kill the buffalo too. And so the dholes have disappeared."

Again and again, at village after village, we heard different versions of the same story: as wildlife diminished, as the forest shrank, as war nipped at their heels and the dam's apocalyptic construction approached, the people diminished too. Not that their numbers were shrinking; in fact, except for the hunter-gatherers, most of the human population of Nakai was growing, we had read in our reports. But their knowledge, their languages, their traditions, their connection to the earth, their sacred compacts with the animals—all were falling away. Increasingly, we had the feeling that we had arrived during the sunset of these cultures, and that soon, the people would find themselves enveloped by the dark.

At Ban Phon Txai, a Tai Meuai village of forty-six homes, a very old, very thin man with a crew cut and few teeth told us that the people name their clans after animals. His family name was Tuong Lo, after the Tuong Lo bird, with its crest of black-and-white feathers. Other families were named after the tiger, or the monitor lizard, and those clans considered these animals the founders of their lineage. They would not hunt or eat their ancestors. "You respect these creatures as if they're your family," he told us. But he could not remember the stories of how these animals founded the lineages. The people and the animals could once talk, he told us. But what they said to one another, he said, no one could now recall . . .

Gary and I wondered if perhaps the people simply didn't want to tell us their stories. After all, we were strangers, and we were asking them to share with us some of the deepest aspects of their culture. Perhaps they said they did not remember only because they were too polite to tell us to buzz off. Sometimes the people were visibly nervous about talking with us. Because of our pale skins and foreign ways, they feared we might have been sent by the "authorities"—the people who planned to flood the villages in a few short years, the people who were ferreting out insurgents. "I tell you, this district one week ago, they were fighting over here, the *resistance*," Panh told us, in an accent that sang "*Allons enfants de la patrie,*" "this is not one hundred percent safe."

Generally, though, when they learned we only wanted to talk about animals, the people welcomed us into their stilt houses to sit beside their fires with them as they struggled to recall what was once central to their lives. But over and over again, in response to our questions, people answered like head-injury victims, vaguely aware they were suffering from some terrible loss, but unable to recall what it was, or even remember how they lost it. Again and again we heard these words: "We do not remember."

*   *   *

The people of Ban Nalie belong to an ethnic group called T'en. The people of the village have distinctive and beautiful pink, round faces. The girls wear long, dangling gold earrings.

"Before," Mo Vong, sixty-two, tells us through Panh as we sit by his fire, "we don't eat the elephant, the tiger, or the bear. Because it was sacred wildlife." But now the people have begun to eat everything. Bun Mee, another village elder, tells us he remembers when bears used to come, to raid the corn in his village. But that was when he was a child. "Now you have to go very far to see bears—to the mountain," he said. In fact, the men gathered at the fireside agreed, all the wildlife is disappearing. Even the *pii-nya-why* and the *pii-com-coy* don't live here anymore.

Mo Vong is one of two shamans, or *Maw*, in the village, and among his duties is to differentiate when a patient has an illness caused by hungry spirits, or an illness that can be healed with herbs. One way to tell is by consulting a set of twenty-nine bamboo sticks Panh called *siem*. Mo Vong shows us some: they are longer than Mo Vong's hands, but they remind me of his fingers, gnarled and dark, they look so much a part of him. To heal an illness, he told us, first you get a shirt from the sick person, a candle, a mirror and some cigarettes, some money and flowers. You make a prayer to the spirits. Then you sort the sticks—almost like shuffling cards, as he shows us—and divide them into three groups, each held between the fingers of one hand. One group of sticks tells of the health of the heart; another of the health of the feet; another of the health of the spirit. The number of sticks that ends up between each group of fingers is guided by the spirit, and tells you the answer you need. It takes many years to learn to read the siem, he tells us, and he is very old. Does he have a young apprentice? we ask. No, he tells us. So who will read them for the villagers when he is gone? This he doesn't know.

The T'en have their own written language, he tells us by his fire. But there is only one book. Would we like to see it? He descends the ladder stairs to fetch it for us.

When he returns, he is bearing an ordinary schoolchild's "One Hundred Pages" brand paper and cardboard notebook. In bold blue script, the last surviving words in the native language have been written in ink by his teacher, a man now long dead. This, he tells us, is the only existing copy.

The book is sacred, he tells us. His eyes loom large and bleary behind thick glasses, and he begins to read aloud. The words are difficult for him; he reads falteringly. He does not read the book often, he explains.

What do the words tell us? At first, in translation, the purpose of the book is unclear. Is it a prayer? Is it a history? Actually it is both, and more. The book, we finally discern with Panh's help, is read at a funeral ceremony, after a buffalo has been killed to nourish the soul along the journey on which it is about to embark. The words in the book, though, are even more critical to the soul than the spiritual meat of the buffalo: this is the set of directions the soul must carefully follow on its long, dangerous quest after death into the afterlife.

The words of the book tell the spirit how to find his way back to the ancestral homeland, Mung Kell-eh—a place somewhere along the Vietnamese and Chinese borders. Only if the dead person can find Mung Kell-eh can he complete his pilgrimage, retracing his ancestors' steps, as they had come from there to Thanh Hoa in Vietnam, and then to Laos. And only then can the soul ascend to Then-Chao, or heaven, and from there help look after his descendants on earth. Without the book's instructions, not only the dead person but also his descendants would suffer.

Without the book, the soul would be literally lost.

And this is the only copy. One tippy cup of tea, one rainstorm, one fire, could obliterate the words from the pages. But the equivalent catastrophe is already under way.

Mo Vong is one of only two people in the village who knows how to read the ancestral language. The other is a person nearly as aged as he. No one else wants to learn the language—not even the four surviving children of his original nine.

"Everyone reads and writes in Lao now," Thao My, another village elder with a neat gray crew cut, explains.

Literacy in Lao was one of the gifts of progress the government and foreign charities wished to bestow on the tribal people. But it is one of many such programs that has backfired miserably, Jim had told us. "Education doesn't prepare you for everything," Jim said. There was one profession for which literacy seemed important in some of these remote Annamite villages, he said: the educated women from the minority ethnic groups were able to become highly successful prostitutes. "These women were in school so much, they lost the opportunity to learn from the village elders," he said. "They were then lured into prostitution, and not unwillingly. They were learning to speak Lao so they could speak to the customers. All the girls had completed secondary school."

But the government and charities insisted that people needed this sort of formal education—like they needed hospitals. But actually, "These people would rather die in their village than go to a hospital," Jim had said. And we knew, from the Hmong, that that was true.

The problem, Jim had told us, was that government and charities, however well intentioned, did not understand the cultures they were trying to "help." They did not understand that in many cases, instead of meeting existing needs, they were creating new ones. "They've equated subsistence with poverty—and not without help from the World Bank and the IMF (International Monetary Fund)," Jim said. "But for many of the Lao and other ethnic groups, enough is sufficient. Why would you want more?" Such had been the case in Cambodia, too: the author of a book published in 1970 had reported with amusement what one farmer said to a group of U.S. aid workers trying to persuade him to raise more rice per paddy with their modern methods. "I have enough for my family," the man replied. "I have seen the King, and he looks well fed, so he must have enough, too. Why bother with more?"

But to Western minds, if you live with just enough of everything, there's something wrong. Enough is not enough, says the voice of progress, the World Bank, the antipoverty charities: you need more! "So the World Bank comes in and says, 'Let us help you.' The villages get electricity, and the people see television. They see these things on TV and now they want them," Jim had told us. "And now you have poverty where there was none before."

Not all the fruits of Western progress are evil, of course. Many are wondrous: were it not for his eyeglasses, for instance, Mo Vong could not read the sacred words of his teacher today. Organizations like CARE save lives by bringing vaccines, vitamins, and emergency rations during famine. Perhaps they could have saved the five children whose deaths Mo Vong still mourns. But even the most high-minded of charities can err dangerously. In seeking to eliminate hunger, they may instead create new appetites.

Westerners see Laotians living in houses made by hand, eating food grown from seed, their children taught by village elders, and their sick doctored in their own homes by learned shamans and cured with plant medicines—and they feel sorry for them. I remembered what an aid worker stationed in Laos had told Stan Sesser, the author of an article on Laos titled "Forgotten Country," which ran in the *New Yorker* magazine: "Life is a struggle," he said. To illustrate this to a fellow Westerner, whose computer-centered culture increasingly imprisons its workers in glass and steel boxes for eight, ten, or twelve hours a day, the aid worker continued the lament: for these Laotians, "most of one's labor [is] consumed in monotonous tasks like carrying water, pounding husks off the rice, and hoeing the soil." Ironically, I would later read in the *New York Times* travel section that city workers are now increasingly seeking vacations on working farms—paying for the chance to help with the daily chores much like those the aid worker found so odious.

And I remembered a story I had read in *The Same Ax, Twice: Restoration and Renewal in a Throw-Away Age*. It is a book about America's hunger to reclaim what our culture is losing: the grace of old houses, the solace of open spaces, the darkness of the night skies, the silences and natural sounds that are now largely obliterated by the noise of machines. In it is a story taken from the Tao, the holy book of a branch of Buddhism based on the teachings of a sixth century B.C. Chinese philosopher.

A learned master, walking in the country with his disciples, came upon a man toiling to water his garden, hauling jars of water from a well. The master told him he should use a shadoof—a wonderful new invention, a long pole weighted at one end to dip a water bucket at the other end with great ease. With the shadoof, he could irrigate a hundred gardens with less effort than he used on one!

But the old gardener only laughed at the master's suggestion. He knew of the new water-moving contrivance, and he chose not to use it. He had learned that such a thing would only impair his spiritual growth. He lived his life in pursuit of "pure simplicity," in accordance with the teachings of the Tao: "When pure simplicity is impaired," he told the master, "the spirit becomes unsettled, and the unsettled spirit is not the proper residence of the Tao."

The learned master was humbled into silence.

*   *   *

Mo Vang closed the pages of the sacred book and smoothed the cardboard cover with his long, aristocratic brown fingers. "I try to teach our language," Mo Vong lamented, "and the young people say why?"

"We are a new generation," Thao My told us solemnly. "We know nothing now."

CHAPTER FIFTEEN

The Coming Flood

Back when the animals and people could talk, Xieng Xioang told us through Panh, a bear used to come and raid the corn the Brou people had planted.

"Why do you eat our corn so much?" the people asked the bear. "You should pay us something to compensate us!"

"But I have nothing," said the bear.

A year later, the bear returned to the cornfield, now with her cub. This time, the people captured her baby. They planned to keep the cub till she was big and then eat her. But as the little bear grew up in the village, the people began to change their minds. The adopted cub never hurt the village children. She didn't even steal food, but waited politely for the people to bring her meals to her. Everyone was impressed with the little bear's intelligence as well as her gentleness. Because the people had the chance to live with a bear among them, they came to understand something they hadn't known before, Xieng Xioang said: "A bear," he told us, "is just like a person." And that's why the Brou don't hunt bears anymore.

Xieng Xioang knew much about the Brou, as well as the other people here. A Phong speaker, he grew up in this district, in a stilt house his parents made by hand, where everyone farmed rice, corn, and tapioca and fished with bamboo spears and nets woven of palm fiber. He knows everyone, Jim had told us: they had worked together on the Nakai-Nam Theun survey. Xieng Xioang would be able to translate languages that Panh could not, and also he would know the current road conditions and which villages we could most productively visit. His help would be crucial, as we had only tomorrow left before we would have to leave the Annamite Mountains.

Although meeting up with Xieng Xioang had been uncertain—he is often away for days, in the forest visiting different villages—the hope that we could find him was the reason for our long drive south to the Nakai Plateau. Although the town of Nakai is only fifty-six kilometers away, we had driven all day from Lak Xao, taking a circuitous route because the direct road was washed out. Panh, Gary, and I had loud, dramatic colds by now. Panh was still ceaseless in his smoking, but when he would get out of the car, he would pause to clear his sinuses by discreetly blotting one nostril with a thumb and shooting the contents of the other to the ground. Lacking his talent, I filled the backseat of the Prada with piles of sodden Kleenex, and sucked foul-smelling lozenges to ease my sore throat. Gary's cold was characterized by what we called a "turbo sneeze." It came on without warning, usually outdoors, often in response to sunlight, and resulted in a sound so impressive and flamboyant that I would often involuntarily step aside as if I might be blown off balance by its stormy gust. Through all this, though, our driver, Boun Jahn was miraculously unscathed.

Although we arrived in the town of Nakai tired and sick, locating Xieng Xioang gave us a lift. We were lucky to find him: he was chief of the Service of Labor and Social Security in Khammouan Province. Xieng Xioang was much in demand now that the dam was under construction and 4,300 villagers would need to be relocated. But when we first met him, I was certain he could not be our man: Jim had told us the guy was more than sixty years old. Instead of a venerable-looking elder, we met a small, smiling, handsome man wearing a blue Nike jacket, with jet-black hair and a full set of strong, white teeth. The only evidence suggesting he might be more than thirty were wrinkles that blossomed at the edge of his eyes when he smiled, which was often.

Xieng Xioang was obviously thrilled to see Panh again. So, although Gary was eager to pepper our host with bear questions, and I was hungry for his stories, we let the two friends catch up. Together they spoke in Lao, as we shared dinner that evening at a little restaurant along the side of the road.

Nakai has a raw, masculine, Wild West feel. Like the American West during its period of "settlement," this is an area in the process of being overrun by speculators, many of them foreign, some of them outlaws. It's a town filled with men and heavy equipment for building the dam, and for taking out the trees that will soon be flooded—and probably many trees that wouldn't. On the drive here, we had passed dozens of trucks heading in the opposite direction, laden with huge logs. When we arrived in the dusty, barren town, one of the logging trucks was broken down at the side of the road. A quick count of the tree rings showed the severed trunks had belonged to trees at least 150 years old.

The restaurant where we ate was surely the Laotian equivalent of a saloon, but instead of swinging saloon doors, a single curtain stood between diners and the red dust of the road. As we walked in through the curtain, a dog walked out, exactly like a human patron. Inside, it was loud and smoky. Several dogs and one puppy patrolled the dirt and cement floor for scraps. I was the only female patron. The male diners talked and drank and smoked as taped Thai music played and a soft-porn video showed slender Asian women who had somehow acquired enormously fat breasts.

The restaurant, like most of the other buildings in this town, was indeed hastily erected, to serve the loggers and truckers and consultants working on the dam. It is one of the biggest growth projects Laos has ever undertaken. Its supporters see it as a remedy for poverty. "Lao PDR is a poor, sparsely populated country, having a rugged terrain, limited infrastructure, and a weak manufacturing base," the World Bank report on the project explains. It then details the litany of Laos's economic woes: subsistence agriculture, a "weak human resource base," increasing inflation, depreciating currency, declining tax revenues. "The country's growth prospects," read the report, "depend to a large extent on the pursuit of sound macro-economic policies, and the sustainable development of the two main resources available to it—timber and hydropower."

With help from the World Bank, a foreign consortium is assisting in the construction and operation of the $1.3 billion project: Électricité de France, Transfield Holdings Ltd. of Australia, and three Thai companies. We met a Bangkok-based Nepali survey consultant at the restaurant who saw the project as little more than a money-grab. He, too, mourned the logs leaving the forest, the villages that would be obliterated by the flood.

"Here in this country, when I see it, it is a pity," he said in perfect, British-accented English. "Everyone wants the pocket to be heavy. The money you get today is the benefit. It is terrible to see it."

We seemed to be a long way from any place or time that the animals and people could talk.

*   *   *

"Eh!" With this incoherent complaint, I roused the scientist from sleep at 2 A.M. As Gary's eyes flew open, I announced to him, "There are ants all over the toilet seat!"

Our last day in the Annamites had begun inauspiciously.

We had spent the night at a picturesque lodge. It had been built, we were told, for a Thai princess. Intricately carved, throne-sized teak chairs and huge coffee tables face the dirt road from the front porch. The view from the back porch was spectacular, overlooking a stream crossed by a bridge also built in her honor. For the moment, the bridge was prevented from collapse by three poles propped against its listing side, placed in the shimmering water.

"The princess, she stayed one night only," Panh told us. That was ten years ago. It appears that may have been the last time the place was cleaned. Gary and I were allotted a little suite of two adjoining rooms and a shared bath, through which roaches audibly scuttled. There was electricity but no running water; to flush the Western-style toilet, you had to scoop water out of a tile basin and dump it in with a bucket. There was no sink. Hanging on a nail was a black beach towel of dubious history and on a teak dresser, a used toothpick. That the roaches had not eaten the mouth detritus still clinging to it suggested the toothpick was of recent vintage.

I'd been wakened in the middle of the night by the pain from my worsening sore throat. Unable to do anything about it, I thought I might as well get up and pee. When I flicked on the fluorescent light in the bathroom, however, the idea lost its appeal. The toilet seat was crawling with many dozens of enormous black ants, running around and around.

Both the thought of nearly having sat on the ants, and the question of what might have attracted them to the toilet seat in the first place, made my original errand lose its urgency. I decided now to share my latest natural history observation with the sleeping scientist.

Gary's reply came instantly, with clarity and resolve, and not a trace of irritation. "I will kill them," he said, and the biologist in shining armor went to work.

*   *   *

When I next awoke, I had better news to share. "I think I am getting better!" I announced to Gary, as if bestowing a thank-you gift for his chivalry. Though his cold was surely uncomfortable, he never complained about it, but worried constantly about Panh's and mine.

"I've heard that before," Gary answered skeptically. In fact, I had repeated that phrase like a mantra every day for the past three. Prior to this, I had insisted "I'm not getting sick." I could no longer hold on to this particular fiction, now that my every cough was followed by an involuntary moan. Two days later, after Gary had shined a flashlight down my raw throat to reveal it was red, swollen, and spangled with white spots, he took me to a Bangkok hospital where we discovered I had strep, and where I was issued an antibiotic so powerful it killed off my gut flora for six months.

But in the meantime, I'd tried to treat my ailment with *Tom Yum Pla*, the spicy fish soup that I not so much tasted as applied, like a poultice, to my mouth and throat. I ate it for breakfast, lunch, and dinner, and for several hours afterward it obliterated all pain, as well as all taste and feeling, and my mouth would run with saliva like blood gushing from a wound.

My sore throat was an apt metaphor for my frustration. As a writer, words are my only power; now I felt powerless in so many ways. Everything seemed tragic and disjointed: the paralyzed moon bear at the zoo owned by the logging company, the T'en people's vanishing language—they characterized the state of the forest and the cultures here, increasingly paralyzed and silenced by the encroaching hand of modern greed.

And again, it felt like everything was going wrong. If there was a new species of bear in the Annamites, it might have been represented by the poor, paralyzed animal at the zoo owned by Phoudoi. But we had not been allowed to pluck hairs from him, even though due to his tameness and disability this would have been all too easy. And now, although we had found Xieng Xioang, he told us at breakfast that we could not make it to the place where the Mlengbrou lived, the group I was especially eager to visit. It was three days' walk from here. Panh, sick and easily winded from four decades of chain-smoking, certainly could not have made the walk; further, it would not have been ethical to bring an unknown sickness to a remote people; and besides, we would soon have to return to the States.

But we did have this day. And thanks to Xieng Xioang, we made the most of it.

The animals may no longer talk to people, Xieng Xioang told us at breakfast, but they still speak among themselves. At least that is the legend that he learned as a child, as he told us at breakfast. For instance, gibbons, monkeys, and the slim-bodied leaf-eating langurs are constantly communicating, as if the three species were all part of an extended family. How do the people know? When the gibbon sees food, he calls—and the monkeys and langurs come running through the trees to share the bounty.

In fact, all the different animals talk together—all but the tiger and the banteng, he told us. They fight with everything! But the legends say that even the tiger obeys the laws of the forest, laws that have been worked out among all the animals. The laws, he explained, keep things in balance: "And here is the proof: if the tiger ate all the wildlife, everything would be finished," Panh translated. "Inside the jungle, if there is a salt lick, there you can see all wildlife there together. Animals, they sometimes fight each other, but always there is a balance. For here, they do not fight, and you may even see tiger and deer together, proof there is a law."

The people, too, once took part in a compact among creatures, he told us. For instance, his people—his mother was an ethnicity he called Kri Phong, and his father, Kri Ngum—came to an agreement long ago. After discussing the matter with the animals, all the parties agreed that the horse, the elephant, and the buffalo would live with the people and help them with their daily lives. The fish volunteered to be the food of the people, so his people became skilled fishermen. "And the tiger, the snake, and the dhole said nothing," he told us through Panh. "This is why the snake, tiger, and dhole are never mixing with people at all."

His people long believed they were the older brothers of the animals, as well as all the other people. A flood myth similar to the Jewish and Christian tale of Noah's Ark pervades many Southeast Asian cultures, in which the people took refuge from the rising waters not in a boat but inside a huge vegetable. In the Kri version, when the water subsided, his people were the first to come out. Because they were first, they were like elders: it was their job to look after those who followed. So the Kri have an ancient tradition of nonviolence toward all other creatures.

Panh corroborated this. "I remember during the French period. When the Kri went into the military, they never went to the field to fight. The grandfathers told them to shoot into the air instead."

But the draft in 1950 brought a change to the culture. The boys drafted into the army were given meat in their rations. At first they were disgusted, Xieng Xioang said. But there was little other food, so they ate what they were given, and gradually they acquired an appetite for animal flesh. "When they came home, they wanted meat," he said. By 1960, everyone in his village ate meat.

There have been many changes since then, he told us. But our cheerful companion was sanguine about change. After all, he has attained a position of high status in the district government. His four sons have all survived. Three are farmers, one is in the army. "Before," translated Panh, "the ancestors knew this was our area. We who stay here, we know how to behave. But now, there is a mix between. The ancestors did not want contact between the different people. Now the ancestors do not speak to us. But today, we are happy. We criticize the ancestors. We used to have to move around and live in the jungle. We are happier now."

But such was not the case at the villages we visited together later that day.

The thirty-seven Brou-speaking families of Khon Kene village have lived here for more than four generations—fishermen, farmers, and hunters. Fishing nets hang inside the neat thatched-roofed stilt homes. They tend to spend more time in the forest than at home, they told us through Xieng Xioang and then through Panh. But this month, December, is the time to stay home; it is the time they burn the fields. We had seen no animals, not even birds, on our long, bumpy drive to the village; but the forest around them, they said, is still full of life. They did not know golden bears, nor did they know of the Hmong's giant mountain bear, but they did know of two kinds, they told us: the larger, the moon bear, called *Jack!-ow*; and the smaller, the sun bear, *Jack!-EE-ow*. Less than a kilometer from this house, a bear came to eat nuts called *co nom* just last year.

The two hundred people of the village like it here, they told us. No one remembers any other home. They don't want to leave; but what can they do? The government people have told them their village will be wiped out in the flood once they build their dam.

"They came to talk with us about it so many times!" one of the men complained to us through our translators. "But that didn't change anything." They will still have to move.

Ban Bouama, too, a village of both Brou and Tai-Bo people, will also disappear in the flood. We drove for an hour along a bumpy track from

Khon Kene to get there, Boun Jahn skillfully crossing several shallow rivers in the Prada. The village has been here more than thirty years. Most of the stilt houses are thatched, but some have shingles; a few have metal roofs. Some are decorated with gifts from previous visitors. The home in which we sat and talked boasted a "Bye, Bye, Polio!" poster as well; all of the children had been immunized. There was also a poster from the Center for Protected Areas and Watershed Management, featuring pictures of endangered animals—animals who will lose their homes, too, when one quarter of the Nakai Plateau is flooded by the dam waters.

The people of Ban Bouama were exceptionally welcoming. They shook our hands with both of theirs outstretched. They seemed delighted to talk with us about animals, and viewed Gary's Rogues' Gallery of Bears with great interest. And one of them immediately recognized the photos of the golden bears.

A Brou wearing a checkered shirt had seen a golden bear in November 1992, he told us. It was at the top of a mountain in Xiangkhouang Province, on the border between Laos and Vietnam, when he had been there with the army. It was a big one, he said—he estimated that if they shot it, it would take more than two strong men to carry it away. But they didn't shoot it, even though they all had guns. They ran away!

"What is this animal?" he had asked his comrades. Villagers at the nearby Hmong village of Ban Tong Peuk later told him it was a particularly dangerous kind of bear. If you shoot it and it doesn't die, they said, it will attack you.

They had never seen a golden bear near this village, though, they told us. They had both sun and moon bears living nearby, which they clearly identified from our picture book. They knew a lot about them: they described the sun bears as the more tree-loving of the two types. They knew when the mothers first brought the babies out of the den: June or July. They knew the bears sometimes built "nests" in the trees. And they described how the bears loved to eat honey, and how when the bees would sting them, the bears seemed impervious, except for the sensitive nose.

The people, too, love honey, they told us. They use smoke to drive the bees away from the nest, so as not to kill them. They also make a prayer to the *pii* or spirit of the tree where the bees live, and offer some of the honey to the *pii* afterward. Likewise, they make an offering—alcohol, plus a sacrificed chicken and pig—to the *pii* of a field before they clear it. They are aware of displacing other lives in order to assuage their own needs, and the *pii* have taught them it is morally necessary to atone for this. Spirits are around all the time, they told us, even though you don't see them. But the *pii* see you, and if you do not behave properly they will retaliate. Sometimes they will send a tiger to discipline the people for wrongdoing.

Like Xieng Xioang's people, they, too, had a legend that the people and the animals could once talk. And remembering this, though they hunt many animals, they honor the compact among the creatures. They never kill a bird who is sitting on eggs. They do not cut down trees to collect the fruit. They do not kill any animal during its birthing season. Why? we asked. "The mother, the father is angry," Panh translated for us after Xieng Xioang. "Please, generosity: you would not want someone to kill your baby!"

What will happen when they move to the new place? we asked. Where would the *pii* who advise them go after the flood? "Perhaps," one of the men told us, laughing, "the *pii* will take a helicopter."

* * *

At the end of the day, we said our grateful good-byes to Xieng Xioang and dropped him off at his office near town. We left Nakai at sunset, in a cloud of brownish dust.

Like the way your vision slowly browns out before you faint, the dust blurred and effaced everything: the jagged limestone mountains, the green flesh of the trees' leaves; the plastic chairs and plastic tablecloths inside the little cement and dirt-floored restaurants; the men trying to repair their broken-down logging truck.

The road, and its dust, seemed to be acting like a giant, dirty eraser: it smeared the outlines of the ducks and chickens in the road, the shapes of the trees and houses. Because of the dust, you could hardly see the glow of the people's fires outside the houses along the road; you no longer felt the shock of seeing so many severed and blackened tree limbs. Perhaps the dust was erasing everything: even the memories of the time when the animals could talk, even the powers of the *pii* and the voices of the ancestors. . . .

No, I thought; the dust does not erase, exactly; it clouds, it blurs, it confounds—like smoke from an opium pipe. The effect, rather than erasure, is to make you think, for a dangerous moment, that you no longer care what is dirty.

*   *   *

But before we left the Nakai Plateau, we begged Xieng Xioang and Panh to let us take a walk in a forest. Boun Jahn drove us to a parklike setting beside a sign reading "Nakai-Nam Theun National Biodiversity Conservation Area." After a five-minute stroll through a very young forest of regenerating saplings, our path was blocked by several cut trees. Here Panh let us go ahead, so he could enjoy another cigarette and talk with Xieng Xioang.

Within a few minutes we passed through an area that Gary called "the Doorway." Once through, suddenly we were in real forest. It was young; the oldest trees were perhaps only a hundred years old, and among them, we found burned stumps and banana trees, evidence of recent cultivation. Panh later told us that only three years before was this area added to the larger protected area. But instantly, once through the Doorway, as if at the behest of some cool, green goddess, the temperature dropped ten degrees. The air smelled for the first time not of dust but of life. The vegetation was now luxuriant: everywhere, the precise triangulated leaves of bamboo, the graceful tracery of vines, the embrace of living wood and breathing leaves soothed our souls.

It was quite different from anywhere else we had visited in the Annamites. We stood quietly and soon understood why: for the first time on the trip, we now heard the voices of birds. They twittered and chattered, uttering waving notes as if from the throats of flutes. It was as if they were singing the melody called forth by the leaves themselves. We counted eight distinct bird calls within a space of five minutes, and spotted some of the singers: one was a drongo, an elegant, insect-eating bird with long, elaborate tail feathers whose shafts are bare of barbs except at the tip, here called *Nok-Say-ow*.

Gary and I waited and let the music refresh us. Finally he said, "So this will be an island."

Actually, we could not know how much of the land over which we had just walked would be flooded by the dam. No one did: the Nepali surveyor we met at the restaurant told us, no matter what the reports claimed, no one really knew how high the water would rise. But surely, some of the mountaintops—if not this one—would become islands amid the dammed waters. What would that mean to the creatures who lived there?

Island biogeography, Gary reminded me, is a study of isolation: the animals here, without the chance to exchange genes widely with their neighbors, would be genetically cut off from their neighbors. Islands, for this reason, are places of transformation, as Darwin showed in his study of the finches of the Galápagos. Because they are cut off, the fauna of islands are also more vulnerable to extinction; if some cataclysm befalls their populations, their numbers cannot be augmented by immigrants from adjacent territories.

But the isolation is also, perhaps, protection. Poachers seeking easy money selling bats to be smoked as local delicacies, capturing bears to sell their gall to pharmacies, and killing tigers so their penises could be made into soup, would find it too difficult to hunt the animals here, once the mountaintops were surrounded by the protective moat of water. Perhaps, for the mountaintop survivors, the deluge would be their savior.

According to many cosmologies, the world begins with water, dies with water, and through the power of water, all life is reborn. The Hindus say the Creator sleeps on a cosmic ocean, dreaming the universes into being. The Jews and Christians say the formless earth began as sea, until the Spirit of God, moving over the face of the waters, called the dry land to appear. The Ngaju Dayak, a head-hunting tribe of Borneo, agree: the Supreme Being, whom they call Ranying Hatala, spoke to the primeval waters in the voice of thunder. But he used a great dragon—essentially a naga—to form the foundation of the earth.

Our gods often use floods to wipe away the sins of the world. Flood myths are among the commonest in human cultures. There are 302 of them by one count. In the Shan myth, an angry Indra first sends hosts of lion-cranes and serpents to eat the impious, and then tries to kill the sinners with a terrible drought. Finally the Thunder God settles on a flood to wipe the slate clean, but seven couples seek refuge in a giant dry gourd. In the Hmong version, a brother and sister are the only survivors of the flood, having sheltered in a large funeral drum. The Kri hid in a vegetable. The Lao, whose lords had escaped by floating to heaven on a raft, emerged after the water had receded from a gourd that grew from the nostrils of a dead water buffalo. From death follows new life, the stories promise—just as the bear rises from her grave-like den, with her cubs in the spring.

We have kept our flood myths alive all these millennia because they speak to us of new beginnings. Humankind needs to remember that even in apocalypse, there is hope for redemption. When the dust settles, we can learn to see clearly again. We can emerge from war to make peace. We can turn from greed to compassion.

The scientist and I drank in the cool of the young forest and watched shafts of light pour down like blessing from the openings in the forest canopy. It produced what photographer friends have called "God Rays"—beams of soft light that painters of cathedral walls bestow upon the images of saints.

It was late afternoon, but it felt like morning.

PART FOUR

The Naga and the Khting vor

WAS THE GIANT bear a real species, or merely a myth?

One of the commonest mistakes people make when describing an unknown wild animal is making it bigger than it really is. This I had discovered years ago when researching one of my nature columns for the
Boston Globe, on the subject of "phantoms of the woods." Minutes after
Vermont's Fish and Wildlife Department released some martins—little
squirrel-sized, tree-dwelling native weasels—a passerby spotted one of
them. He phoned in a report of "a thing the size of a cocker spaniel."
Likewise, numerous reports of roaming panthers in New England turn
out to be house cats. An injured "eagle" was really a black-backed gull.
Strange creatures, seen under emotional circumstances, tend to become,
in our imaginations, much larger and more exotic than they actually are;
they are the source of so many "Big Fish" stories. We were well aware that
could be the case with reports of our giant bear.

Then again, a surprising number of "phantoms" have turned out to be
real. Such was the case with the manlike ape of the Congo described in
the nineteenth century, which proved to be the gorilla. In New England,
DNA testing of hairs found in the feces supposedly left by giant cats have
shown that mountain lions, indeed, again roam the north woods. Even

stranger eyewitness reports have proved true. Twelve people reported seeing a kangaroo hopping around Massachusetts in 1989, and authorities later captured a loose wallaby—possibly an escaped illegal pet. An armadillo showed up outside of Boston (it had hitchhiked in a trailer carrying a horse to Tufts' veterinary clinic from Florida). A flamingo was found wading in a Vermont pond (it had blown in on a spring storm).

Eyewitness accounts alone can't prove the existence of a strange or new animal. This is why science demands physical evidence: a live or dead specimen, a skin or a skull, a photograph or a video, or DNA. But even this may not be definitive, as we were soon to discover, shortly after our return to the States, with the new goatlike mammal known only from its horns, classified with the scientific name of *Pseudonovibos spiralis* and known in Cambodia as the Khting vor.

*   *   *

Our friend Sun Hean had been fascinated by the reports of this animal. It had first been noted by scientists in December 1993, when German and Austrian scientists had procured several distinctive sets of horns in a market in Ho Chi Minh City in Vietnam. They later obtained more from Cambodia. Amber to black, round to laterally flattened, the lyre-shaped horns curl conspicuously backward at the tip and are corrugated with thirteen to twenty-one ringlike ridges along the entire length. In 1994, the team announced their findings in the prestigious journal *Zoologische Abhandlungen, Staatliches Museum fur Tierkunde* of Dresden: "A New Bovid from Vietnam and Cambodia."

What animal went with the horns? Was it a new kind of wild ox? A mountain sheep? A wild goat? Or was it a kind of antelope? Museum curators and taxonomists around the world joined the debate. Robert Timm, the mammal curator at the University of Kansas, realized he already had two sets of horns of the new animal in his collection. Donated along with many other specimens then of greater interest in 1930, the seventy-year-old horns had been presumed to have belonged to a female kouprey from Binh Thuan Province of Vietnam. Male koupreys' massive horns sweep outward at an obtuse angle and are frayed at the tip; females' are more delicate and spiral upward, in the same shape as the Khting vor's. However, kouprey horns lack the distinctive annulations, Timm pointed out, which these had. Based on his careful observations, he concurred with the majority of other scientists: to him, it looked as though this was not only a new species but a new genus, and was probably a new kind of wild ox.

Then in 1999, the year we had begun our search for the golden moon bear, molecular data reclassified the missing animal. Isolating the mitochondrial DNA from horn fragments, Austrian and German scientists compared their sequences with those of wild sheep, oxen, antelope and goats. They determined, to everyone's surprise, that the Khting vor was most closely related to sheep and goats.

Meanwhile, teams of biologists dispersed to the forests of Southeast Asia to try to find the animal. Our friends George Schaller and Hunter Weiler were among those looking for the creature, and we'd have done so, too, had Sun Hean been free the previous summer as the three of us had hoped. Scientists from around the world purchased more horns from markets in Vietnam and Cambodia.

"To my knowledge, this is the only wild mammal on the face of the earth that we know positively exists but have never seen," Hunter Weiler told the *New York Times*. Species accounts of the animal, based on eyewitness descriptions collected from local hunters, such as those Kimchhay had amassed, appeared in IUCN references and textbooks published by university presses. Based on verbal accounts, its range was described, and maps appeared showing the provinces of Cambodia and Vietnam where the animal was supposed to live. The creature was awarded an official conservation status by IUCN: it is listed as endangered, and thus at least in theory is internationally protected.

But then in early 2001, just as we returned to the States from our third expedition, we found the mysterious Khting vor facing a fate worse than extinction. It may never have existed at all.

* * *

While we'd been in Laos, Sun Hean had kindly added our names to the growing list of scientists and conservationists discussing the Khting vor in an e-mail conversation. When we returned, we soon learned that Arnoult Seveau of the Zoological Society of Paris had just spent seven months scouring Cambodian forests and unsurprisingly, like the other scientists before him, caught no glimpse of the animal. When he returned to France, however, he happened upon four sets of antique horns, which he recognized instantly as those of the Khting vor. They had been collected by the French colonial Edmond Marchand in Indochina in 1925. These were subjected to a very rigorous DNA extraction technique. This time, scientists used as their samples bone from the skull fragments to which the horns connected. DNA extracted from the bone of museum specimens, they argued, is less subject to disintegration or contamination than the keratin of the horns. In a previous study, the Austrian and German researchers, whose results had classified the animal as a new kind of goat or sheep, had just finished extracting DNA from six populations of chamois, using the same lab where their Khting vor samples were sequenced. This, asserted Seveau's colleague and coauthor, molecular scientist Alexandre Hassanin, may have contaminated their samples, accounting for the unexpected classification.

But Hassanin and Seveau's results were more surprising yet. Their findings were unambiguous: the nucleotide sequences of the Khting vor matched exactly with those of the Asian domestic cow.

The astonished researchers next tried to figure out how the horns of a cow had taken on such a strange shape. Their conclusion: "humans had created them." Their scenario matched what the market vendor had told our friend Gerry Schroering in Cambodia: the originally smooth horn sheaths had been carved to obtain the ripples. The lyre-like twist in the upper part of the horns had been created by torsion, probably after softening and heating.

This would not be the first time that scientists had been victims of a hoax, Gary noted. "This situation is very similar to that of the Yeti in the

1950s," he observed. Scientific papers were published. There were plenty of sightings. The Yeti was even given a scientific name—*Dinanthropoides nivalis:* Terrible Ape of the Snows. One specimen was analyzed at the Field Museum, collected by no less a figure than Sir Edmund Hillary (who had built a new school for a monastery in Nepal in exchange for borrowing the venerated scalp for scientific analysis.) Field Museum scientists determined the hair and skin had belonged to a takin or serow—both goatlike bovids often hunted for food in the Himalayas—and molded on a conical wooden form so that it resembled a scalp.

Likewise, the famous 1934 photo of the Loch Ness monster was faked. The black-and-white photo of the brontosaur-like neck rising from the Scottish lake had been created by mounting a whittled piece of wood to a child's toy submarine—a trick to which one of its perpetrators confessed just before his death more than six decades later. "Some of these Khting vor horns even look like the fake Loch Ness Monster neck!" Gary observed.

"Scientists aren't used to having people deliberately fool them," Gary said. "A cop may be good at figuring these things out. A magician would be good at it. But a scientist just doesn't think that way. They are used to dealing with the natural world, not with human artifice."

But Gary, like a detective from one of his beloved whodunits, threw himself with gusto into the e-mail discussion group and offered up plausible ways the mystery had come to be.

How to account for all the sightings? Banteng, gaur, kouprey, and wild cattle often graze together and may even hybridize. They are often difficult to distinguish from one another at a distance, especially without field glasses. In Khmer, "khting" simply means "gaur." Richard Melville, a retired trustee of Johns Hopkins University, noted two names for the gaur: when he had hunted in Cambodia in his younger days, locals had called the gaur both Khting vor and Khting pouh. Possibly, Gary suggested, "vor" may have been used as a modifier to describe differences in the horns. Perhaps, like the golden moon bear, and possibly the giant bear as well, the Khting vor was a striking variant of a known species.

What about the Kansas City horns? After all, everyone supposed the animals they came from had been shot by the donor, American Richard L. Sutton. But this may have been an erroneous assumption. The tag on these horns noted they were from Suoi Kiet. Gary looked up the location in an old Indochinese encyclopedia from the early 1930s, and found it to be right along a railroad line that Sutton, Junior may have taken while on a trip to procure tiger bait. There was a thriving market there. The horns were probably purchased as curios.

But why would anyone purposely create horns for a nonexistent animal? "Because all the specimens used in this study were collected in 1925 in Indochina," Seveau and Hassanin wrote in a February 2001 article in *Les Comptes Rendus de l'Academie des Sciences de Paris,* "we suspected that ancient worship traditions, rather than scientific forgery, could explain the occurrence. . . . However, the reasons motivating such ethnic practices remain a real mystery." This, Gary solved too: he had read, in an article published well before the Khting vor's authenticity was questioned, that the people of India had long believed that the spiral-horned mountain goat, the markhor, eats snakes—almost certainly what fostered confidence in the magical properties of the horns. "I'll just bet that this is another cultural theme exported from India," he said. Had a sudden demand for markhor horn arisen in Southeast Asia, what was the local vendor to do? Medieval European druggists faced a similar problem when unicorn horn was in high demand as an antidote to poison. Traders solved it for them by selling the spiraling tusk of an Arctic whale, the narwhal, and billing it as the actual horn of a mythical beast. In Southeast Asia, suppliers for the local apothecary trade may have been similarly inspired to provide a substitute for the product in demand—either by manufacturing one, or by using the horns of an unusual kouprey or gaur.

Solving any mystery always brings Gary great delight. It all tied up so neatly, every unexpected element falling into place like the last, whirlwind pages of a good whodunit. I admired his detective work. But I found the conclusion deeply unsettling. It wasn't so much that scientists had been led astray; on our bear quest, we had already seen firsthand how easily and innocently misunderstandings can happen. What disturbed me so deeply was that the Khting vor was a not a miracle of evolution, but an invention of commerce. I was beginning to feel that in Southeast Asia, commerce reigned supreme: the marketplace both extinguished real species and created fake ones, undermining both science and story, fooling the biologists and mocking the gods.

But happily, this isn't always the case. Sometimes, too, a real creature arises from the deep ocean of Mystery and shows its face to science.

* * *

I had wandered into small travel agency in Thailand when I saw it: a framed black-and-white photograph showing a dozen American GIs lined up for the picture. Before them stretched a huge but slender water monster, more than twenty feet long, which they held rather like a team of Amazon explorers might display a huge anaconda. But though it was long and slender, this was no snake. A strange, deflated, rufflelike fin extended from the top of the head down the back to the tail. It was clearly some kind of monstrous fish.

All over Thailand, Laos, and Cambodia we had seen creatures like this before: they adorned the balustrades of all the temples, were painted on the walls, were depicted in mosaics. In art, unlike in death, the finny top-knot was erect like a dragon's crest, the mouth gaped open, and the eyes glowed with glass or marble. Such beauty and awesome strangeness befitted a magical creature—the one who gave birth to the land of Cambodia, who built the great capital of the Kingdom of a Million Elephants, and who continues to dwell among the peoples of Southeast Asia, blessing the life-giving waters of their rivers.

As if there were ever any doubt of the identity of the creature, beneath the photo was a caption printed in English: "Queen of the Nagas, Seized by American Army at Mekong, Laos military base on June 27, 1973."

I rushed to show Gary. "Wait till you see this!" I told him.

He recognized the fish at first glance. "Oh!" he said, "it's *Regalecus glesne!*"

He had read about these creatures when he was in college, in a big Time-Life picture book on oceans. *Regalecus glesne* is the Latin name for the giant oarfish, so named for its elongated, oarlike belly fins. A rare, deepwater, fragile giant, its long, deep narrow body can weigh six hundred pounds and stretch more than thirty feet long. Later, when I would read more about it, I was struck by how local artwork captured the features of the living creature—in ways the photograph of the dead specimen could not. Indeed, the giant oarfish does erect a crimson, plumelike crest on the head, just as the temple decorations show. It swims in a serpentine motion, as it seems to do as it glides down temple banisters. The artists, too, were wise to show the naga's jaws agape: *Regalecus glesne* belongs to the piscine order Allotriognathi, or "strange jaws," so named because the distinctive, protractile mouth is worked with a different system of muscles and bones than in other fish.

This astonishing giant has inspired fear and gratitude among peoples who have glimpsed it in waters throughout the world. One source mentioned it may have inspired the Latin poet Virgil's famous exclamation, "*Horresco referens!*"—horrifying memory!—about monsters sent to strangle Laocoön and his sons: "Their breasts rise among the billows, their bloody crests tower over the waves . . . their burning eyes shine, red with blood and flame; and their tongues, like a dart, flicker in their mouths, which they lick, hissing." In Norwegian waters, where the scientific type specimen was found (in Glesnaes), fishermen called it King of the Herrings. If anyone injured one of these giants, it was believed the herring would, in retribution, avoid their nets.

In Laos, the old legend is still told of a naga who lives in a hole by the holy spire of Vientiane's That Dam stupa, who will rise up and defend the Laotian people if they are threatened. I could only hope that in modern Southeast Asia, beset at once by the terrors of war and the market-greed of new peace, the people would remember the ancient powers of their deepest, wildest places, and summon the courage and foresight to bring about redemption.

EPILOGUE

Angkor: Forgetting and Remembering

The great limestone terraces and tiered towers of Angkor Wat comprise the largest religious edifice in the world—a universe in stone, evoking eternity even as it seems to crumble into jungle. Yet the legends say it was built in one night.

At the command of Indra, the Hindu thunder god, a heavenly architect presided. Nagas showed the workers where to find gold, pearls, and precious stones to line the walls. Magical servants of the god, called *devati* and *devi,* lifted the giant limestone blocks into place. Their fingerprints are still there, the people say. Look: our guide, Yosha, points out the perfectly rounded holes, left by the fingers of angels.

Twenty-nine-year-old Yosha first entered Angkor Wat in 1989. It was on the Khmer New Year's Day, April 14. "I came with my parents for the celebration at the pagoda," he says in his soft, British-accented English, each word stretching as if it is melting in the heat. "At that time," he said, "the temple was very quiet, and the jungle look very secret. Inside, very quiet—more than I can say."

I envied him that quiet. Angkor now receives more than 250,000 visitors a year, making Cambodia's Siem Reap an international tourist destination.

How did it feel to be alone in the temple? I wondered. Yosha, looking studious and thoughtful in his wire-rimmed glasses, paused for a moment. His words came slow and deliberate as a sleepy carp moving in a still pool. "I felt very, very great," he said. "How can my ancestors build a temple as big as this?"

But the fingerprints of angels are not the only holes in the walls of this greatest of Khmer temples. I was particularly eager to see the carvings of beautiful celestial nymphs called apsaras—there are more than 1,500 of them lining the walls of just one gallery, each unique in her face and dress and posture, poised forever in a single gesture of her dance of timeless joy. The first one I examined was at the edge of a doorway to the west entrance. Between her upturned hand and her tilted head was a two-inch crater. It had been made by a bullet.

On my fourth journey to Southeast Asia, I have come to a vandalized temple to try to reconcile opposites. After two years of travels with a scientist, I have come to this desecrated but still holy place to contemplate beginnings and endings, animals and people, science and story, heaven and earth.

Yosha grew up a few miles from Angkor, in the same district. When he was young, his mother eagerly awaited the eclipse. In the dark of the moon, the most auspicious time for her prayer, she would splash him with water, tap his chest three times, and utter her deepest wish for her son: "Don't grow tall." The tallest boys, she knew, would be taken first for the Khmer Rouge army.

Yosha did not grow tall, but still, he was taken away, in 1985. The genocidal army in which he was forced to fight had already desecrated the nation's greatest temples. In 1971, Khmer Rouge guerrillas occupied the temples of Angkor. They lit fires in the galleries, looted its treasures, decapitated statues, and sold the heads on the black market to finance the war.

They were not the first—nor the last—to sack the place. We soon saw that Angkor Wat's Gallery of a Thousand Buddhas has scarcely a handful left. Long ago, they were stolen away—by the Chams of what is now Vietnam, by the Siamese of what is now Thailand, in a series of sieges that preceded the mysterious abandonment of the entire city of Angkor in 1431, to be embraced by jungle until its rediscovery a century ago. Yet even now, the looting hasn't ceased. You can buy pieces of Angkor's gods on any day at Bangkok antiques dealers.

Many of the stalwart lions guarding the entrance of Angkor Wat have no faces; none still have their tails. They remind me of the crippled moon bear at Lak Xao, of Motola the elephant with her three remaining feet. Few of the freestanding statues here have heads. Buddhas, apsaras, nagas, kings, and gods have been torn from walls and pedestals—some by vandals, some by soldiers, some by collectors, some by time.

And yet, the historians tell us when Angkor Wat was built, at the command of King Suryavarman II in the first half of the twelfth century, it was dedicated to the Hindu god, Vishnu—the Preserver. He is the one who ordered Creation, who maintains and organizes heaven and earth. Yet the Preserver himself constantly changes form: often he is shown in a human shape but with four arms. Sometimes he is lying on Annata, the Grand Serpent of Time. But in the great cycles of eternity, he has also appeared in the form of animals: a turtle, a fish, a wild boar. In one incarnation, the god was an ordinary shepherd.

Inside the entry tower of Angkor Wat, he assumes yet another shape. His ancient stone torso is now topped with a new head—that of Buddha, to whom the temple was rededicated by subsequent kings. In his new incarnation, he is still adored. Incense smolders at his feet, fruits and flowers ripen into decay.

And throughout the temple, at all times of day, we would find, to our astonishment, monks in saffron robes and nuns with shaved scalps carefully tending headless Buddhas—the decapitated statues clothed magnificently in saffron silk, their stone feet perfumed with offerings of incense, fruit, and flowers. With Yosha, I, too, lit candles at their feet.

* * *

Hope, horror, avarice, blessing: "The stark disjunctures" so evident at Angkor, wrote the author of one guidebook, "are almost too sharp to countenance."

But that is precisely why I have come here.

Ostensibly, I am still looking for bears. While Gary teaches his spring courses at Northwestern, my companion, Dianne Taylor-Snow, and I scour the temple galleries for ursine images. We find apsaras, crocodiles, deer, birds, three-headed elephants, winged bird-monsters, monkey-princes, fish, trees, chariots, demons —but no bears. I inquire after live bears in the area. People have brought bears here for sale on temple grounds. A few years back, I was told, one person was hawking a moon bear cub like a postcard vendor, asking the equivalent of two hundred dollars. We found there is a sun bear in captivity nearby, to amuse guests at a hotel.

But what I am really looking for is something else. For millennia, bears have been honored as teachers of healing, revered as symbols of resurrection, deified as the goddess who cradles rebirth. And this is what brings me to this temple: what I am really looking for is redemption.

The scientific studies we began here in Cambodia have produced a wealth of new information. Gary's work has brought to global notice a beautiful bear no one knew existed before. Not only is the golden color form new to science; so are the pandalike variants, and the brown color phases along the spectrum. As I wander the maze of Angkor's stone courtyards and galleries, a scientific paper, listing Sun Hean and me as coauthors, is in press at the *Natural History Bulletin of the Siam Society*.

And although the DNA sequencing on some of the samples will not be done yet for months, much later we will find it to reveal more than a dozen distinct haplotypes. These fall into four major lineages, which will begin to reveal the outlines of the refuges that may have harbored them during the last glaciation.

As for a third species of bear, proof of its existence is still outstanding. The DNA data will provide some valuable leads. It could still be out there, awaiting discovery. So productive has been our work, and so promising its many leads, that Gary intends to focus on the zoology of Southeast Asia for the rest of his professional career.

But despite the satisfaction of such scientific success, my heart is haunted with memories: the nine-hour motorcycle ride through the Cardamom wilderness, when every animal we saw was dead. The bears confined to tiny cages in Phnom Penh and the Elephant Mountains. The markets with their live and dead illegal wildlife. The trucks full of severed tree trunks. The starving animals in the zoo owned by the wealthy logging corporation. The T'en reduced to one last book only two people could read.

When Gary and I began our quest, it was our fervent hope that our work would help save Southeast Asia's bears and forests at a critical turning point in the area's history. Today the peoples of these nations will decide the fate of war's unexpected boon: the survival of some of the largest, richest, and most pristine forests in this part of the world. Now at peace, will the people be able to forge a prosperity that does not rape their precious wilderness, eradicate their rare and beautiful animals, erase unique cultures like the T'en?

Even among the markets chocked with corpses of endangered animals and mountains laced with land mines, there are reasons for hope: smart, scrupulous, and motivated people like Sun Hean and Preecha Rattanaporn, in positions of power in their nation's governments. (Preecha has in fact received a promotion, to head of the Thai Royal Forest Department's Wildlife Conservation Division, which we hope will hasten plans to restore moon bears to Thailand's national parks.) Nongovernmental organizations, like Gary van Zuylen's TSCWA and Hunter Weiler's Fauna and Flora International and Cat Action Treasury, accomplishing the humane and conservation work for which governments can't or won't pay. Foreign scholars and researchers who, like Gary and myself, hope to contribute to worldwide efforts to preserve the gems of Southeast Asia's natural heritage.

Even more influential than government or science, Buddhism's deep roots in the region hold hope for developing a humane and ecologically sustainable economy. Its temples have long served as sanctuaries for animals and as nurseries for trees. Teaching nonviolence, respect for all living creatures, and control of craving or desire, Buddhism presents its "cool joyfulness" as an alternative to the "hot happiness" so popular in the Western world. As the participants who gathered for a regional seminar "Toward an Environmental Ethic in Southeast Asia" held in Cambodia in 1997 pointed out, Buddhism offers a model for development. The Dalai Lama calls it a Compassionate Economy, based on need, not want, and on reverence and gratitude toward humans, animals, and nature.

And finally, there is the miracle of Angkor itself. Though a contemporary of Chartres, Angkor Wat is more than a gathering place for the faithful. It was built, École Française Khmer scholar Claude Jacques tells us, as a palace to call a god to earth—an earthly model of a cosmic world, built not merely to depict, but to materialize the divine.

Even Cambodians themselves were at first incredulous to learn that their ancestors built Angkor. After its ruins were discovered in the jungle, explorers speculated on who could have created such splendor. Indians, many scholars thought—for some of the inscriptions on the stone are Sanskrit. Others thought it was the Chinese. Portuguese and Spanish explorers, who had glimpsed the ruins before Henri Mouhot popularized their majesty in 1860, suggested Alexander the Great, or the Romans, or the Jews. But today there is no question. The credit for the splendor of Angkor belongs to the people of a nation now crippled, lawless, and impoverished—people who, remembering their ancient reverence for life, now face the opportunity to show the world the way to a new and compassionate economy, a new way to call heaven to earth.

But even here, in this holy of holies, rings the siren song of consumption. Yosha, like his country, has embarked in peacetime on a new beginning. Today, his focus is on learning better English, to become a better tour guide and earn a better living. Each week he invests a precious dollar of his salary in English lessons with a tutor. He has even learned to sing a song in English. At our request, he sang it for us:

> "Oh Lord, won't you buy me
> a Mercedes-Benz,
> My friends all drive Porsches,
> I must make amends . . ."

* * *

Before entering Angkor Wat for the last time, we noticed a large tree on its southwest lawn. A huge, welcoming creature, its trunk thirty feet around, it bears the heart-shaped leaves of the Bo, the species of ficus beneath which the Buddha attained enlightenment.

The tree is a hub of life. Large red ants course along scent trails, like platelets in blood vessels seen under a microscope. Four, foot-tall brown termite nests stand like the temple's sentinel lions at the tree's base. Birds twitter hidden among the spreading branches. And looking closely, we see that the tree is not one, but two: another species of ficus, having landed as a seed perhaps a century ago, is spreading its great spotted roots down over the Bo trunk, enveloping its host, embracing the old with the new.

At the tree's base, someone has erected two crude, miniature shrines. Both were made out of square tins for cooking oil, one side of each bent to create peaked roofs. Each shrine shelters an altar made of a single brick, in front of which people make offerings to the spirits that live here. In front of the spirit house is a can that had once held sardines, anchoring a bristle of spent incense, probably burned that morning.

"I wonder who is the spirit that lives here?" I say aloud. I wonder if the spirits will survive this strange, new, materialistic age—and if they do, if the people will remember how to listen. I wonder if, as Gary suspects, golden bears can be found throughout Southeast Asia—and if so, whether the last of them will be doomed to die in zoos. I wonder whether an unknown species of bear really is still out there, in the unexplored forests—and if there is, whether it will survive to be discovered.

Just then, a rare breeze stirs the heart-shaped leaves of the Bo. "It's talking to you," says Dianne.

Struggling with hope and despair, caught in the mystery of eternity and the unknown of tomorrow, I strain to understand that whispered answer.

Science and Moon Bears

A Scientific Addendum by Gary J. Galbreath, Ph.D.

When I began this venture with the intrepid Sy Montgomery, we intended to learn the identity (color phase, subspecies, or species) of the blond moon bear. Along the way, other objectives were added: resolving the mystery of *Pseudonovibos*, elucidating past biogeography of moon bears using mitochondrial DNA variation, helping conserve the moon bear, and investigating the possibility of an unknown species of dark bear. We have made progress on all fronts.

First, blond moon bears definitely represent a color phase never before reported in the scientific literature. They are discussed by me, Sy, and Sun Hean, in a paper in the *Natural History Bulletin of the Siam Society*. We have also demonstrated the presence in Southeast Asia of brown-phase moon bears, heretofore only known from far to the west. Moon bears are commonly pictured as temperate-climate creatures, but we have found them dwelling in remarkably "tropical" habitat. Our blond female and dark cub from the Elephant Mountains may be the most southerly ones scientifically recorded.

We have helped demonstrate that *Pseudonovibos* is probably a myth, despite its formal scientific recognition. Horns of the wild ox called the gaur vary in size and shape. Both in Vietnam and in Cambodia, such variation has allowed a belief that more than one type of gaur exists: thus the Khmer distinction between the vine gaur (Khting vor) and the serpent gaur (Khting pouh). Most scientifically published "*Pseudonovibos*" or "Khting vor" horns are actually zebu or buffalo horns that have been artificially twisted and carved, like those described to us by the resourceful Gerald Schroering, and I know of none that are convincing as horns of a new species.

Whether a third species of bear exists in Southeast Asia has not been resolved, but it is possible to partly sort wheat from chaff. In 1900, Flower noted that bears larger than sun bears were being reported in Siam, and mentioned a sloth bear specimen at the Siamese Museum. We may never know whether it was an imported sloth bear or simply a misidentified moon bear, but this report may have engendered a belief among French hunters that sloth bears occur in Southeast Asia. In 1906, Thomas described *Ursus arctos shanorum,* a dark grizzly supposedly from the Shan States of Burma; I suspect that this specimen really came from much further west, in the Himalayas. In 1916, Gyldenstolpe added the moon bear to Thailand's known fauna, and in 1917, Eberhardt noted its presence in North Annam. Since about 1920, the scientific world has accepted only two species of bear (sun and moon) as existing in Southeast Asia.

But, as noted by Sy, not so for some hunting writers! De Monestrol in 1925 contrasted moon bears reported from high mountains of northern Indochina with supposedly smaller ones elsewhere; for the latter he used the scientific name of the sloth bear. The account of *shanorum* may have been partly responsible for Bordeneuve's 1925 listing of an Annam grizzly, along with sun, moon, and sloth bears. In 1939, Cheminaud's inaccurate descriptions of sloth and moon bears he had supposedly hunted in Laos added to the confusion. As late as 1949, Devariaux listed sun, moon, sloth, and grizzly bears as existing in what is now southern Vietnam! In sum, this French literature concerning multiple bear species does not inspire confidence.

Local people in Nepal, and perhaps in Sichuan, recognize two types of moon bear differing in size, as did Hmong we interviewed in northern Laos. (Shuttong Vang's account in Skokie proved to be a fairly accurate summary of Hmong beliefs, but not surprisingly some information, such as lack of a chest patch in the dog bear, was incorrect after so many years away from Laos.) Is the large Hmong horse bear a different species from their pig bear? A conservative view would be that the great within-species size variation typical of bears has encouraged such beliefs. Sy Montgomery and I have seen much variation in moon bear body size, in length of the mane, and in size and shape of the pale chest patch.

It is plausible that at times during the Pleistocene, the area comprising Southeast Asia and southern China was the main refuge of moon bears. We have obtained DNA samples from western Cambodia, northern and southeastern Thailand, and northern Laos, and we intend to obtain additional samples. The data sort into several groups of DNA haplotypes with undeniable geographic patterning. These data may be used in planning the release of captive moon bears back into the wild. And they allow us to hypothesize dispersions and population constrictions of these wonderful, shaggy beasts over the terrain of Southeast Asia during the last quarter million years. All in all, quite a trove of information for our efforts!

Selected Bibliography

Following is a list of some of the books, reports, and scientific articles most helpful to my research and some books on related topics that readers might particularly enjoy.

Animals

Ayer, Margaret. *Animals of Southeast Asia.* New York: St. Martin's Press, 1970.

Bartlett, Thad Q. *Feeding and Ranging Behavior of the White-Handed Gibbon in Khao Yai National Park, Thailand.* Ph.D. dissertation, St. Louis: Washington University, 1999.

Brown, Gary. *The Great Bear Almanac.* New York: Lyons and Burford, 1993.

Bordeneuve, J. *Les Grandes Chasses en Indochine: Souvenirs d'un Forestier.* Saigon: A. Portail, 1925.

Cheminaud, Guy. *Mes Chasses au Laos.* Paris: Payot, 1939.

Corvanich, Amnuay. *Thai Elephant.* Bangkok: Forest Industry Organization, 1995.

De Camp, L. Sprague. *Elephant.* New York: Pyramid Publications, 1964.

Domico, Terry. *Bears of the World.* New York: Facts on File, 1988.

Duckworth, J. W., and S. Hedges, compilers. *Tracking Tigers: A Review of the Status of Tiger, Asian Elephant, Gaur and Banteng in Vietnam, Lao, Cambodia and Yunnan (China) with Recommendations for Future Conservation Action.* Hanoi: World Wildlife Fund Indochina Programme, 1998.

————, R. E. Salter, and K. Khounboline, compilers. *Wildlife in Lao, PDR: 1999 Status Report.* Vientiane, Laos: IUCN/The World Conservation Union/Wildlife Conservation Society/Centre for Protected Areas and Watershed Management, 1999.

Fair, Jeff, with photographs by Lynn Rogers. *The Great American Bear.* Minocqua, Wis.: Northwood Press, 1990.

Gittleman, John L. editor. *Carnivore Behavior, Ecology and Evolution.* Ithaca, N.Y.: Cornell University Press, 1989.

Herald, Earl S. *Living Fishes of the World,* Garden City, N.Y.: Doubleday, 1967.

Herrero, Stephen. *Bear Attacks: Their Causes and Avoidance.* New York: Lyons and Burford, 1985.

Heuvelmans, Bernard. *In the Wake of the Sea-Serpents.* New York: Hill and Wang, 1968.

Holldobler, Bert, and Edward O. Wilson. *The Ants.* Cambridge, Mass.: Belknap Press of Harvard University Press, 1990.

Kaniut, Larry. *Alaska Bear Tales.* Anchorage: Northwest Books, 1990.

Mallon, D. P. and S. C. Kingswood, compilers. *Antelopes, Part 4: North Africa, the Middle East and Asia: Global Survey and Regional Action Plans.* Gland, Switzerland: IUCN, 2001.

Maurice, A. *People and Wildlife in and Around Saigon 1872–1873.* Bangkok: White Lotus Press, 1997.

Millet, F. *Les Grands Animaux Sauvages de l'Annam: Leurs Moeurs, Leur Chasse, Leur Tir.* Paris: Librarie Plon, 1930.

Mills, Judy A, and Christopher Servheen. *The Asian Trade in Bears and Bear Parts.* Baltimore: World Wildlife Fund, 1991.

Monestral, H. de. *Les Chasses et la Faune d'Indochine.* Hanoi: Imprimerie d'Extreme-Orient, 1925.

———, H. de. 2nd ed. *Les Chasses et la Faune d'Indochine.* Hanoi: Imprimerie d'Extreme-Orient, 1931.

———, H. de. 3d ed. *Chasses et Faune d'Indochine.* Saigon: Portail, 1952.

Nowak, Ronald M., and John L. Paradiso, editors. *Walker's Mammals of the World, vol. 1, 4th ed.* Baltimore: Johns Hopkins University Press, 1983.

———, Ronald M., and John L. Paradiso, editors. *Walker's Mammals of the World, vol. 2, 4th ed.* Baltimore: Johns Hopkins University Press, 1983.

Nowell, Kristin, and Peter Jackson, compilers. *Wild Cats, Status Survey and Conservation Action Plan.* Gland, Switzerland: IUCN, 1996.

Rabinowitz, Alan. *Chasing the Dragon's Tail: The Struggle to Save Thailand's Wild Cats.* New York: Doubleday, 1991.

Roberts, T. J. *The Mammals of Pakistan.* London: Ernest Benn, 1977.

Sanderson, Ivan, *Living Mammals of the World.* Garden City, N.Y.: Doubleday, 1961.

Servheen, Christopher, editor. *Bears: IUCN/SSC Action Plan.* Gland, Switzerland: IUCN/World Conservation Union, 2000.

Sun, Hean, Seng Kim, Keo Omaliss, Heng Neathmony, and Colin Poole. *The Birds of Cambodia,* Phnom Penh: European Commission Support Programme for the Environmental Sector in Cambodia with the Wildlife Protection Office, Royal Government of Cambodia. 1998.

Taylor-Ide, Daniel. *Something Hidden Behind the Ranges: A Himalayan Quest.* San Francisco: Mercury House, 1995.

Stirling, Ian, editor. *Bears: Majestic Creatures of the Wild.* Emmaus, Pa.: Rodale, 1993.

Vrba, Elisabeth S., and George B. Schaller. *Antelopes, Deer and Relatives: Fossil Record, Behavioral Ecology, Systematics and Conservation.* New Haven: Yale University Press, 2000.

TROPICAL FORESTS

Earl of Cranbrook, *Wonders of Nature in Southeast Asia.* Kuala Lumpur: Oxford University Press, 1997.

Forsyth, Adrian, and Ken Miyata. *Tropical Nature.* New York: Macmillan, 1984.

Neal, Marie. *In Gardens of Hawaii.* Honolulu: Bishop Museum Press, 1965.

Terborgh, J. *Diversity of the Tropical Rainforest.* New York: Scientific American Library, 1992.

Veevers-Carter, W. *Riches of the Rain Forest.* Singapore: Oxford University Press, 1991.

Whitmore, T. C. *Tropical Rain Forests of the Far East.* Oxford: Clarendon Press, 1984.

TRAVELERS' ACCOUNTS AND TRAVEL GUIDES

Aoyagi, Kenji. *Mekong: The Last River.* San Francisco: Cadence Books, 1995.

Carne, Louis de. *Travels on the Mekong.* Bangkok: White Lotus, 1995.

Cranmer, Jeff, and Steven Martin. *Laos: The Rough Guide.* London: Rough Guides, 1999.

Delaporte, Louis, and Francis Garnier. *A Pictorial Journey on the Old Mekong: Cambodia, Laos and Yunnan. The Mekong Exploration Commission Report (1866–1868) vol. 3.* Bangkok: White Lotus, 1996.

Eliot, Joshua, Jane Bickersteth, and John Colet, editors. *Vietnam, Laos and Cambodia Handbook.* Chicago: Passport Books, 1995.

Garnier, Francis. *Travels in Cambodia and Part of Laos: The Mekong Exploration Commission Report (1866–1868) vol. 1.* Bangkok: White Lotus Co. Ltd. 1996.

————. *Further Travels in Laos and Yunnan. The Mekong Exploration Commission Report (1866–1868) vol. 2.* Bangkok: White Lotus, 1996.

Hollinger, Carol. *Mai Pen Rai.* Boston: Houghton Mifflin, 1965.

Parkes, Carl. *Thailand Handbook.* Chico, Calif.: Moon Publications, 1997.

Pattison, Gavin, and John Villiers. *Thailand.* London: A. & C. Black, 1997.

Pham, Andrew X. *Catfish and Mandala.* New York: Farrar, Straus and Giroux, 1999.

Philpots, Robert. *Reporting Angkor: Chou Ta-Kuan in Cambodia.* London: Blackwater Books, 1996.

Rooney, Dawn. *Angkor.* Hong Kong: Odyssey Publications, 2001.

Sepul, Rene. *Luang Pabang.* Vientiane, Laos: Raintrees, 1998.

Stewart, Lucretia. *Tiger Balm: Travels in Laos, Vietnam and Cambodia.* London: Chatto and Windus, 1992, 1998.

Ta-Kuan, Chou. *The Customs of Cambodia.* Bangkok: Siam Society, 1992.

Yamashita, Michael. *A Journey on the Mother of Waters.* New York: Takarajima Books, 1995.

Young, Robert. *The World's Most Dangerous Places.* New York: HarperCollins, 2000.

SOUTHEAST ASIAN PEOPLES

Bernzatzik, Hugo Adolf. *The Spirits of the Yellow Leaves.* London: Robert Hale, 1951.

Chamberlain, James R. *Nature and Culture in the Nakai-Nam Theun Conservation Area,* unpublished ms. 1997.

————. *A Proto-Tai Zoology,* Ph.D. dissertation. University of Michigan, Ann Arbor, 1977.

Edmonds, I. G. E. *The Khmers of Cambodia.* Indianapolis: Bobbs-Merrill, 1970.

Fadiman, Anne. *The Spirit Catches You and You Fall Down.* New York: Farrar, Straus and Giroux, 1997.

Kira, Tatuo, and Tadao Umesao, editors. *Nature and Life in Southeast Asia.* vol. I. Kyoto: Fauna and Flora Research Society, 1961.

Mabbett, Ian, and David Chandler. *The Khmers.* Oxford: Blackwell, 1995.

McKinnon, John, and Wanat Bhruksasri, editors. *Highlanders of Thailand.* Singapore: Oxford University Press, 1986.

Ponder, H. W. *Cambodian Glory.* London: Thornton Butterworth, 1936.

Rovenda, Vittorio. *Khmer Mythology.* London: Thames and Hudson, 1997.

Segaller, Denis. *More Thai Ways.* Bangkok: Post Publishing, 1998.

Seidenfaden, Eric. *Thai Peoples.* Bangkok: Siam Society, 1963.

Thierry, Solange. *The Khmers.* Paris: Kailash Editions, 1997.

CURRENT SOUTHEAST ASIAN HISTORY

Chandler, David. *Facing the Cambodian Past.* Chiang Mai, Thailand: Silkworm Books, 1996.

Heidhues, Mary Somers. *Southeast Asia: A Concise History.* London: Thames & Hudson, 2000.

Kremmer, Christopher. *Stalking the Elephant Kings.* St. Leonards, New South Wales, Australia: Allen and Unwin, 1997.

Osborne, Milton. *The Mekong: Turbulent Past, Uncertain Future.* New York: Atlantic Monthly Press, 2000.

Stuart-Fox, Martin. *A History of Laos.* Cambridge: Cambridge University Press, 1997.

Ung, Loung. *First They Killed My Father: A Daughter of Cambodia Remembers.* New York: HarperCollins, 2000.

PREHISTORIC CREATURES

Eisenberg, John F. *The Mammalian Radiations: An Analysis of Trends in Evolution, Adaptation and Behavior.* Chicago: University of Chicago Press, 1981.

Kurten, Bjorn. *Pleistocene Mammals of Europe.* Chicago: Aldine, 1968.

———. *The Cave Bear Story: Life and Death of a Vanished Animal.* New York: Columbia University Press, 1976.

Lillegraven, Jason A., Zofia Kielan-Jaworowska, and William A. Clemens, editors. *Mesozoic Mammals: The First Two-Thirds of Mammalian History.* Berkeley: University of California Press, 1979.

RELIGION, MYTHOLOGY

Boyes, Johnathan. *Tiger-Men and Tofu Dolls: Tribal Spirits in Northern Thailand.* Chiang Mai, Thailand: Silkworm Books, 1997.

Coomaraswamy, Ananda K. *The Dance of Shiva.* New York: Noonday Press, Farrar, Straus, 1957.

Estes, Clarissa Pinkola. *Women Who Run with the Wolves: Myths and Stories of the Wild Woman Archetype,* New York: Ballantine, 1992.

Gyallay-Pap, Peter and Ruth Bottomley, editors. *Toward an Environmental Ethic in Southeast Asia: Proceedings of a Regional Seminar Organized November 5–7, 1997, by the Buddhist Institute in the Kingdom of Cambodia.* Phnom Penh, Cambodia: Buddhist Institute, 1998.

Johnson, Charles, editor. *Dab Neeg Hmoob: Myths, Legends and Folktales from the Hmong of Lao.* St. Paul, Minn.: MacAlester College, 1989.

Jumsai, Manich M. L. *Understanding Thai Buddhism.* Bangkok: Chalermnit Press, 1998.

Knappert, Jan. *Mythology and Folklore in Southeast Asia.* Selangor Darul Ehsan, Malaysia: Oxford University Press, 1999.

McNeely, Jeffrey A., and Paul Spencer Wachtel. *Soul of the Tiger: Searching for Nature's Answers in Exotic Southeast Asia.* New York: Doubleday, 1988.

Mitchell, A. G. *Hindu Gods and Goddesses.* New Delhi: UBS Publishers' Distributors, 1993.

Rigg, Jonathan, editor. *The Gift of Water: Water Management, Cosmology and the State in South East Asia.* London: School of Oriental and African Studies, University of London, 1992.

Shepherd, Paul, with Barry Sanders. *The Sacred Paw: The Bear in Nature, Myth and Literature.* New York: Penguin, 1992.

Zimmer, Henrich. *Myths and Symbols in Indian Art and Civilization.* Princeton, N.J.: Princeton University Press, 1974.

OTHER BOOKS

Jumsai, Manich M. L. *History of Thai Literature.* Bangkok: Chalermnit, 2000.

Mansfield, Howard. *The Same Ax, Twice: Restoration and Renewal in a Throw-Away Age.* Hanover, NH: University Press of New England, 2000.

Moore, Christopher G. *Heart Talk.* Bangkok: Heaven Lake Press, 1998.

Sayasithsena, Tham. *Victory Arch: Construction˙Significance˙Prestige.* Nongkhai, Thailand: Matthai Press, 1995.

Thai Phrase Book and Dictionary. Oxford: Berlitz, 1994.

Zajonc, Arthur. *Catching the Light: The Entwined History of Light and Mind.* New York: Oxford University Press, 1993.

SOME KEY REPORTS AND SCIENTIFIC PAPERS

Brandt, John H., Maurizio Dioli, Alexandre Hassanin, Richard Melville, Link Olson, Arnoult Seveau, and Robert Timm. 2001. "Debate on the authenticity of *Pseudonovibos spiralis* as a new species of wild bovid from Vietnam and Cambodia." *Journal of the Zoological Society of London* 255: 437–44.

Galbreath, Gary J., Hean Sun, and Sy Montgomery. Summer, 2001. "A New Color Phase of *Ursus thibetanus* (Mammilia: Ursidae) from Southeast Asia." *Natural History Bulletin of the Siam Society* 49, no. 1: 107–11.

Hassanin, Alexandre, Arnoult Seveau, Herbert Thomas, Herve Bocherens, Daniel Billiou, and Bui Xuan Nguyen. 2001. "Evidence from DNA that the mysterious linh duong (Pseudonovibos spiralis) is not a new bovid." *Comptes Rendus Acad. Sci. Paris, Science de la Vie* 324: 71–80.

Heng, Kimchhay, Ouk Kimsan, Masphal Kry, Sin Polin, and Uch Seiha. Narrative by Hunter Weiler. 1998. "The Distribution of Tiger, Leopard, Elephant and Wild Cattle in Cambodia: Interim Report 1998." Compiled by Cambodia Tiger Survey Interview Team, Cambodia Wildlife Protection Office, Phnom Penh.

Nisbett, Richard E., Kaiping Peng, Incheol Choi, and Ara Norenzayan. April, 2001. "Culture and Systems of Thought: Holistic vs. Analytic Cognition." *Psychological Review* 108, no. 2: 291–310.

Peter, W. P., and A. Feiler. 1994. "Ein neue Bovidenart aus Vietnam und Cambodia (Mammalia: Ruminantia)." *Zoologische Abhandlungen, Staatliches Museum für Tierkunde Dresden* 48:169–76.

Pocock, R. I. 1932. "The black and brown bears of Europe and Asia. Part II." *Journal of the Bombay Natural History Society* 36(1): 101–38.

Waits, Lisette P., Jack Sullivan, Stephen J. O'Brien, and R. H. Ward. 1999. "Rapid radiation events in the family Ursidae indicated by likelihood phylogenetic estimation from multiple fragments of mtDNA." *Molecular Phylogenetics and Evolution* 13: 82–92.

Weiler, Hunter, Roth Bunthoeun, and Uch Seiha. 1998. "Tiger Conservation Workshops and Hunter Interviews in Koh Kong and Pursat Provinces." Organized by Cat Action Treasury.

RESOURCES

Here is a short list of organizations and agencies working to protect bears in Asia and around the world, and to conserve wild lands, creatures and cultures in Southeast Asia. Readers are urged to contact them to find out more and to offer support for their many excellent conservation and research projects.

Thai Society for the Conservation of Wild Animals
32 Prathum Court, 85/3-8 Soi Rajaprarop Makkasan, Bangkok, 10400 Thailand
www.tscwa@bigfoot.com

The Thai Society for the Conservation of Wild Animals works with the Thai Royal Forest Department to care for well over 100 sun and moon bears and hundreds of other animals rescued from poachers, confiscated from or donated by illegal owners, or living homeless on the streets. In addition to numerous projects throughout Thailand, the organization works in Laos with that nation's largest zoo to comfortably house confiscated bears. It is hoped a reintroduction project will soon begin to return some of these captured bears to the wild.

World Society for the Protection of Animals
Western Hemisphere Office
P.O. Box 190, 29 Perkins Street, Boston, MA 02130-9904
www.wspa-international.org

An international society, WSPA investigates and alleviates animal cruelty worldwide. It has sponsored investigations of the illegal trade in animal parts and launched a major campaign to rescue bears held captive on bile farms. WSPA has provided critical support for a number of other organizations, including the Thai Society for the Conservation of Wild Animals.

Wildlife Conservation Society
New York Zoological Society

185th Street and Southern Boulevard
Bronx, NY 10460-1099
www.wcs.org

This well-respected organization, an arm of the former Bronx Zoo, sponsors wildlife studies and conservation programs in Thailand, Laos, Cambodia, and many other countries, including the landmark work of George Schaller, Alan Rabinowitz, and their colleagues. WCS helped establish more than 130 major protected areas in Asia, Africa, and Latin America. Its tiger conservation programs in Cambodia, Burma, and Thailand benefit all the animals who share the tiger's habitat, including bears, and its work includes educational campaigns to curb the use of endangered animal parts in traditional Chinese medicine.

World Wildlife Fund/TRAFFIC USA
1250 24th Street NW, Washington, DC 20037
www.wwf.org

World Wildlife Fund is an international organization working for conservation in more than 40 countries. TRAFFIC USA is the wildlife trade monitoring program of WWF-US. Among its many excellent projects, WWF has sponsored major investigations into the Asian trade in bears and bear parts. Its Indochina Program address is:
World Wildlife Fund Indochina Program
53 Tran Phu Street, Ba Dinh District, Hanoi, Vietnam
hanoi@wwfvn.org.vn

Animals Asia Foundation
   U.S. Office:
PMB 506, 584 Castro Street, San Francisco, CA 94114-2594

   Hong Kong Office:
P.O. Box 82, Sai Kung PO, Kowloon, Hong Kong
www.animalsasia.org

Devoted to the needs of wild, domesticated, and endangered species in Asia, this organization is based in Hong Kong with offices in the United Kingdom, New Zealand, Australia and San Francisco. Among other projects in 2000, AAF signed an agreement with the Chinese government to phase out its 247 "bear farms," where the animals are held in tiny cages and catheterized to obtain their bile. Until then, about 6,500 sun and moon bears remain incarcerated in such facilities.

Cat Action Treasury
c/o Kristin Nowell
P.O. Box 202, Los Gatos, CA 95031
www.felidae.org

Established in 1966 to fund high-priority cat conservation projects around the world, Cat Action Treasury has sponsored and organized many of the landmark studies of Cambodian wildlife conducted in concert with the Wildlife Protection Office. The organization works closely with the Cat Specialist group of IUCN, of which Kristin Nowell is a member.

Hunter Weiler is CAT's representative in Cambodia. You can write to him at:

PO Box 1585, Phnom Penh, Cambodia
or
#22 EoA Street 334, Phnom Penh, Cambodia

IUCN/The World Conservation Union
Rue Mauverney 28, CH-1196, Gland, Switzerland
www.iucn.org

The International Union for the Conservation of Nature and Natural Resources (also known as the World Conservation Union) is a union of sovereign states, governmental and nongovernmental agencies working to conserve biological diversity. Its Species Survival Commission is a volunteer network of over 7,000 scientists, field researchers, and conservation leaders from 188 countries working to save, restore, and manage species and their habitats. IUCN/SSC Action Plans are considered among the world's most authoritative sources for species conservation, assessing the conservation status of species, and specifying conservation priorities. To obtain a list of the reports available write or e-mail:

IUCN Publications Services
219C Huntingdon Road, Cambridge, CB3 0DL U.K.
iucn-psu@wcmc.org.uk

Center for Khmer Studies
P.O. Box 9380, Wat Damnak, Siem Reap, Cambodia
www.crp.cornell.edu/projects/cks

The Center for Khmer Studies is an independent institution for the study, research, and teaching of Khmer civilization. Located within Wat Damnak in Siem Reap, it has a fine library that is open to the public and offers the community a forum for research seminars and an exchange of ideas and knowledge.

Cambodia Wildlife Protection Office
40 Norodom Boulevard, Phnom Penh, Cambodia
wpo@forum.org.kh

This fledgling governmental organization writes and enforces wildlife protection laws and conducts research into both the conservation status of wild species and the human use of these species.

North American Bear Center
P.O. Box 161, Ely, MN 55731
www.bear.org

Run by maverick bear biologist Dr. Lynn Rogers, the North American Bear Center sponsors studies and conservation projects for American black and grizzly bears. During the winter there is often a live den-cam you can watch on the Internet, showing bears in their dens, sometimes with cubs.

International Bear News
(The Newsletter of the International Association for Bear Research
   and Management)
10907 Northwest Copeland Street, Portland, OR 9722-6145
E-mail: Ibanews@bearbiology.com

An association of professional bear biologists from around the world working to learn more about bears and how to protect them and their habitats.

Free the Bears Fund Inc.
P.O. Box 673, Mona Vale, New South Wales 2103, Australia
www.freethebears.org.au/savethem/contact_us.html

This organization funded the construction of Mary's Bear Home at Lop Buri Zoo. The organization works to free bears from the horrid conditions of overcrowded bear parks in China and Japan and to rescue them from bear bile farms.

ACKNOWLEDGMENTS

During the four expeditions to Southeast Asia to research this book, many dozens of kind people shared information, talents, and contacts. I am most grateful to Dr. Gary J. Galbreath. I could not have invented a scientist more thorough and knowledgeable, nor a traveling companion more cheerful and patient.

For shepherding us safely through his native Cambodia despite biting bears, unexploded land mines, unseen bandits, and tangled bureaucracy, we are both indebted to Sun Hean, the dedicated and resourceful deputy director of Cambodia's Wildlife Protection Office. We extend our thanks to the staff at the Wildlife Protection Office, especially to Heng Kimchhay, who accompanied us to the Elephant and Cardamom mountains. Hunter Weiler, His Excellency Chhun Sarreth, and David Ware provided us valuable assistance and welcome in Phnom Penh.

Gary van Zuylen, director of the Thai Society for the Conservation of Wild Animals, was a most generous and informative host at Banglamung, on multiple trips through Bangkok, and on our travels together to northern Thailand. Special thanks to his dedicated staff working both in Thailand and Laos; to his colleagues and friends in the Thai Royal Forest Department; and particularly to our host in the Salaween, Preecha Rattanaporn.

For sequencing the nucleotides of the DNA we collected in Southeast Asia and helping to interpret the data, Dr. Lisette Waits played a crucial role in the unfolding of this story. We are grateful to her and her staff for welcoming us to the lab during our fascinating visit there.

Forbes Lewis, who we met in Vientiane, was an excellent source of advice. He introduced us to Gerry and Tina Schroering, who generously shared their home and library. Gerry in turn introduced us to ethnolinguist Dr. Jim Chamberlain. His findings, insights, suggestions, and friendship informed our understanding of the peoples and language of the region. We are also grateful to Jim for introducing us to Panh Phomsombath, who ably served as our translator and guide in the Annamite Mountains.

For translation and cultural guidance elsewhere in our travels, we also thank Sangphet Unkeaw, Pranee Thongnoppakun, and Samkait Reinpathomsak. We are grateful to Jaa Bet and Na La for welcoming us into their home during our stay at Bo Kreit, and to the Black Lahu and Hmong who shared with us their knowledge about bears.

Dianne Taylor-Snow, who has accompanied me on so many travels, served as a collaborator on my fourth trip to Southeast Asia. I thank her for her wonderful companionship and photographs.

Closer to home, I am indebted to Eleanor Briggs, a talented and intrepid photographer who has, for years, shared with me her extensive experiences in Cambodia and Vietnam, and who introduced me to Sun Hean. Thanks to Judith Stout for providing the occasion for that meeting.

*   *   *

The following trusted friends and colleagues carefully read all or parts of this manuscript as it was being written. I thank them all for their advice and encouragement; I thank them, too, for averting errors. Any that remain are my responsibility. My deep thanks to:

Dr. Gary Galbreath, Dr. Jim Chamberlain, Selinda Chiquoine, Gretchen Morin, Joni Praded, Howard Mansfield, Dianne Taylor-Snow, Elizabeth Marshall Thomas, Ranida Touranont, Gary van Zuylen, and Dr. Lisette P. Waits. I thank my agent and friend Sarah Jane Freymann, my wonderful editor at Simon & Schuster, Denise Roy, and my production editor, Gabe Weiss.

*   *   *

This book would have remained imprisoned in a broken computer were it not for the technical assistance of Ray and Beth Cote of Appropriate Solutions of Peterborough, New Hampshire. I also thank my friends Selinda and Ken Chiquoine who allowed me to take over their home and computer equipment to print out the manuscript.

*   *   *

For their special help with this project, I also gratefully acknowledge:

Dr. William Burger; Dr. Francine Cuthbert; Dr. Lisa Dabeck; Dr. Richard Estes and Runi Estes; Dr. Richard Frechette and the staff of Monadnock Family Care; Joel Glick; Dr. Ian Glover; Laura O'Mara James; Suthep Janthavawong; Ben Kilham and his human and ursine family; the late Colonel Clyde Layne; Dr. Johan Lindsjo; Carnig Minisian; Dr. Richard Melville; Glynn Ellington Perera; Lieutenant Colonel Wirat Phupiangjai; Dr. George Rabb; Dr. Lynn Rogers; Panit Sanpote; Dr. George Schaller; Dr. David Smith; Corina Sutel; Dr. Kristina Timmerman; Chris Van Valkenburgh; Leonie Vejjajiva; Dr. Penny Walker; and Xieng Xioang.

* * *

In addition, I acknowledge the help of the following institutions:

Cambodian Office of Forestry and Wildlife; Field Museum of Natural History; Harvard University; Northwestern University; Siam Society; Center for Khmer Studies; Tulakhom Zoo; Lop Buri Zoo; Thai Royal Forest Department; and the World Society for the Protection of Animals.